FIGURE SKATING'S GREATEST STARS

FIGURE SKATING'S GREATEST STARS

STEVE MILTON

FIREFLY BOOKS

A FIREFLY BOOK

Published by Firefly Books Ltd. 2009

First printing

Publisher Cataloging-in-Publication Data   (U.S.)
Milton, Steve.
    Figure skating's greatest stars / Steve Milton.
[   ] p. : col. ill., photos. (some col.) ;   cm.
Summary: A celebration of figure skating and its athletes, including pioneers,
legends and current stars, told through profiles and essays.
ISBN-13: 978-1-55407-324-5
ISBN-10: 1-55407-324-3
1. Skaters -- Biography. 2. Figure skating -- Pictorial works.
 I. Title.
796.91/2/0922 dc22   GV850.A2M54 2009

Library and Archives Canada Cataloguing in Publication
Milton, Steve
    Figure skating's greatest stars / Steve Milton.
Includes index.
ISBN-13: 978-1-55407-324-5
ISBN-10: 1-55407-324-3
    1. Figure skaters--Biography. 2. Figure skating. I. Title.
GV850.A2M535 2009   796.91'20922   C2009-900763-0

Published in the United States by
Firefly Books (U.S.) Inc.
P.O. Box 1338, Ellicott Station
Buffalo, New York 14205

Published in Canada by
Firefly Books Ltd.
66 Leek Crescent
Richmond Hill, Ontario L4B 1H1

Cover and interior design: Kimberley Young
Factual proofing: Karen Cover, World Figure Skating Hall of Fame

Printed in China

The publisher gratefully acknowledges the financial support for our publishing
program by the Government of Canada through the Book Publishing
Industry Development Program.

CONTENTS

GREATEST STARS AND LEADING LEGENDS

How does a figure skater become one of that elite group of athletes recognized around the world as a "greatest star"? There is no specific blueprint, no foolproof plan that works for everybody and the criteria for greatness has changed over time. Figure skating has always been an uneasy blend of science and art; of athleticism and aesthetics; of purposeful power and elegant ease; of the feminine and the masculine; of apparent abandon and disguised restraint; and of the East and the West. It is because of these inherent contrasts that it is difficult to distinguish what separates a star performer from the rest of the herd. It is also because of these contrasts that figure skating is one of the most fascinating of all athletic pursuits.

The title "greatest star," as it applies to the figure skaters covered on these pages, has been bestowed by the author. This book tracks figure skating history through the athletes who were, and are, most responsible for the direction the sport has taken. So, a skater's impact on the sport was a major factor in awarding him or her the delineation as a "star."

Compared to other major sports, figure skating has not yet enjoyed the same level of sustained celebration of the men and women who have made the sport what it is. The World Figure Skating Hall of Fame in Colorado Springs has been the leader in recording and publicizing the history and glory — and some of the warts — of the sport, but figure skating writers and broadcasters tend to deal with current events, and make little reference to the history of the sport.

Other sports have been much better served. Millions of North Americans are aware

A contemporary skater carves the ice, mapping the graceful movements
that have shaped figure skating since the beginning.

that Abner Doubleday is the accepted founder of baseball, that Ty Cobb was its earliest mega-star, that Babe Ruth was its defining and history-altering player and that Mickey Mantle was its post-war face. Skating, however, though more than a century and a half has passed since Jackson Haines turned a pastime into a sport and spectacle, still lacks the basic public awareness of its history. And, although the general public may not be aware of it, skating has its own Doubledays, Cobbs, Ruths, and Mantles in Haines, Gillis Grafström, Sonja Henie and (take your pick) Dick Button or Peggy Fleming.

It was a wrenching process to separate the 63 skaters and pairs who made it into this book from the other magnificent athletes who skated in the various eras. For that reason, those selected have not been ordered from 1 to 63. As John Updike famously wrote of transcendent athletes, "Gods don't answer letters" and in the same vein, these Legends don't need registration numbers.

All the exceptional skaters featured in this book have entered the wider public consciousness in one manner or another: by their remarkable stretch of dominance; by their pioneering style; by their technical innovation; by their impact on a major skating country; by their sustained influence within their discipline; by their roles as signposts of a new era; by their ability to compel others to take up the sport; and by their personification of the skating ideals of their time. And all are worthy of legendary status.

What is often most striking about any catalogue of "greatest stars" that spans many eras are those who are left off the list. The exclusions tend to generate as much criticism and debate as the selections do. Athletes the likes of Willy Böckl, Ronnie Robertson, Vladimir Kovalev, the incomparably exciting and funny Isabelle Brasseur and Lloyd Eisler; as well as pre-World War II pioneers like Cecilia Colledge and Megan Taylor, and young champions from the turbulent 1990s like Alexei Urmanov, Ilia Kulik,

Ever the showman, Lloyd Eisler looks skyward and thanks the heavens for the free skate performance he and Isabelle Brasseur delivered to win the pairs bronze at the 1994 Lillehammer Olympics.

Oksana Baiul and Tara Lipinski, were all tremendous skaters worthy of the praise and championships they won. But, for reasons ranging from being just one of many superb skaters in a very deep field of great skaters, or to careers that were prematurely ended, these athletes were left off the list.

And even though victory is the ultimate goal in all competition, and most of the greatest stars presented here (and many of the names above) have been world and/or Olympic champions, some haven't. Jackson Haines predated major skating tournaments, but international competition started because of him. Toller Cranston never finished higher than third on the big-time international stage, but there can be no disputing that he has had the most enduring stylistic impact of his, and perhaps of any, generation.

Werner Groebli and Hansruedi Mauch were unknown by their given names, but as Frick and Frack they motivated thousands of youngsters to take up figure skating, including many who later became world champions. They did this by being part of a legion of professional skaters during the 1940s-to-1960s era of touring shows. Other long-touring pros such as Richard Dwyer, Freddie Trenkler and dancers Rona and Cliff Thaell also spread the gospel to the furthest corners of two continents. But Frick and Frack were the ones who entered the North American lexicon.

And the mere mention of Janet Lynn, whose best world finish was second, still evokes the image of what chief rival, and fellow legend Karen Magnussen refers to as "ethereal skating." Magnussen and Beatrix Schuba regularly beat Lynn, but Lynn's heartbreaking style prompted young Americans to stampede to their local arenas to see if they could glide across the ice like her.

In all sports, stars are born at the convergence of opportunity and ability. There is a similarity between the indomitable character traits of the Greats in one era to those of another era. In figure skating, there has been a remarkable chain of personal inspiration from one star to another. The audience that watched Jackson Haines in the 1860s included those who became the champions of the first international competitions two decades later. Their audience, in turn, included the first formal world champions. Sonja Henie's tours inspired a number of future North American stars who, after meeting her in person, further committed themselves to the sport. Carol Heiss recalls being at the Dartmouth Winter Carnival as a nine-year-old when Barbara Ann Scott presented Heiss and her sister Nancy with lapel pins

in the shape of tiny silver blades. Those pins proved to be symbolic relay batons: Heiss herself met other future champions at rinkside at local carnivals she skated. Donald Jackson, the world's first triple Lutzer, saw Scott skate live and himself passed the torch to Axel king Brian Orser, a nine-year-old soloist sharing a dressing room with Jackson at the 1971 Midland Skating Club carnival.

There have been countless other such moments of pivotal personal contact, but their frequency and impact are lessening. In the current big-money era, it is very rare for a young skater to meet a star in a local club show. The skating muse is now most-commonly transferred via television. It may be less intimate, but it also reaches a larger pool of potential superstars.

Woven around the 63 biographies of these greatest stars are essays and sidebars that analyze some of the most important themes and moments in skating's history. They provide the wider context for the individual skaters.

Decade after decade skating fans have celebrated the best and brightest that the worlds' skating nations have had to offer. I hope you will enjoy this tribute to skating's heritage and that it will help you to appreciate the next groundbreaking routine, the next genre-altering moment and the next legendary performance. Looking back gives us the understanding to move forward.

Steve Milton

THE MEN

The list of men's world champions in figure skating stretches all the way back to 1896, making it one of the longest and most enduring histories of global titlists in all of sport. The first winter-sport gold medal in Olympic Games history even went to a figure skater, when Ulrich Salchow won the figure skating event staged at the 1908 Summer Games in London. So, it's not surprising that the greatest male skaters in history are a diverse group, crossing a wide spectrum of athletic and artistic gifts: from the solitary expressionism of John Curry's haunting performances to the exuberant populism in Kurt Browning's vast repertoire; from the architectural precision of Gillis Grafström to the abstract body sculptures of Toller Cranston.

But no matter how different their styles, how different their eras, the legends of men's skating had one thing in common: they all could draw on a reservoir of mental toughness. For some, such as Elvis Stojko, that competitive strength was a career hallmark. For others, it was present in only their biggest moments; or, as with Cranston and Jackson Haines, their toughness was displayed in their dogged determination to do things their way, no matter how strong the resistance from others. That emotional and mental fortitude is imperative because singles figure skating is often said to be the loneliest and most pressure-packed pursuit in sport. The men's single skater competes with no other opponents or teammates on the playing field for a longer such stint than in any other sport. He's in a confined space in close proximity to thousands of knowledgeable fans. He's trying to maximize the speed and power of male skating, while harnessing both artistry and control. He must make the extraordinarily difficult appear routinely easy.

Many of history's greatest men's figure skaters — from Salchow and Grafström, through to Dick Button and Scott Hamilton — established competitive dynasties. Others managed to win only one or two major titles, while still others like Haines and Cranston won none at all. But every one of these legends made an enormous lasting impact on his sport that can still be felt today.

Brian Boitano performing his classic spread eagle during his gold-medal-winning
free skate at the 1988 Calgary Olympics.

PIONEERS AND TRENDSETTERS — *Skaters through to the 1950s*

Dick Button

Watching the perfection of barrel-chested Dick Button shift the balance of men's skating power to the United States, it must have been shocking for mortified Europeans to learn that he was once told his body type would prevent him from ever succeeding at the sport. Nobody, it turned out, ever succeeded so thoroughly.

Button ushered in a golden age of American skating. But the United States has still never produced a men's skater equal to the groundbreaker from Englewood, New Jersey. In the minds of many skating experts he's the finest men's skater who ever lived. Even those who might favor another contender, such as Ulrich Salchow, Gillis Grafström, Kurt Browning or Jackson Haines, routinely regard Button among the top two or three.

Button's legacy extends from his on-ice mastery to his off-ice contributions, as he was a pioneer of televised skating commentary in the U.S., founder of the popular and self-sustaining world professional championships and promoter of other TV events that have prolonged and enhanced many careers.

On the ice is where Button had the greatest impact. North Americans had the advantage of training time, facilities and coaching during World War II, since figure skating in Europe was almost completely shut down. When the World and European Championships resumed in 1947, two teenagers, Dick Button and Canada's Barbara Ann Scott, demonstrated just how far the New World had advanced the sport.

When he took the 1946 U.S. title at the age of 16, Button was the first American man to win the novice, junior and national championships in three successive years. He had begun training in earnest just four years earlier, after an instructor at Riverdale Skating Rink said he could never be an elite skater.

Button's quick ascent was fuelled by his coach, former ski-jumper Gus Lussi, who studied the physics of the sport intently and applied the science to Button's skating, particularly in the jumps and spins. His precise methodology allowed room for Button to experiment with a variety of new jumps, but also gave him the discipline and control to excel at compulsory figures.

When 18-year-old Button won the first of his five straight world championships in 1948, he was the youngest man ever to claim the title and the first American, in any skating discipline, to climb to the top of the podium. His serial victories instilled American men with enormous confidence and gave them cachet on the world scene. In the Button-initiated period from 1947 to 1959, American men won 12 world championships, nine silver medals and five bronze, sweeping the podium an astonishing three times. It wasn't until 1960 that a man from another country (France) won the world title.

Button won both the 1948 and 1952 Olympics, making him the only American ever to repeat as

---

OPPOSITE: Dick Button warms up in Oslo, Norway, at the 1952 Olympics. He won the gold medal to defend his 1948 Olympic title.

Button after his performance at the 1948 St. Moritz Olympics. Button won the event, becoming the first American to win an Olympic figure skating gold medal.

Dick Button leaps during practice at the 1948 Olympics in St. Moritz, Switzerland.

Olympic figure skating champion. He is also the youngest man, at 18 years, six months and 18 days old, ever to win the Olympic skating gold, 20 months and 14 days junior to second-youngest winner, Alexei Urmanov, the 1994 champion.

After being shaded by veteran Swiss skater Hans Gerschwiler for the 1947 world title, Button never lost another event. He became so dominant that after the 1948 Olympics, only twice did a judge not rank him first in both the figures and free skate. He won seven straight national titles, a string not duplicated since then, and he and Carol Heiss are the only singles skaters of the post-war era to win five consecutive world titles.

Button's five world titles are third on the men's list behind only Salchow's ten and Karl Schäfer's seven; but neither Salchow or Schäfer wanted, or needed, to turn professional as early as Button did. (Almost every skater in the sport's pioneer competitive years had the financial means to afford the luxury of competing as an amateur for as long as he or she wanted.) And Button is the only man who has ever held, or ever will hold, the U.S., Olympic, World, North American

and European titles simultaneously. After his and Barbara Ann Scott's victories in 1948, the European Championships were closed to non-Europeans and in the early 1970s the North American tournament died because of widespread suspicion of partisan judging.

Button raised the technical bar so high that at the end of his amateur career, the sport was almost unrecognizable to those who had seen it before World War II.

His incomparable flair derived not just from the new jumps he introduced to the world, but also from the circumstances. Just one day after completing his first double Axel in practice, Button landed the world's first double Axel in the 1948 Olympics, when by doing so he could have jeopardized his safe lead. Four years later, at the 1952 Games, he led Austrian Helmut Seibt after figures, and then confidently landed the world's first triple jump, the difficult triple loop, in the free skate.

He was the first skater to do the flying camel, and his flying sit spin became universally known as the Flying Button. He was constantly adding rare double-jump combinations to his repertoire and at the 1948 Europeans, he landed five combinations of either two double jumps or a double jump with a spin. Only one other skater, fellow American John Lettengarver, attempted any such double combination. And he and four-time world and

American runner-up Jimmy Grogan were the only men's skaters immediately after the war to use connecting steps as part of their choreography.

When he stormed onto the scene with the new "American style" at the 1947 Worlds in Stockholm, some European critics took solace in pegging Button as an athletic rather than all-round skater. But he understood and excelled at figures too. He was also deeply connected to his music. Through eight years of study, he had become an accomplished pianist by the age of 18, playing only classical music, and as a teen he always skated to music he could also play on the piano.

British author T.D. Richardson described Button as "a superbly built athlete of immense strength, as lithe as a panther. He trains as few athletes have ever trained . . . in order to attain such exceptional brilliance."

Button's discipline extended to the classroom. Rejected by Yale, where administrators didn't want him trying to balance studies and competition, Button went to Harvard to study law. He was awarded an athlete's letter every year, even though figure skating was not a varsity sport. And while training for the 1952 Olympics, he submitted his graduating thesis from Europe. After his amateur career ended in 1952, he toured professionally during vacations while completing his law degree.

Two full generations have grown up learning skating techniques and detailed plot lines from his incisive, often critical, but always fair television commentary. For more than half a century Button has been without equal as figure skating's American emissary.

Gillis Grafström

Gillis Grafström, the first truly interpretative skater of the 20th century, believed that figure skating was art on ice.

An eclectic Swede, whose international career spanned 18 years, from 1914 to 1932, he won championships seemingly at will and entered only those events he considered important. Grafström was a skater so in advance of his time that his contemporaries could win only when he made a huge mistake, or was absent.

He never bothered to enter a European championship, and competed only four times at the World Championships (winning three), but he had a burning passion for the Olympic Games: Grafström is still the only man to win three Olympic titles, and might have had a fourth, but in 1932 in Lake Placid, at the age of 38, he skated a wrong compulsory figure and later banged into a photographer during the free skate, giving Austrian Karl Schäfer the win. He still managed to win the silver, however.

Grafström was the first major musically-creative skater of what was then called "the modern era." American Olympic medalist and writer Maribel Vinson Owen, herself a legend in the sport, said that even in the latter stages of his career, Grafström skated "almost superhumanly to music."

He influenced every skater of his generation to treat music as more than just background accompaniment. It was widely reported at the time that his 1932 Olympic free skate signaled a new era in skating choreography that was built specifically, and in detail, around the music.

A portrait of the multi-talented Grafström dated 1930, two years before he retired from competitive international skating.

The veteran Grafström at the 1932 Lake Placid Olympics, his fourth and last. It would be the only Olympics he entered he would not win; he placed second.

Grafström was skating's early Renaissance man: a professional architect, a poet, a painter, a skating innovator and an art collector.

In 1930, he and his wife Cecilie Mendelssohn-Bartholdy began their legendary collection of skating art and artifacts by touring the antique shops of Holland, where skating first became a social and artistic force. At one point, Gillis and Cecilie owned the three oldest skating books in print. Before

Grafström's untimely death from blood poisoning in 1938 at the age of 44, the couple had spent a small fortune on what became known as the Skating in Art collection. The majority of the collection was donated by the Grafströms, in two parts, to the World Figure Skating Museum: the first part was donated to the Museum while at its original Boston location, while the rest went to Colorado Springs when Cecilie officially helped open the Museum's new home there in 1979.

Like a painter, Grafström knew that art was a combination of technique and creativity, and he approached skating from that angle. He was equally adept at figures and free skating, using the discipline of one as the foundation for the other.

"He is ideal," wrote Nathaniel Niles, an American who competed against Grafström in his first three Olympic Games. "He skates in as correct form as I have ever seen, in absolutely his own way. All his movements seem most natural yet in no part is his style incorrect. In free skating, his good form becomes free and full of life."

Grafström finished second at the 1912 Swedish Championships, but didn't attend the World Championships until 1914 in Helsinki, where he finished seventh. There were no global championships during the next seven years because of World War I, but when the competitions resumed in 1922 at Stockholm, he won. He entered the Worlds only twice more — in 1924 and 1929 in England — and won both.

But he was a fervent believer in the Olympic ideal, and two years before he won his first world title, Grafström won the gold medal when figure skating made its second appearance at the Summer Olympics in 1920 at Antwerp. During the event, he broke a skate blade and didn't have a spare. He finished the competition wearing old-fashioned skates with curlicue toes, which he had found at a downtown shop.

He also won the first separate Winter Games — then called International Winter Sports Week, and retroactively named the First Olympic Winter Games — in 1924 at Chamonix, France, fighting off the effects of influenza to soundly beat Austrian Willy Böckl (who would go on to win the next four world

Haines in 1867, three years after having made his first trip to Vienna where he introduced what became known as the International Style of figure skating.

championships in Grafström's absence). Grafström won gold again at the Olympics in 1928 in St. Moritz before his incredible string was broken, when he was 38 years old, with a silver at Lake Placid in 1932.

Grafström's Olympic three-peat, along with Ulrich Salchow's 1908 Olympic gold at the London Summer Games, gave Sweden a sweep of the first four men's Olympic championships, and other than Grafström's 1932 silver, the country hasn't won an Olympic medal of any hue, in any figure skating discipline, since then.

When Austrian Karl Schäfer succeeded Grafström as Olympic champion and the dominant force in men's skating, he did it by appropriating Grafström's fluidity and musical artistry. Grafström's elements and body positions advanced the sport immeasurably. He pioneered the forward inside spiral and flying sit spin; diagrammed several new compulsory figures; and invented a bevy of unique foot and ankle exercises that helped provide his unique softness, which allowed his knees to look less rigid.

Once Grafström had introduced high art and musical interpretation to men's skating with such illumination, there could be no turning back.

Jackson Haines

Is it possible to be the lightning rod, and also the lightning?

Because it was possible for Jackson Haines. He is arguably the most important individual in the history of figure skating.

The flamboyant New Yorker was both the messenger and most of the message during an 11-year odyssey of skating evangelism through the northern half of Europe in the middle of the 19th century that signaled the beginning of figure skating's move from its elite primness to something far more expressive and accessible.

Haines was the father and champion of the "International Style" of skating, which opposed, and often mocked, the mathematical rigidity of the British and American schools. He embodied and entrenched the skating dualities that exist to this day: he was athletic and artistic; graceful and theatrical; noble and populist.

He performed in England, Germany, Russia, Hungary, Scandinavia and, most importantly, Austria, and stimulated skating growth in each country. Word of Haines' European fame spread back to North America, which eventually wore down resistance to more expressive skating.

Haines' separate visits to Vienna in 1865 and 1870 were seminal periods in skating history. He used live music to accompany his exhibitions, opening the possibilities for skating to be enjoyed by people as both spectacle and activity. As spectators, witnesses were enthralled by the master skater; as participants, skaters were no longer just tracing figures, but instead were dancing on ice. After his two visits, countless Austrians were inspired to try skating at their numerous local rinks.

Haines grew up in New York longing to be a dancer and entertainer. Some histories say he taught ballet before turning his attention to figure skating. There is no doubt he began applying ballet principles to a serious sport that had been focused entirely below the knee, the torso remaining erect, the arms pinned to the sides.

In his skating exhibitions throughout North America, the small and muscular Haines began experimenting with body positioning. He brought the arms and upper body into play for both artistic and athletic effect. He borrowed ballet's arabesque and it evolved into the spiral, one of skating's enduring and most evocative elements. And, although the spread eagle had been used sporadically before, Haines made it a signature skating move. He also invented the sit spin, another durable figure skating staple.

These motion-filled innovations were all too much for the conservatism blanketing American skating, where the fascination was with carving two-footed "grapevines" and numbers on the ice, so Haines set out for London. He was disappointed there, too, as his "fancy" skating, with its pirouettes, forward-leaning spirals and ballet moves was considered slightly effeminate and an affront to skating discipline.

Although London was not a success, Haines was idolized everywhere else in Europe and became a major star. His greatest conquest was Vienna, and the city famous for music embraced his dancing on blades, especially to its own waltzes. The citizenry took to the ice to emulate him. Haines' expressive form of skating became known as the Viennese Style, which became the International Style, the base model for today's skating. Some of the Austrians he taught became the earliest stars and organizers of the sport, including Leopold Frey, winner of the first major skating competition, The Great International Skating Tournament, held in Vienna in 1882.

Little is needed to boost Haines' reputation. In 1865, he invented the two-plate skate blade, which was screwed right into the boot, freeing himself, and those who followed, to expand into an infinite number of new moves. In just 11 years, he revolutionized the embryonic sport, infusing it with music, artistry and romanticism.

Where would figure skating have gone without him?

David Jenkins

Thirty years before the world's first official triple Axel was ratified by the International Skating Union,

David Jenkins was landing plenty of them in practice.

But he didn't need anything as radical as the triple Axel to win, his older brother Hayes Jenkins recalled, so why risk it in competition? Jenkins was able to complete about half the triple Axels he tried in practice, but he wanted at least 80 percent consistency from any jump he'd include in his program.

"I gave up practicing the triple Axel in 1958 when I was 21," the Olympic and three-time world champion explains. "Today, they have to take so many risks to win, but back then, there were no Russian men skating, no Chinese men, no Japanese men to speak of. So the depth of competition wasn't pushing things for us."

Still, Jenkins was a rarity in an era of double jumpers, having three triples in his arsenal by the time he capped his amateur career with the 1960 Olympic championship at Squaw Valley, California. He already had performed a triple Salchow and triple loop when he won the 1957 World Championship, succeeding his brother who had retired after four world titles, and in 1958 he added the triple flip, a jump far more advanced than anyone else was considering in competition. It would be several more years before the flip would come into widespread use in the men's division.

"I think I could be credited with, or be found guilty of, extending the athleticism in men's skating," Jenkins wryly says. "Style came very late to me. I skated like a hockey player...and I wanted to."

Jenkins was the third sibling in a skating family behind Hayes and Nancy. He and Hayes were coached in Colorado Springs by Edi Scholdan, one of the many great talents lost in the 1961 crash of Sabena Flight 548, which killed the entire U.S. figure skating team. After David Jenkins won the 1953 U.S. men's junior title, he graduated to the senior ranks to compete directly against his brother Hayes, and in 1954 and 1955 he finished second to Hayes at the Senior Nationals.

Hayes made his first world title defense in 1954 in Oslo, with David just missing the podium in fourth. For the next two years, '55 and '56, Hayes, runner-up Ronnie Robertson and David finished

U.S Junior champion David Jenkins in 1954. Jenkins would go on to follow in his brother Hayes' footsteps, becoming both world and Olympic champion.

David (left) gliding with his older brother Hayes Alan Jenkins in Oslo at the 1954 World Championships. David finished fourth, Hayes claimed first.

1–2–3 at the Worlds, marking the last time one country swept the men's medals. They were also the only world championships in which two brothers have stood on the podium together.

"He always looked after me, the burden was on him," David says. "I got awfully nervous, but never for me. For him. We travelled together and roomed together, it was great."

It was even greater at the 1956 Olympics in Cortina, where Hayes won the gold medal and David took the bronze behind his brother and Robertson.

"The U.S. hadn't won much at those Games, so it was a huge day when we won," David says. "And it meant so much to the family to have my brother on the top step and me on the third."

Coach Scholdan, though, knew Jenkins had to increase his artistry in order to move up two places, even with his brother and Robertson retiring from amateur ranks. So for the entire 1956 summer training session, Jenkins was not permitted to practice any jumps. With that deprivation, his skating rounded out "and by the time I was winning, I had developed a lot of style."

Jenkins won the 1957 world title right in Colorado Springs, and made a successful defense the next year in Paris.

"In those days, it inspired me what a big deal skating was in Europe," he said. "They'd get 20,000 for a competition where usually we'd have 1,000 or 1,200 people in the U.S., except in Boston where we could fill the Garden."

He was accepted into the medical school at Case Western Reserve University in Cleveland in the fall of 1958, and planned to retire. But the 1959 Worlds were back in Colorado Springs and the Nationals in

Rochester, New York, so he had to miss only four days of school to defend both titles.

"I wouldn't make a compromise with medical school," said Jenkins, who still trained under his Colorado-based coach. "I fought everything about the skating life. I wanted a normal life and I made it my battle cry.

"When I got hurt badly in the Olympic year, in a peculiar mental way I was relieved, because then I didn't have a conflict between skating and medical school."

In training during the fall of 1959, Jenkins severed the tendon that facilitates movement of the lower leg. The wound required 34 stitches and he was locked in a cast for weeks.

He was able to resume training only seven weeks before the 1960 Olympics. Yet he prevailed over figures specialist Karol Divin and dynamic Canadian free skater Donald Jackson to win the gold medal, the fourth straight Olympic title by an American man, but the last one for 24 years.

"It was the first Olympics televised in the U.S.," Jenkins said. "And CBS didn't even have a sports department, so I was interviewed on TV by Walter Cronkite and Dick Button, and on radio by Bing Crosby."

"I've never had any elation quite like it, and I tried to figure out if I was elated because I won, or because I could get back to medical school."

Instead of heading to Vancouver for the World Championships two weeks later, Jenkins returned immediately to classes, and the longest domination of men's skating by one country came to an abrupt end. After 12 consecutive years of American gold medalists, France's Alain Giletti won at the 1960 World Championships. Over the next 21 seasons, American men would win only three world titles.

Jenkins did take a one-year leave from medical school a year later, accepting a lucrative contract from Ice Follies in order to finance the rest of his studies.

"In those days if you went professional you were sort of a pariah in amateur skating," he says. "I didn't feel welcomed back until the 1970s."

Like his older brother Hayes, David Jenkins is not accorded nearly enough recognition by the current generation for his Olympic championship, three world and four national titles, and for pushing the sport toward more, and harder, triple jumps.

Hayes Alan Jenkins

Dick Button was the five-star general of a dramatic power shift in men's skating after World War II, but the campaign was continued and amplified by a smooth and effortless skater from Akron, Ohio.

Because Hayes Alan Jenkins predated the television era and performed only periodically after winning the 1956 Olympics and Worlds, he is not celebrated nearly as loudly as a four-time world champion should be.

But during his championship run, which immediately followed Button's, Jenkins was equally unbeatable. He didn't lose a competition from

Hayes Alan Jenkins skating figures in front of judges at the 1956 Olympics in Cortina d'Ampezzo, Italy. Hayes led an American sweep of the podium.

1953 through 1956, when he edged ultra-athletic countryman Ronnie Robertson at both the Olympics and Worlds, and then retired to continue his law studies. He toured professionally for two summers in Europe, when school was out, and helped finance his first year of law school by appearing in club carnivals every second weekend.

Jenkins' ability to accept the torch passed on by Button solidified the transfer of power — to win, and to dictate style — from Europe to North America. In both 1955 and 1956, his final two years of competition, Hayes Jenkins led a U.S. sweep of the men's podium ahead of Robertson and the younger Jenkins' boy, David.

"They called it the American School of Skating, because we learned to skate without the influence of the Europeans, although we did have ex-Europeans as coaches," Jenkins says. "We developed a more athletic kind of skating. It became less of a stylized sport. Sonja Henie started the trend, but Dick continued it. So North America did revolutionize the sport in that sense.

"We did have a bit of an unfair advantage. You're talking about skaters like Dick and myself who were

learning to skate while Europe was being torn apart [as a result of World War II]. That really hit home when I first went to Europe in 1949 to compete. For instance, we'd be in Austria and they would have no toilet paper."

Jenkins says he was "in awe" of Button's ground-breaking athleticism but also wanted to leave his own mark on the sport. Jenkins' skating was athletic but in a more subtle way, and he strove to blend his technical moves with his musical accompaniment.

"I tended to be not as dramatic as Dick in an athletic sense," Jenkins says. "I wouldn't call myself artistic, and certainly not in comparison to today, but I was very conscious of the music I skated to."

His artistry led one journalist of the era to write that Jenkins' jumps "almost sneak up on you."

Jenkins and his older sister Nancy Sue began skating on Saturday afternoons when he was seven, and they eventually competed in pairs and ice dancing together. David, three years Hayes' junior, was soon joining the family at the rink.

When he was 15, Hayes won the 1948 National Junior Championship, and in 1949 he finished third behind Button and perpetual runner-up Jimmy Grogan in the Senior Nationals, earning his first of eight straight trips to the Worlds.

Jenkins finished sixth in his 1949 Worlds debut, third in 1950, fourth in 1951, and third again in 1952. He came fourth at the 1952 Olympics — "the worst spot to finish, and you never know if you're going to get back."

Then he leapfrogged Grogan to win the Worlds in 1953 and never lost again.

"Jimmy and I had the same coach [Edi Scholdan] and often roomed together," Jenkins said. "When I won my first Worlds he said to me, 'If I couldn't win, I'm glad it was you.'"

Throughout his international career, Jenkins was an honors student with an eye on postgraduate work. When he made the 1952 Olympic team, he was in his first year at Northwestern University — the first-ever Olympian from Northwestern — but he found it

hard to get to the old Chicago Arena for practices. So the following year he moved to Colorado Springs to work with Scholdan, and attended nearby Colorado College.

"I had an excellent coach and it was never a question of sacrificing college for skating," he said.

His younger brother spent the first summer training with him in Colorado Springs. David Jenkins followed his older brother's path and made the U.S. world team in 1954. They are the only brothers ever to stand on the same Olympic podium and to win medals at the same world championships.

"We've talked about that a lot since then," Hayes Jenkins said. "For us, it was an incredible feeling at the 1956 Olympics. We had been competing against each other for three years and never had any trouble with it. We always wanted each other to do well."

Another world teammate was Carol Heiss, who celebrated her 16th birthday during the 1956 Games and who'd been on the U.S. team since 1953. Heiss and Hayes Jenkins struck up a friendship, and when he was in his first year at Harvard Law School, the year after retiring from skating competition, they began dating. They married after she won the 1960 Olympics, and have raised three children.

Jenkins is often remembered as an expert in compulsory figures, but he was also a subtly exquisite free skater. And the reality is that as the "American School" deepened the domestic talent pool, he made a concerted effort to master figures, out of necessity.

"The first time I won the Worlds it was based on my free skating," he recalls. "But as I started to defend it, it was against Ronnie Robertson and my brother, and they were both excellent free skaters. So I needed to build up a margin in figures.

"At the Olympics in 1956, that margin was only razor-thin, so it came down to free skating there too."

He edged Robertson by one point for the Olympic title, won his fourth straight Worlds, and then left school figures for school books and a very successful career in international corporate law.

In the modern era, Button is the only male skater to surpass Jenkins' haul of an Olympic gold and four world championships, and only Scott Hamilton and Alexei Yagudin have managed to equal it. His career should be regarded with the same reverence.

Four-time world champion Hayes Alan Jenkins combined with fellow Americans Dick Button and David Jenkins for 12 straight World gold medals.

Axel Paulsen, the father of figure skating's most daunting physical element — the Axel jump.

Axel Paulsen

If figure skating's early organizers hadn't been quite so elitist, Axel Paulsen might have accelerated the sport's technical evolution by a hundred years.

The well-traveled Norwegian never won a major figure skating contest and, after the International Skating Union was formed in 1892, never even competed in one. Strict rules against professional athletes — reflecting ancient apprehensive tensions between figure skating and speed skating — meant that Paulsen could not compete as an amateur figure skater because he had won prize money, and lots of it, from speed skating races.

But it was Paulsen who gave figure skating its most majestic jump and the one which even the uninitiated can easily recognize without a reference book. In many places in Europe, the jump with an extra half-turn is called an Axel Paulsen, but generally it's referred to as an Axel.

In technical terms, the Axel is a jump that takes off from the forward outside edge of one foot and lands on the back outside edge of the other. To the layperson, it is the jump that travels the farthest in the air, and the only one that the skater enters while facing forward. The necessary extra half-turn means that a triple Axel actually has three-and-a-half revolutions.

Vern Taylor broke the triple Axel barrier in 1978, but it was Brian Orser one year later — followed closely by Brian Boitano, Alexander Fadeev and Jozef Sabovcik — who popularized the jump and made it a necessary part of an elite male skater's repertoire. During the early part of their era, the triple Axel became a synonym for any athletic move, in any sport, that was challenging and dangerous.

Of figure skating's six standard jumps, the flip, loop and toe loop are named for the methodology, and the Lutz, Salchow and Axel are named for the inventor. Alois Lutz, an Austrian who first landed his demanding look-over-the-shoulder jump during the 1913 season, didn't win any world medals nor gain any other skating notoriety, and was swallowed up long ago by the mists of time. Even the most educated skating fan would have trouble coming up with his first name, or even that a Lutz was named after a person. But Ulrich Salchow and Axel Paulsen remain part of common skating vocabulary; Salchow because of his dominating presence as a champion and administrator, and Paulsen because his jump was impossible for the non-athletic and because he enjoyed an international reputation as a showman and a racer.

When the Great International Skating Tournament, the first major figure skating competition, was organized in Vienna in 1882, Paulsen arrived from Christiana (now Oslo), with his speed skates. Jackson Haines' protégé Leopold Frey won, and Paulsen finished third, but what impressed observers was a single jump that contained an extra half-revolution and looked like it flew forever. It was a major announcement to the world that the airborne potential of this new competitive sport might prove to be almost limitless.

Paradoxically, the jump that epitomizes athleticism and power was not introduced as part of the four-minute free skate. According to historian James Hines,

Ulrich Salchow, the most decorated men's world competitor in figure skating history.

it was delivered by Paulsen in the now-defunct "special figures" segment, an ill-defined category somewhere between compulsory figures and free skating. Other technical moves that eventually made their way into free skating, including certain spins and spirals, also made their competitive debuts in the special figures.

And Paulsen performed the figure skating feat in his speed skates, as opposed to a ruse he would use in America, where he'd don figure skates and bet speed skaters that he could beat them while he skated backwards and they skated forwards.

After leaving his mark on figure skating, Paulsen sailed for Canada in 1883, promoting his patented "tube" skates, his greatest contribution (besides several championships) to speed skating. The skates were lighter than before, with longer blades, and weren't significantly improved by anyone for a century. While in North America, he set a course record in New Brunswick, established the American 15-mile record

and won the first intercontinental speed skating championship in Brooklyn, New York, in 1885.

With his brother Edvin, he performed exhibitions of speed and athletic bravado all over Europe, spreading interest in skating. In March 1885, on the frozen Christiana Harbor, he beat Dutch champion Remke van der Zee in front of 30,000 delirious spectators. Royal dignity prevented the Norwegian King from attending, but messengers quietly kept him up-to-date.

Although he is considered one of the greatest speed skaters of all time, it is in figure skating where his first name is spoken at every competition.

Ulrich Salchow

The ringing irony is that free skating wasn't even Ulrich Salchow's strong suit.

Yet the multitalented Swede, the first superstar of figure skating's competitive era, is best remembered for creating the elegant jump that is a free skating staple, and one of the first two jumps any serious young figure skater is taught. Skating outsiders, who may watch the sport only during the Olympics, often make jokes about a sow-cow, because that's how the uninitiated hear "Salchow."

By sheer statistics alone, Ulrich Salchow would qualify as one of the top five skaters of all time. Only Sonja Henie has matched Salchow's 10 world championship titles, and only two other men (Karl Schäfer with seven, Dick Button with five) won even half as many. He captured nine European titles, was the first Olympic men's champion, and at the age of 41, finished fourth overall at the 1920 World Championships, the first global event after a seven-year hiatus caused by World War I — and nine full years after he'd retired from regular competition.

From the 1897 World Championships, just the second ever held, until he retired in 1911, he entered 24 World, European or Olympic Championships and won 20 gold medals, three silvers and a bronze. But Salchow's reach and influence extended far beyond his extraordinary competitive résumé.

It was he who welcomed Madge Syers — and, by extension, women — to world competition by reportedly giving her his gold medal at the 1902 Worlds after she finished as runner-up. This unconfirmed story does have historical cachet as Salchow made a similar gesture to Dick Button in 1947 after Button finished second at the Worlds in Stockholm. The Swede invited the American to take his pick of any of the myriad of trophies he'd won during his storied career.

In 1925, Salchow was elected president of the International Skating Union, succeeding Viktor Balck, the sport's first great administrator, who had run the organization for 30 years. Before Salchow was unseated as president for the 1937 season, after several internal disputes, he had significantly modernized the old-world ISU.

Under his guidance, the number of competitors at major events increased substantially. In the 15 years that spanned Salchow's first and last medals at the Worlds, only four times did he compete in a men's field that had more than four competitors, and twice there were only two. Women's entries peaked at seven, and pairs skating often had only two or three teams. But by 1938 competition numbers had increased to 13 pairs, 12 women and 10 men at the Worlds.

Salchow was also instrumental in bringing the World Championships to another continent, as the competition made a huge impact in both New York (1930) and Montreal (1932), stimulating a North American skating boom. And perhaps because he'd seen the potential for disastrous judging controversy during his competitive career, Salchow also added more definition and structure to judging rules and processes. They still had a long way to go, though, as subsequent scandals and unfair judging revealed.

Salchow didn't limit himself to running the ISU for 12 years. He spent 13 years as president of the Swedish Boxing Association and a dozen as president of the AIK Stockholm, Sweden's premier football (soccer) team. For four of those years he simultaneously held all three posts, giving him the unusual trifecta of being the leading Swedish voice in soccer, figure skating and boxing.

Salchow may never have had the lasting impact he did in the sport had his parents not moved the family from Denmark to skating-friendly Sweden when he

The muscular-legged Salchow in an undated portrait.

was young. He was interested in many sports, and competed in cycling, bobsledding and sailing, but he loved figure skating.

He was the first skater from Sweden to religiously study and practice compulsory figures, and he became a master at them. His body control and inner composure were perfectly suited for the precise tracings, and many other skaters copied his style of body movement during figures. He also excelled at "special figures" when that hybrid discipline was part of major championships in the late 19th and early 20th centuries. But Salchow didn't enter that branch of the competition at the 1908 Olympics, the only time special figures were contested at the Olympics. Russian Nikolai Panin won that gold medal.

Because his muscular legs were heavy and short, Salchow didn't have the natural grace and flow of some other free skaters, but his programs were thoughtfully assembled and, as one contemporary magazine wrote, "he could free skate with much power and sureness."

At 13, Salchow won the 1891 Swedish junior title, and then tied for first at the senior level in 1895 and 1896 before winning outright in 1897, the same year he debuted at the World Championships with a silver medal behind winner Gustav Hügel of Austria.

That was the beginning of skating's first big rivalry, a three-way affair among Salchow, Hügel and the gold medalist at the first-ever Worlds, Gilbert Fuchs. Each man earned at least one victory over each of his rivals, and only once did all three skaters compete in the same event: the 1901 Europeans — with Hügel taking first, Fuchs second and Salchow third.

But while both Hügel and Fuchs were great skaters, neither of the two had nearly the longevity and legacy of Salchow.

After finishing second to Hügel three times in four years, Salchow won his first world title, with Fuchs as runner-up, in 1901. This would mark the beginning of an incredible 10-year run where the only time that Salchow didn't win the Worlds was when he skipped the 1906 event in Munich for fear of biased judging that would favor the German Fuchs. (Biased or not, Fuchs ended up winning the gold in Munich.)

Less than a year after Salchow won the first

Olympic skating gold, as part of the 1908 London Summer Games, he introduced a then-daring jump, which took off from the back inside edge and landed on the back outside edge of his other foot. The Salchow jump was born and christened at the 1909 World Championships in Salchow's adopted hometown of Stockholm and has enjoyed a long and productive life, advancing from the inventor's single all the way to quadruple, first landed by American Tim Goebel 89 years later.

With no skating at the 1912 Olympics, there were no horizons left for Salchow to conquer and he retired after winning the 1911 Worlds over German Werner Rittberger, right in Berlin.

But, as a challenge, he came back for his commendable fourth-place finish at the 1920 Games. That became an unofficial passing of the torch because in Salchow's beloved compulsory figures, only one man was able to beat him: fellow Swede and soon-to-be legend, Gillis Grafström.

Karl Schäfer

It seems that with every major development involving figure skating and music, Austria somehow plays a role.

The Viennese, in the middle of the 19th century, went wild over Jackson Haines' new spins to musical accompaniment. Austrian aristocrat Lily Kronberger brought her own orchestra to the 1911 World Championships and opined on "feeling" the music and interpreting it, rather than having it play in the background like a separate entity.

And in the 1930s, a well-rounded athlete from Vienna who would become his country's all-time favorite skater, imported Kronberger's musical notions into men's skating.

Karl Schäfer won seven world championships (second only to Ulrich Salchow's 10), eight European titles and two Olympic gold medals. He succeeded the venerable Gillis Grafström as the world's leading male skater, and although Grafström had linked performance to musical interpretation, it was Schäfer who really popularized the concept.

Schäfer actually handed Grafström his last defeat when he beat the brilliant but aging Swede at the 1932 Olympics. Schäfer, the youngest man in the field at 22 years old, won because of a huge lead in compulsory figures after Grafström traced the wrong pattern on the first figure.

Partly because of the nature of that win, Schäfer is often described as a figures expert, but his true legacy was his use of double jumps and the manner in which he matched his skating to what the music was telling him. Most skaters of the time had usually designed their free skating programs without music, and then asked the on-site competition orchestra to play a standard waltz or 10-step while they showed their routine.

But the animated Austrian was different.

"Schäfer says he has no real program," American judge Joel Liberman wrote after the 1932 season which, with the Olympics in Lake Placid and the Worlds in Montreal, made Schäfer and Sonja Henie enormously popular in North America. "He just introduces elements from his vast pool of them, as the music allows. His rather casual program depends upon execution and surprise more than pattern. Every move with Schäfer must be a novelty."

Schäfer sprinkled his routines with dance steps, innovative spins and a liberal dose of double jumps. As early as 1925, when he was in his mid-teens, he was seen practicing double loops and double Lutzes at competitions, when no one had officially landed either.

His new-wave fusion of art and athletics made sense, considering his background.

Growing up not far from the famous outdoor artificial ice rink built by Eduard Engelmann, Schäfer excelled at many sports, particularly swimming and tennis. But he was guided toward skating by a local coach who directed him to Engelmann, who became his coach. Schäfer was so athletically gifted that, at 18, he competed in both the summer and winter Olympics of 1928, making the finals of the 200 meter butterfly swim and finishing fourth in men's skating singles.

He played both the saxophone and violin very well and later in life led his own dance band. In figure skating, he found the perfect vehicle for his highly developed musical sensibilities and a broad athleticism one observer called "impetuous."

After he won the 1936 Olympic and World Championships, Schäfer had run out of challenges in the amateur skating world, and retired. He married

Karl Schäfer in the mid-1930s. Schäfer blended art and athletics so sublimely his performances seemed almost casual.

his coach's daughter, Christine Engelmann, whose sister Helen was an international-caliber skater and whose cousin was the iconic champion Herma Szabo.

He turned professional, cashing in on his American popularity by appearing in several U.S. club carnivals and touring the country with American legend Maribel Vinson in their own revue called Gay Blades. After two years Schäfer returned to Europe performing with skating coach Herta Wachter in the Karl Schäfer Ice Revue, a forerunner to the famous Vienna Ice Review.

After World War II, Schäfer helped rebuild the famous Engelmann rink, which had fallen into disrepair, and taught skating there for 10 years. Schäfer later lived and taught in New York from 1956 to 1962, before returning home to coach Austrian skaters. Schäfer died in 1976 in Vienna, the place where figure skating and music always met.

AGENTS OF CHANGE — *Skaters from the 1960s through the 1970s*

Robin Cousins

Any discussion about compulsory figures should begin and end with this damning evidence: because of those boring, demanding carvings, Robin Cousins of England never won a world championship.

Cousins crowned the end of the artist-influenced 1970s with his 1980 Olympic championship. But, although he was three times the world free-skating champion, and took two silver medals and a bronze at the Worlds, the treacherous figures, worth 30 percent of the total mark during most of Cousins' amateur career, usually sabotaged his bid for world gold on opening day.

The restraint of figures, generally traced in front of only judges, was simply not meant for a Renaissance man like Cousins, who loved to perform and always kept the interests of the audience in mind.

"Despite the Olympic gold, I still bitterly regret not having won a world championship," Cousins concedes. "Not for want of trying, mind you."

In 1978, Cousins skated one of the best free programs of his life, rebounding from his poor figures into a deadlock with the eventual winner Charles Tickner of the U.S. and runner-up Jan Hoffmann of East Germany. The tie-breaking procedure went all the way down to the majority of fourth-place votes, and ultimately relegated Cousins to the bronze.

In the 1970s, two older skaters, fellow Brit John Curry and Canadian Toller Cranston, were revolutionizing the men's division with their groundbreaking, but different, brands of creativity.

Cousins, also an accomplished artist, was more upbeat and more a man of the people than either Curry or Cranston — and he was more of a natural athlete. From the time he debuted with a 10th place finish at the 1975 Worlds, his energetic technical abilities were beyond those of most of his peers, and he was the only skater to land five triple jumps at the 1976 Olympics.

"My favorite skater was Robin Cousins," says Brian Orser. "I loved his athleticism and his speed. I loved his free-form skating. I loved the magical quality of his blade, whether he was going slow or fast, in footwork or in spins. I loved his big single Axel and I used it myself later, to advertise the height you can get. He was a great example to pattern yourself after."

Cousins unleashed fast and varied spins and had, arguably, the best sit-spin ever, increasing the visual impact and the difficulty with an acute forward lean. He and Hoffmann were easily the most powerful jumpers of their era. Cousins never saw the technical elements as being divorced from the overall program, and it was this sense of flowing connection that won him the 1980 Olympics, Britain's second in a row after Curry's 1976 win.

"You cannot differentiate between the sport and art," he said, "because the idea is to make the sport like an art."

Robin Cousins in 1980 displaying his Member of the Order of the British Empire (MBE), which he was awarded after winning both the 1980 Olympics and European Championships.

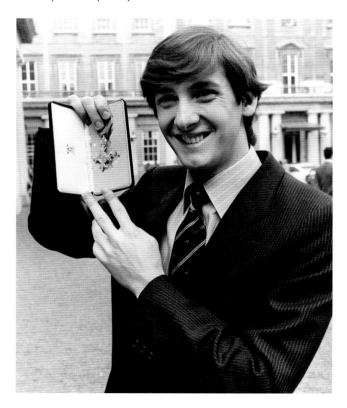

1980 Olympic champion Cousins, flanked by silver medalist Jan Hoffmann of East Germany (left) and bronze medalist Charlie Tickner of the U.S.A. Hoffmann and Cousins would trade places a month later at the Worlds.

Therefore, he says, he got into skating not for the competition but "because I could play at being Gene Kelly. When I was a kid I wanted to *be* Gene Kelly."

Cousins came to skating during a family vacation in Bournemouth, England. While shopping, the seven-year-old and his mother ventured into the local rink to escape a warm day. They bumped into a coach, and paid for a lesson, which whetted Cousins' appetite. When a rink opened in his hometown of Bristol, he started taking private lessons.

He won the national novice title as a 12-year-old, but at the same time nurtured a myriad of other artistic interests: he studied dance, was proficient at ballet and sang in school and church choirs. But at 13, he dedicated himself to skating and a year later won the 1972 junior title (after, prophetically, finishing last in figures). Thus qualifying for the Senior Nationals, Cousins came in a surprise third, and was named to the British team for the 1973 Europeans. He finished 15th, but made a lasting impression with the majestic lift of his jumps.

Cousins made his Worlds debut as a 17-year-old in 1975, finishing 10th. He moved up a spot

the next year, but at the 1977 Worlds in Japan, the effects of earlier knee surgery forced him to withdraw before the free skate, when he was sitting in sixth place. With coach Gladys Hogg absent because of an aversion to flying, Carlo and Christa Fassi were mentoring Cousins at the time, and he decided to move to Denver to work with them the next season.

While in Denver, Cousins boarded with Paul Wylie's family for three years. In appreciation, Cousins choreographed the program that helped Wylie win the 1980 World Junior Championship.

Under the coaching of the Fassis, Cousins began his three-year tenure as the world's best free skater, but because of figures had only bronze and silver medals at the Worlds and three European bronzes to show for it, until he won both the Europeans and Olympics in 1980. It rankled Cousins that he didn't deliver his best free skate in winning the Olympics, so he promised to skate cleanly at his final Worlds. Although he was too far behind in figures to win, Cousins delivered a performance for the ages, earning three 6.0s in a brilliant adieu.

His post-amateur career has been a creative, eclectic palette. He toured with Holiday on Ice, and headlined countless other skating shows and broadcasts. He has choreographed for the world's best skaters (including himself), directed and produced innovative TV skating specials, had his own critically acclaimed theatre-on-ice company, has sung and performed in the musicals *Cats* and *The Rocky Horror Show* and sung with the Nottingham Philharmonic Orchestra during Queen Elizabeth's Golden Jubilee Celebrations. He's also been the senior judge for the wildly popular *Dancing on Ice*.

In fact, it wasn't until after he turned professional that he invented his famous layout back flip. While trying a conventional back flip, Cousins inadvertently kept his legs straight. With his slender, six-foot-long body, the flip was an artistically impressive and physically dangerous happy accident. And it wasn't the stopping point for the always-reaching Cousins, as he later combined it with a triple toe loop.

He once said that winning three free skating gold medals at the Worlds was as important to him as his Olympic title, and that admission dovetails with incisive British journalist Chris Hilton's description of Cousins in his prime: "God made him to skate free, electric, boneless, defying all laws of gravity, to leap great distances, and to lift whole audiences to their feet."

Toller Cranston

Seven different men won the figure skating World Championships in the 1970s, but one who didn't influence the sport far more than any of his peers.

Toller Cranston was the most fascinating male skater of the 20th century. His awe-inspiring creativity arrived on the world scene without advance warning and, initially, there was no room in the staid sport to accommodate it. His entire amateur career was a battle for artistic and athletic acceptance, a battle which wasn't fully won until long after he'd turned professional.

In the end, the outspoken Canadian created a safe place in men's skating for innovative artistry. He was steadfastly true to his creative process and was vigorous in defending it, often to the point of alienating officials and judges. He had no tolerance for skating's restrictive traditions, especially the draconian compulsory figures. He never won or finished second in a world or Olympic championship, but he was the world free skating champion (combined short and long program finishes) three times.

After finishing ninth at the 1972 Olympics, he called skating "an expensive practical joke," and although he softened his public stance somewhat over the years, that sentiment was never far below the surface.

Cranston was a contemporary of John Curry of Britain, another revolutionary skater, and the two combined to pull the sport back from a headlong rush toward simple athleticism. Although both were pensive, often moody, artists who wore their hearts on their sleeves, there were at least two important differences between the Brit and the colorful Canadian.

For one, Curry finally overcame his competitive jitters, while Cranston was unable to completely transcend his. Curry won the 1976 Olympics, while Cranston's bronze in that event — he won the short program and was second in the free skate — was only his second podium appearance in nine world and Olympic championships. He also won bronze at the 1974 Worlds.

For another, Curry used classical ballet and form to break down artistic barriers, while Cranston was notably avant-garde, employing what some European writers of his time labeled "shock tactics" to chip away at accepted skating notions.

When Cranston debuted at 13th in the world in 1970, male skaters were still expected to be somewhat stately, holding their upper bodies erect and their hands near their sides in what was cynically called the Penguin Syndrome. Cranston challenged that convention with all four limbs. He was the master of the flamboyant, in dress and in performance, holding a leg or an arm at unusual and evocative angles. He peppered his free skating with demonstrative stag jumps, sideways toe-pick runs and unpredictable

The artistic Toller Cranston performing at the 1976 Innsbruck Olympics. Cranston claimed the bronze, his only Olympic podium finish.

variations on standard spins. Unbridled free skating was his calling card, the standing ovation his sign-off.

"One can only dream of being able to move one's body as artistically as that," 10-time world champion Irina Rodnina wrote of Cranston in her autobiography. "Toller, however, was unable to demonstrate his highest efficiency in important competitions. The simplicity of his movements and his way of passing on his feelings to the public by his gestures are indescribable."

Cranston brought the artist's eyes to figure skating, because he *is* an artist. From the age of 16, without parental or governmental funding, he financed his skating career through his paintings, many of which hang in the homes of the world's most famous skaters. His art, like the man himself, is bold, personal, intricate, fanciful and without exact precedent. He compares the self-discipline necessary to produce good skating to that required by painting.

While Cranston often referred to himself as an

Cranston, receiving his star on Canada's Walk of Fame in 2003 for his influence and numerous achievements in both the arts and figure skating.

artist who skates rather than the other way around, he would bristle at being tagged only as an artist. He liked the athleticism of skating, and considered himself the Renaissance man of the sport. Although many insiders disliked this self-aggrandizement, there were many important skating people who agreed with it.

"His creativity was immeasurable," marvels 1960 Olympic champion Carol Heiss. "He was non-traditional, but he was also traditional: he had wonderful edges and good jumps."

Cranston grew up in the northern Ontario town of Kirkland Lake, which was better known for producing NHL hockey players than figure skaters. He showed interest in ballet at an early age and transferred that interest to figure skating. When he was 10, the family moved to Montreal, where Cranston met coach Eva Vasak who nurtured his artistic interests.

Cranston finished third in the Canadian Junior Championships in 1963 when he was 14, and won the title the following season. In the senior ranks his radical style met with resistance and he could not reach the podium until his fifth year, finishing third. But he was gaining a legion of fans. When he did not qualify for the 1968 Olympics — Canada's representatives eventually finished 7th, 16th and 22nd — there were public criticisms of the judging at the Canadian Nationals.

In the summer of 1968, Cranston landed in Toronto with Ellen Burka. The venerable coach, who had taken her daughter Petra to the top at the 1965 World Championships and was also coaching national men's champion Jay Humphry, was the perfect mentor for the mercurial young skater. She encouraged his passion for art, both on and off the ice, and Cranston boarded at her home for many years.

Cranston debuted at 13th in the Worlds in 1970, moved to 11th, and then shot up to fifth in 1972, after the Olympics. But his figures' results almost always kept him off the podium, despite his free skating wizardry, and on the rare occasions he found himself in a position to contend for the title, he did not deliver his best performance.

As a professional skater, Cranston was released from figures and the other artificial constraints he abhorred, and his creativity had freedom to grow. He took great artistic chances with his programs, and

John Curry holds his gold medal from the 1976 European Championships. He went on to win gold at both the 1976 Worlds and Olympics.

usually succeeded. Added to the scores of skaters, of both sexes, who tried to emulate him during his amateur career were countless others who were inspired and influenced by his touring performances and TV work.

Cranston has written books, had a broadcasting career that was cut short by his propensity to tell the truth — often a blunt truth — as he saw it, and has designed programs for elite skaters. Lucinda Ruh, Christopher Bowman, Lu Chen and Yuka Sato have all been choreographed (and some coached) by Cranston and all of them were noted for that little something extra in their programs.

In his autobiography, the never-modest Cranston wrote that he sometimes wonders if he is the reincarnation of Jackson Haines. Like Haines, he was considered ahead of his time on his own continent

and was an adored celebrity in Europe before he was accorded the same status at home.

When Cranston signed with Holiday on Ice after his 1976 season, he was asked to design the publicity posters for their Paris show. The artwork was plastered on large billboards around the city, with the company-added description of Cranston as "Le Patineur du Siecle," [The Skater of the Century].

It may have been hyperbole, but three decades of his fans don't think so.

John Curry

There was a time when the International Skating Union wanted to make one of John Curry's signature spins a mandatory element in the men's short program. The idea failed because hardly anybody else in the world could actually do the spin.

During the first half of the 1970s, Curry, the creative genius from northern England, joined with fellow artistic rebel Toller Cranston to provoke a much-resisted upheaval in men's figure skating. Despite skating authorities, particularly those from eastern Europe, who overtly preferred a more athletic, masculine skating style, the two outsiders imposed their own dance influences on the sport: Cranston via free-form modern dance; Curry through the firmest principles of ballet.

Had the massively talented Curry been blessed with more self-confidence, he could have dominated skating from a very early age, but as his Birmingham clubmate Bernard Ford recalled, "He told me in the 1960s, 'Every time I skate I feel like I'm going to fail.' He couldn't quite put it together."

When he did put it together, the world was treated to unprecedented brilliance. After having won only one world championship medal (bronze in 1975), and two European medals (bronze and silver) Curry swept the 1976 triple crown: the Europeans, Worlds and Olympics. His Olympic performance at Innsbruck, one of the greatest ever, was so clearly superior that the judges from Canada and the Soviet Union were suspended for national bias after opting for Toller Cranston and Vladimir Kovalev, respectively.

Like many artists, Curry was detached from the mainstream, sometimes to the point of being cold

Curry illustrating great skating lines while practicing at the 1976 Innsbruck Olympics.

and short with his legion of fans. But when he won the Olympic championship, a wave of Currymania swept the British Isles. His was the first Winter Olympic medal of any hue for Britain in 12 years and the first Winter Games gold, ever. And no British man had won the world championship since Graham Sharp in 1939.

But Curry's real impact had nothing to do with wins and losses, although the gold medals in the final season of his amateur career lent extra authority to his unique style. His influence came exactly where he had hoped it would: he had chosen figure skating at the age of seven because it was the closest sport to ballet, which his father refused to allow him to pursue.

"I want skaters to see my skating and be inspired by it," he once said. The mission was accomplished.

Carlo Fassi, who coached him to the Olympic title, said upon Curry's untimely death in 1994, "He completely changed skating, turning it into a real art."

Curry's first coach in Birmingham doggedly insisted that his students bend at the knee, push hard into the ice and keep their backs ramrod straight, all techniques that came from classical dance and which stayed with Curry throughout his career.

He moved to London at the age of 16 to train with disciplinarian Arnold Gerschwiler, who had just taken Sjouke Dijkstra to her world and Olympic titles. Curry spent his first winter impoverished, working in a supermarket just to afford the gas meter. But he finished third at the British Nationals in 1968, was an alternate to the Olympic team and in 1970, won his first British title. A mistake-filled 14th place debut at the 1971 Worlds foreshadowed Curry's long struggle with landing jumps in critical situations.

Like Cranston, Curry had trouble finding judging acceptance for his artistic brilliance. He once complained to *Sports World* magazine, "The bias in judging really is a pain. Of nine judges at [the 1973] European championships, five came up to me afterwards to say that, without a doubt I was the best. They had all put me fourth but now they were saying I was the best. What do you say to that?"

In 1974, Curry felt encouraged by his first major international medal, a bronze at the Europeans, but made several free skating errors to finish seventh at the Worlds. At that point, he seriously considered quitting skating to concentrate on dancing. An American philanthropist Ed Mosler had started paying for him to train in the U.S., and so Curry went to Gus Lussi in Lake Placid to improve his jumps, and to Carlo Fassi in Denver to improve his figures and gain the technical consistency that he had lacked. Lussi also deconstructed one of the most riveting aspects of Curry's singularity: jumping counterclockwise, like most skaters, but spinning clockwise. Because spins are the stepping-stones to jumps, Lussi got them going in the same direction to increase the chances of consistent performances.

All the moves paid off with a world bronze medal in 1975, and that summer Curry took a course in positive thinking, to help stabilize his confidence and allow him to move past missed jumps and marred routines.

With a new confidence, and his brilliant lines, easy gracefulness, expressiveness and sense of music, Curry dominated the 1975–76 season, the most important stretch of the Olympic quadrennial. Despite a thinly-disguised campaign against him by the Soviets, Curry won a 5–4 split for the European gold when the Czech judge broke with the Eastern bloc, and he sailed into the Olympics as favorite. At the 1976 Innsbruck Games, Curry refused to let nerves swallow him and, had he not drawn to skate first in the final group of skaters, his gold-medal-winning performance would have earned a slew of sixes.

After winning his world title, Curry began an eclectic professional skating career. He starred in some of the very first TV skating specials. And he developed the first British show to lay ice down on theatrical stages, blending dance and his boyhood fascination with the stage into *Theatre on Ice*, which had a critically acclaimed three-month run at London's Cambridge Theatre. He moved to the U.S. in 1978 and developed an ice show which played at the Kennedy Center and the Metropolitan Opera House in New York. He also turned to non-skating roles, dancing and singing in the Broadway production of *Brigadoon*, playing in an off-Broadway comedy and even some pantomime in Liverpool.

In 1987, however, he was diagnosed HIV-positive and returned to England, living reclusively with his mother before complications from AIDS took his life in 1994. He was just 44.

But Curry's elegant artistry and long struggle to forge his own way within a sport resistant to change continue to influence skaters born in the wake of his death.

Donald Jackson

With appreciative nods toward Dick Button, the Protopopovs and all the others who've delivered

virtuoso performances under intense pressure, Don Jackson's Carmen at the 1962 World Championships in Prague stands as one of the two greatest competitive programs in skating history (the other being Torvill and Dean's Bolero at the 1984 Olympics in Sarajevo).

And there was one major difference between those two virtuoso deliveries.

"No one expected me to win," said Jackson, who was nicknamed the King of Blades for what happened on March 15, 1962.

The 21-year-old *had* to deliver the performance of his lifetime to capture the first world championship by a Canadian male. Jackson trailed hometown favorite Karol Divin of Czechoslovakia by an almost impossible 45 points after compulsory figures.

Divin had already performed solidly in his free skate and, just before Jackson went on, he asked his coach, Sheldon Galbraith, if there was any chance for him. "Don, there's room at the top," said Galbraith, uttering six of the most indelible words in Canadian sports history.

Jackson then unleashed a free skate that was so stunningly far ahead of its time, that any of its individual components would have been remarkable, let alone the staggering sum of them all: Jackson landed the first triple Lutz ever seen in international competition. The jump was so difficult that another one was not landed at the Worlds for a decade. His speed was blinding, the trademark Jackson footwork airy and lightning fast, and his spins were a blur. He did a double flip with his hands over his head, a jump which had never been seen before, and a delayed double Salchow, another rarity, and a single Axel with his arms crossed, even upon entry.

The five-minute program, the signature segment of ABC's inaugural televised broadcast of the World Championships, contained 22 jumps — 3 triples, 10 doubles and 10 singles — or one every 13 seconds, each of them with a difficult variation. All of it delivered with his traditional energy and playful enthusiasm, punctuated by the broad, almost-impish Jackson smile.

The crowd knew what it had seen and roared for the final two minutes of the routine, and stood for the end of it.

The performance was so overwhelming it

provoked two of skating's most magnanimous acts of sportsmanship. Before the marks were posted, Divin sought out Jackson in the dressing room, called him the true champion and promised to give him his gold medal if the judges saw it differently. And in the stands, Divin's mother told Jackson's mother, Pat, "if anyone beats my son, I'd be proud for it to be your son."

Donald Jackson received a new record of seven perfect 6.0s, one for technical prowess — where there should have been more — and a half-dozen more from the nine judges for artistry. The record stood until Torvill and Dean shattered it in an era of more liberally distributed sixes.

When Jackson was 14, he starting training at Ottawa's Minto Skating Club under famous coach Otto Gold. Growing up in Oshawa, Ontario, he took up skating (on hockey skates) at age eight for a winter carnival. His first figure skates were white women's skates dyed black. After seeing Don Tobin, the male soloist in Barbara Ann Scott's touring show, Jackson vowed to become a skater "just like that."

"And I wanted to do what Barbara Ann had done by bringing glory to Canada."

Jackson caught a career break when two-time world silver medalist Ede Kiraly moved from Hungary to coach in Oshawa, and fanned Jackson's passion for speed and jumping. Although it took a lot of financial juggling for his working-class family, Jackson proceeded from one top coach to another, following Kiraly with Gold, and Gold with famed Pierre Brunet in New York. He left Brunet in 1962 for Sheldon Galbraith, a Canadian icon.

Through it all, he worked diligently on his weak point, compulsory figures. He developed so much balance and edge feel because of that, his footwork was the best of his generation and he could rescue jumps from impossible mid-air angles. In six world championship appearances, he never fell.

Jackson was training in New York in 1961 when he caught a cold just before the World Championships in Prague, and his temperature rose to 103 degrees. Brunet advised him to convalesce for a couple more days in New York, so Jackson cancelled his seat on Sabena Flight 548 that was carrying the 18 members of U.S. figure skating team to Brussels, where they would catch another flight to Prague. That cold saved

Jackson's life. The Boeing 707 bound for Brussels crashed during its landing approach, killing all 72 on board, including the entire U.S. team, plus family members and coaches. Jackson didn't know about it until his mother called frantically the next day. The World Championships were cancelled, and Prague was rescheduled as the 1962 host.

While Jackson has come to be identified with that single night of awe in Prague, his career has been broad and distinguished.

He could have won the world title in Vancouver two years earlier in 1960, but had dropped behind in figures yet again and his winning free skate was not enough to overcome the deficit behind France's Alain Giletti. A month earlier, in February, Jackson had won a bronze at Squaw Valley, the first Olympic medal for a Canadian male skater.

With his 1962 victory, and Don McPherson's the next year, men's skating gained a front-row foothold in Canada, although it would be 24 years before another Canadian man won. That man, Brian Orser, performed as a child with Jackson during a carnival in Midland, Ontario.

Jackson became hands-on in Canadian skating after finishing a seven-year career with Ice Follies, during which he skated 420 shows per year. He still appeared in larger productions, but also spent years skating in Canadian club carnivals, staying with a local family, giving small-town skaters a chance to meet a world-class star, and teaching seminars. On his 50th birthday, he landed a triple Salchow for a TV commercial. And in the mid-1980s, he was hired as director of skating for Ottawa's prestigious Minto Club, a position he still holds.

It was while training in New York that Jackson came to an important realization.

"The Americans were really dominant in skating and Canadians said 'Hey, we came second to the Americans!' and that was supposed to be good.

"It wasn't good enough for me. I thought, 'We can be just as good.'"

And he proved it.

The King of Blades, Donald Jackson, fresh off his spectacular 1962 World Championship gold-medal performance.

BREAKING THE LIMITS — *Skaters from the 1980s through the 2000s*

Brian Boitano

There was a time when the top step of the men's Olympic podium was covered in stars and stripes. Male skaters from the U.S. won the first four Olympic gold medals after World War II, in synch with their 12 straight world titles.

But no man from the U.S. has won the Olympic championship since Brian Boitano's brilliant Calgary skate more than two decades ago. He and Scott Hamilton, who won the previous Games (1984 in Sarajevo), are still the most widely known American male skaters.

In fact, since the late 1990s, Boitano has found a niche in U.S. popular culture, well beyond the boundaries of sport. In the animated movie *South Park: Bigger Longer & Uncut* (made by the creators of the TV series *South Park*), a caricature of Boitano is seen in cutaway clips as a superhero fighting the forces of evil while the movie sound track plays the original song, "What Would Brian Boitano Do?"

Boitano has also won an Emmy for his performance in *Carmen On Ice*, has been part of the halftime show at a Super Bowl, dominated professional skating competitions when they multiplied outrageously in the middle 1990s, and was such a convincing spokesman for the reinstatement of professionals for the 1994 Olympics that the one-time window of return became forever branded as the Boitano Rule.

Boitano emerged from the Calgary Games as the "victorious Brian," triumphing over Canadian Brian Orser by one-tenth of a point in one of the greatest Olympic men's events in history. Unlike so many heavily hyped Olympic showdowns (including the fizzled "Battle of the Carmens" at the same Games), the Battle of the Brians lived up to, and even surpassed, its advance publicity. And it made the unknown Boitano a household name.

"1988 changed my life," Boitano acknowledged.

Brian Boitano, the 1986 world champion, skating at the 1988 World Championships. Boitano reclaimed his title from 1987 champ, Brian Orser.

"Nobody knew who I was in March of 1987. Nobody."

By then, Boitano had won bronze, silver and gold medals at the World Championships, and four straight U.S. crowns, but still flew under the national radar.

He was not anonymous inside skating circles, however, winning a bronze medal at the 1978 World Junior Championships and establishing himself as the premier jumper in the U.S.

In 1982, he became the first American to land a triple Axel, and he would go on to join Orser, Jozef Sabovcik and Alexander Fadeev in forging the mid-1980s' technical revolution that carried the men's division right through the millennium.

But, as Boitano admitted, until he lost his 1986 world title to Orser in 1987 (in Cincinnati where he had "home ice" advantage), he was primarily a technician. He had the triple Axel and an extremely difficult variation of the triple Lutz with his hand lifted over his head, still known as the Tano Lutz. He landed textbook, monster jumps with frightening regularity, possessed strong lines and depended for artistry on a majestic, unforgettable spread eagle.

After he failed in his attempt to land the world's first successful quad at the 1987 Worlds — an echo of the previous year when Orser fell attempting the world's first triple-triple combination involving an Axel — Boitano recognized that he needed more than his precise athleticism for the Olympic year. He later described his pre-1988 skating as "a bit robotic."

Boitano and Linda Leaver, still his coach and the only one he has ever had, sought the aid of Canadian choreographer Sandra Bezic. Bezic helped him reach out to the audience instead of shrinking from it; she helped him become more self-assured in his presentation — and she also found the perfect Napleonic-themed Olympic vehicle for his erect, proud style.

"I felt at my peak. I think the timing of my amateur career was exactly right," he once said. "In 1988, I was skating exactly the way I wanted to, but because of the Battle of the Brians, I felt I might have to put in four more years. I knew I had to be perfect to be even close to beating Brian Orser."

programs. Although he eased off in later years, Boitano had raised the bar so high for himself and other skaters that professional skating of the 21st century requires much better technical preparation than in previous eras and is, therefore, a better spectacle.

Boitano's other contribution was his leadership in having professionals reinstated into the 1994 Olympics, which was one of the major factors in blurring the lines between amateur and professional skating. Soon the word "amateur" was removed from skating rules for the first time in more than a century, and replaced by "eligible," and the International Skating Union eventually provided significant prize money at its major competitions. The former "amateurs" were becoming better performers and the former "professionals" were skating at a higher technical level.

Ironically, Boitano had his worst finish (sixth) in three Olympics in his reinstatement Games, after he fell on a triple Axel in the short program. It is a testament to his technical proficiency that it was just the second major mistake he'd ever made in a short program. And it is a testament to his belief in competition that taking the season off pro skating cost him about a million dollars.

"I didn't think about the money," he said. "It wasn't as important as the desire to compete."

Kurt Browning

Figure skating has never seen anyone quite like Kurt Browning. There is a wholeness to Browning's skating and career which, like the very sport itself, results from opposing forces living in harmony rather than conflict.

He was a brash, exuberant hockey player from

And he was perfect, with Orser only a minor glitch away from the same perfection. It was the closest result in men's Olympic history, and is credited as the first major step on the road toward figure skating's unprecedented North American popularity in the mid-1990s.

After he won his second world title, a month after his Olympic triumph, Boitano had the cachet to start his own professional touring show, rather than join an existing one. And despite his commendable amateur career, his two most important contributions to the sport came after he turned professional.

In the pros, he set a standard for technical excellence that nobody before him had even considered. He'd land perfect triple Axels and Tano Lutzes night after night. He won five straight world professional championships and just to finish second, his opponents had to elevate the content in their a mountain village who conquered the world and became an urbane artist, equally at home with classical ballet as with hip-hop.

He was the only skater to win a world championship with compulsory figures and without them, and he did it twice each. He could be as subtle in his artistry as he was explosive in his technical elements. He thought a lot, and he talked a lot. He could learn, and he could teach.

Browning arrived into the world of figure skating's elite with a hailstorm of dynamic athleticism, credited with the world's first successful quadruple jump and the first short program with two triple Axels. But he became identified with sublime artistry and convincing characterization. In both the latter years of his amateur stint and his pro career, he didn't play at acting, he *was* Gene Kelly, bluesman, rocker, ballet dancer, cowboy, clown, Bogey. He was the best skater of his era at taking any genre of music and owning it completely. In the early 1990s, several musicians marveled that he had the most natural (if then latent) grasp of music that they'd ever seen in an athlete.

In three Olympics, due to injuries or early falls, an extremely disappointed Browning never finished higher than fifth, but he ranks with Dick Button as one of the most complete male skaters in figure skating's second 50 years.

Toller Cranston called the four-time world champion a "magic mushroom," a true skating genius, sprung from an unlikely environment that was more likely to lead him toward becoming a cowboy or hockey player. In fact, Browning preferred hockey to figure skating as he was growing up on a ranch just outside Caroline, a village in the foothills of Alberta's Rocky Mountains.

"My first skating carnival was in grade two and I played a skunk," he recalls. "But I had hockey skates. I remember being mad at figure skates because I couldn't skate on them. So I was determined to get better on them."

That was a self-challenge that appealed to the consummate competitor inside Browning. During his early world championship runs, Browning was, he admitted, not the most consistently diligent trainer. But he had enormous innate ability, a tremendous competitive drive and an uncanny sense of occasion.

Kurt Browning in his 1994 Casablanca Olympic free skate as Humphrey Bogart's character, Rick Blaine.

At the closing ceremonies of his first Olympics in Calgary in 1988, Canadian legend Don Jackson, who pioneered the triple Lutz, said to Browning, "Go to Worlds and land the quad. It will change your life."

"It was just a couple of seconds, but it was a big influence," recalls Browning, who did exactly as Jackson ordered. And found that his life *did* change. He caught the judges' attention, vaulted into the public eye and in 1989 won his first world title, over heavy favorite Viktor Petrenko, American Christopher Bowman and a few others vying to own the next Olympiad. He won again in compulsory figures' 1990 swan song at Halifax, surging from behind in the free skate to become the first Canadian singles skater to repeat as world champion. In 1991, he became only the second man in 20 years (after his soon-to-be-mentor Scott Hamilton) to win three straight world titles.

He was the front-runner heading into the 1992 Olympics at Albertville, but a back injury and a fall in the short program kept him in sixth place. He considered turning professional, but instead opted for a change of scenery, moving from longtime Edmonton coach Michael Jiranek to Louis Stong in Toronto. Browning and choreographer Sandra Bezic came up with the perfectly-crafted Casablanca routine, the most sophisticated amateur singles program of the era and, arguably, of all time and Browning won his fourth World title in 1993, tying him for fourth in all-time wins, behind Ulrich Salchow, Karl Schäfer and Button.

Browning ended up fifth at the 1994 Olympics, pulling up from a disastrous 12th in the short program. On TV afterward, he told Canadians he was sorry for letting them down. Newspaper editorials across the country argued that he hadn't let anyone down and didn't need to apologize. The class and humility with which he treated his second successive Olympic heartbreak won over those few Canadians who weren't already ardent supporters. One fan group collected jewelry from across the country, had it melted down and re-crafted, and presented Browning with a 1.35 kilogram gold medal when Stars on Ice made its spring stop in Halifax.

After the 1994 season, Browning joined Scott Hamilton full time in Stars on Ice and, just as he credited studying Brian Orser for accelerating his amateur career, quickly absorbed the nuances of the professional world from the man who redefined tour skating. His outgoing personality, quick-witted playful humor and small-town sense of family served the tightly-knit Stars tour well, and when Hamilton retired from touring, it was a seamless transition to Browning's marquee leadership.

Unfettered by the restrictions of amateur skating, Browning unleashed a string of innovative programs which, in their entirety, covered every style of music

Browning in the 1992 Albertville Olympics. The four-time world champion never reached an Olympic podium.

and performance. His *Gotta Skate* TV specials are masterful fusions of live musicians and polished skaters, and his *You Must Remember This* is routinely rated as one of the top TV skating specials in history, highlighted by Singin' in the Rain, a Gene Kelly tribute number Browning skated while water drizzled on him from above.

Before a packed Stars on Ice crowd at Toronto's Maple Leaf Gardens in 1995, Browning proposed to Sonja Rodriguez, a principal dancer with the National Ballet of Canada. They were married in 1996 and have two sons. Collaborating with Rodriquez and making celebrity appearances with the National Ballet has extended Browning's artistic reach even farther.

When he was inducted into the World Figure

Skating Hall of Fame in 2006, Browning, who has remained approachable and down-to-earth despite his successes, laughingly recalled what his rancher and trail-guiding father, Dewey Browning, once said to him about skating:

"You're the luckiest guy in the world because you're doing for a living what you did as a kid. And if you let it go to your head, I'll kick you with my cowboy boots on."

That kick never came.

Scott Hamilton

Scott Hamilton is the greatest engineer in figure skating history. The 1984 Olympic champion has spent his adult life building bridges: between audience and skater; between artistry and athleticism; between professional and amateur, and between his era and those to follow.

Hamilton was an elite athlete and entertainer with the common man's sensibilities. And, unlike virtually all other American male skaters, he was able to transcend skating and become a mainstream celebrity. Since the 1930s, only the American female champion skaters had been thought able to capture the country's imagination, but with his gregarious and generous nature, his commitment to innovative entertainment, his renowned sense of humor and his longevity in the public eye, Hamilton became a striking exception.

Further enhancing his popularity, Hamilton repeatedly triumphed over misfortune and transformed hardship into advantage. In 1997, at the age of 39, he was diagnosed with testicular cancer. He left Stars on Ice for surgery and chemotherapy and returned a few months later to a thunderous audience ovation. And then in 2004, he underwent radiation treatment for a benign, non-cancerous tumor near the pituitary gland.

Through both frightening situations he maintained

Stars On Ice performers Katarina Witt, Scott Hamilton, Kristi Yamaguchi and Kurt Browning at the Harley Davidson Café in New York City in 1995.

Scott Hamilton skates with the American flag after winning the men's gold medal at the 1984 Sarajevo Olympics.

years. The condition eventually corrected itself, although Hamilton never grew to more than 5-foot-3. But when he started figure skating at the relatively advanced age of nine, he found his diminutive body, narrow hips and lightness were actually assets.

When Hamilton was 18, his adoptive mother died of breast cancer. While battling the disease, she had returned to school to earn her master's degree so she could become an associate professor to help finance her son's skating. In her honor, Hamilton rededicated himself to his sport. He nearly had to quit for lack of funds before his friend and philanthropist Helen McLoraine sponsored him for the rest of his career.

Hamilton's skating had such a light touch that the feathery landings on his jumps sounded like ice cream being scooped. His rapid, electric spins distanced him from the other male skaters of his era, most of whom were more concerned with their arsenal of big triple jumps. Even before turning professional, he was taking significant artistic risks, changing his motif, "so that you're new every year. There's not going to be one of these guys that come in with this kind of a trendy kind of gimmicky program that's going to overshadow you."

Don Laws, who began coaching Hamilton in 1980, said his star student made figure skating an entertaining athletic sport and "never left either one of those things out. He has given skating a characterization that is very personal. He could turn out many faces, do a variety of acts and entertainment due to his acceptance of change and development. But he remained himself, throughout."

Hamilton won the 1976 U.S. Junior Nationals and two years later finished third in Seniors, qualified for the Worlds and finished 11th. He was fifth at the 1980 Olympics, with fellow Americans Charlie Tickner and David Santee third and fourth respectively. But as his free skate drew to a close, the Lake Placid crowd rose to its feet in the only standing ovation of the evening, foreshadowing the unparalleled connection Hamilton would establish with his audience through his final four years of amateur competition and his brilliant 17-year professional career.

He won his first world championship at Hartford in 1981, surpassing Santee, and then was able to fend off a rising tide of superb athletic skaters — Brian

his characteristic good humor and positive attitude, and the resultant publicity helped raise millions of dollars for cancer research.

"Everything I've ever accomplished in skating and in life has come out of adversity and perseverance," he understates.

Hamilton was adopted by two educators in Bowling Green, Ohio, when he was six weeks old. By the time he was two, he had developed a nutrition malabsorption syndrome, which kept him in hospitals for a large portion of his developmental

Hamilton after winning the 1984 Olympic gold, the first men's Olympic figure skating gold for the United States since David Jenkins' 1960 Squaw Valley win.

Orser, Alexander Fadeev and Jozef Sabovcik leading the charge — for the next three years.

Hamilton was the last man to win four straight world singles championships and his 1984 Olympic victory was the first by a U.S. male skater in 24 years. He went undefeated in his final four seasons in the amateur ranks, but his most enduring influence on the sport came after he turned professional.

Hamilton had spent only two years with the touring show Ice Capades, before it was sold to new ownership, the International Broadcasting Corporation, which felt that only a female lead had the power to attract large audiences. Hamilton and his agents, the International Management Group, rendered that notion laughable and founded Scott Hamilton's American Tour, which soon was renamed Stars on Ice.

"All skating, no Smurfs," was Hamilton's quick description of the new concept.

Revolving around star power, high-level individual acts, a couple of ensemble numbers, and Hamilton's

engaging personality and wide-ranging repertoire, Stars on Ice quickly became the dominant force in professional skating. It cast the die for other such skater-based revues and has remained the king of the genre.

At the core of Stars' success was Hamilton's irrepressible, self-deprecating humor, and his unprecedented sense of knowing what audiences want even before they know they want it. He didn't hoard that knowledge, but passed his entertaining skills on to everyone on tour. When he was ready to step back, Kurt Browning was there to take over as the leader after learning at Hamilton's knee.

"It's what you make of it," Hamilton explained, describing how his post-amateur career had evolved. "You can peak in your eligible career or you can make your own set of rules and guidelines and start anew in your professional career."

Hamilton had hoped to tour for four years as a pro, and expected the limit would be six years, but he remained a major attraction for 17 winters.

On his farewell tour in 2001, an opening number featured a boy who represented a young Scott Hamilton, reflecting upon the journey of life. Among those who played the role were the sons of Charlie Tickner and Mark Cockrell, both of whom had competed against Hamilton. In passing the torch, he had built yet another bridge: from one generation to another.

Brian Orser

Brian Orser's revolutions were the gateway to a new era in figure skating, and made him the most pivotal male skater of the 1980s.

Others may have won Olympic gold medals, others may have won more world championships, others may have steered the professional world to new heights, but it was the refined and principled Orser who turned men's skating in a direction that could never be reversed.

When Orser landed a triple Axel at the 1979 Canadian *Junior* Championships to storm from ninth place to the top of the podium, he singlehandedly snatched men's skating from its technical doldrums. Officially, Canada's Vern Taylor had been credited

with the world's first successful triple Axel at the World Championships the year before, but Orser did the second. And, soon, the third, fourth and fifth.

Because of Orser's consistency with the new jump, within four years the only skater who could attain a podium spot without the Axel was the unassailable Scott Hamilton. By the time Orser retired with one world championship, four silver medals and one bronze, plus two Olympic silver medals — he is the only men's single skater in more than half a century to be on the world podium for six successive years — he and several others were doing two Axels in the free skate, mounting triple-triple combinations and flirting with the quad.

And, on the final day of Orser's amateur career, teammate Kurt Browning landed the first quadruple jump, a Salchow, emphasizing how quickly technical evolution was compressing. The gap between the first triple Lutz and the next jump up the scale, the triple Axel, was 16 years. But it took only 10 years to progress from the first triple Axel to the first quad.

"I know I had an impact, but it wasn't just me, it was the whole era," Orser said. "I think my colleagues and I helped make skating much more popular than it was at the start of the decade [1980s]. Maybe because most of us were around for quite a while. I just wanted to jump all the time, and be a pioneer at it."

Doug Leigh, the only coach Orser had throughout his trendsetting amateur career, recalled, "I knew right away he'd be good. He had no fear when he approached jumps, even when he was young. He wasn't lost in the air, he had an awareness factor. And he woke up the judges."

Ironically, by the time he turned professional Orser had become known more as an artist than a technician. His maturation as a showman compelled other skaters of the late 1980s, particularly Brian Boitano, to seriously upgrade their presentation skills.

He also had a subtle, but significant, impact on Canada's training structure. Doug Leigh was a budding 20-year-old coach when Orser joined him as a nine-year-old. The two began putting in hundreds of miles per week on the road as they hopped between Leigh's central base in Orillia, and other small central Ontario towns — as many as three per day — to find ice time. When he started landing the triple Axel, national skating officials told him that unless he moved from Orillia to Toronto or Ottawa or another large center for further training, his career would die on the vine.

OPPOSITE: Brian Orser in the mid-1980s. He is the only Canadian skater to be on a world podium for six successive years.

Orser at the conclusion of his free skate at the 1988 Calgary Olympics; he finished second to Brian Boitano in a 5–4 judging split.

But Orser believed in his young mentor and stayed in Orillia. Leigh's Mariposa Club became one of the most renowned skating schools in the world. Buoyed by that, local coaches throughout Canada began to be able to keep their young stars at their home clubs much longer.

Orser's only world championship, in 1987 at Cincinnati, was the most important in men's Canadian skating history. It was just the third world title won by a Canadian man, and the first in 24 years, but in an 11-year span, beginning with Orser's triumph, Canadian men would climb to the top of the world podium a stunning eight times. Orser had shown Canadians that they could win.

"I just assumed that the judges and everyone else was going to give me respect because I was Brian Orser's teammate," Kurt Browning says. "And I skated that way, because I felt I had an advantage. I recognize, now that I'm older, that that sort of mentality was huge."

Had it not been for his shortcomings in the now-dead compulsory figures, Orser would have won the 1986 and 1988 world titles and also the 1984 Olympics, where he dominated Hamilton in the short program and free skate, but could not overcome a seventh place in figures. And 1988's Battle of the Brians at Calgary — in which Orser lost to Boitano by one-tenth of a point in the closest men's result in Olympic history — was a seminal moment in figure skating's rise to mainstream status.

"The Olympic thing still haunts me sometimes," Orser says honestly, "but the country really rallied behind me."

Orser was Canada's flag-bearer for the 1988 Olympic Games and, arguably, no single Canadian athlete has ever been under as much pressure as he was that week as the country's only real gold medal hope in the only Winter Olympics it had ever hosted. The drive he showed in his high-wire confrontation with Boitano, and the sportsmanship with which he accepted his defeat, endeared him to fans everywhere. He carried that vast support into the touring ranks with Stars on Ice and became the symbol for smooth, gentlemanly performance.

Just to prove that he hadn't forgotten his roots, when he was 40 years old he opened his technical program at the 2000 Goodwill Games by landing a triple Axel.

Orser retired from touring in 2007, by which time he'd already choreographed programs for a number of eligible (amateur) and professional skaters and spent time as a national coaching consultant in Canada. He had always said he'd stay away from full-time coaching, but in 2007, South Korean Yu-Na Kim, impressed by what Orser had done with her as a consultant, asked him to be her full-time coach.

"And it turns out I really love it," says Orser, who is the first Canadian world champion to also be the full-time coach of a world champion. "Everything I learned through skating, I apply to my teaching. The experience speaks for itself."

Loudly and clearly.

Evgeny Plushenko

Natural talent oozes from his every pore. And once Evgeny Plushenko gained the maturity to know how to use it, he became one of the most decorated men in skating history.

Plushenko started elite competition at such a young age — winning a 1998 world championship bronze medal when he was just 15 years old — that he is one of the only skaters in the modern era to be ranked as the favorite, or co-favorite, at two different Olympics. He won silver in 2002 at Salt Lake, behind longtime club, national and international rival Alexei Yagudin, and then won gold at Turin in 2006, a men's event that was more coronation than competition as Plushenko skated without equal. He became only the fourth male skater ever to win an Olympic championship who also medaled in another Games.

His résumé overflows with medals, mostly gold. To go along with his Olympic gold and silver medals, Plushenko has three gold medals, one silver medal and one bronze medal at the World Championships, five golds and three silvers at the European Championships and five golds, three silvers and one bronze at the Grand Prix Final — all before his 24th birthday. Seven times he won the difficult Russian Championships, missing a string of eight straight only because he skipped the 2003 Nationals with an injury.

Guided by the colorful and politically savvy coach Alexei Mishin, Plushenko became the master of skating's bold statement. His jumps and spins were big and dramatic and approached with unapologetic flair. His artistic side, which at first leaned heavily toward classical, broadened to include humor and pathos as he became more confident and as he was no longer the youngest puppy in the pack.

Plushenko is the third-youngest men's world champion in figure skating history, taking the 2001 title in Vancouver four months after his 18th birthday. He has almost always been the youngest, and — thanks to his extraordinary timing and flexibility, and the power built by an early skating coach who was a weight lifter — almost always the best.

Growing up in the southern Russian city of Volgograd, he landed his first triple jump when he was just seven, and had mastered all six triples by the age of 13. By then he was living in St. Petersburg training with Yagudin, and 1994 Olympic champion Alexei Urmanov. The economic and political wreckage of the old Soviet Union had forced the closing of the Volgograd arena (it reopened as a car dealership), so Plushenko's parents put him on a train for St. Petersburg. His mother joined him later, but they were so poor that Mishin, his coach, had to pay most of their rent for a tiny apartment they shared with another family.

Mishin, one of the great wisecracking storytellers in skating, loves to describe 11-year-old Plushenko's arrival at the famed Yubileyny Sports Palace in St. Petersburg: "He looked like a cheap chicken, very green and very blue and no fat....very ecological!"

But beneath Plushenko's rawness, Mishin, like everyone else, saw a vast reservoir of uncommon gifts. Plushenko was a fearless jumper, but he also had an artistic sensibility and long elegant limbs. And there rarely has been a male skater with such flexibility. Plushenko had seen a young female skater in Volgograd do the back-wrenching Biellmann spin and wanted to try it. In a Biellmann spin, a skater reaches back and grabs the skate of an extended leg and brings it as far up in the air, behind the back, as it will go. Improper use can lead to back problems and Plushenko's mother allowed him to perform it only after he promised that he would practice the proper technique, every day. He got so good at the spin that he could do it rotating in either direction, and became the first man in the world to perform it in

Evgeny Plushenko performs his gold-medal winning routine at the 2004–05 ISU Grand Prix Finals.

competition. He made it his signature artistic move.

His other signature moves were his outrageous jumps.

By the time Plushenko arrived on the elite stage, most of the major triple- and quadruple-jump milestones had been reached, so he worked on doing the jumps higher and more dramatically, and later on refining combinations.

When he was 16, he stunned the audience at Japan's NHK Trophy competition with the world's first quad-triple-double combination (toe loop/toe loop/loop), a nine-rotation monster he would go on to land successfully more than two dozen times. In 2002, he trumped himself by turning the double loop part of the combination into a triple, for the world's first quad-triple-triple.

At the 2001 Worlds in Vancouver, he landed a four-jump string of quadruple toe loop, triple toe loop

Plushenko executing the difficult Biellmann spin at the 2006 Turin Olympics. The spin is a very rare feat in men's skating.

In his earliest years on the world stage, Plushenko was an unrefined leaper capable of bad decisions during competition. Named to the Russian team for the 1998 World Championships when Ilia Kulik withdrew after his Olympic victory, he fell on an opening quad, panicked and rewrote his entire program, racing down to the other end for an unplanned quad, which was also a failure. It was a weak field, though, and he finished third in that world debut. Two years later at Nice, he was enjoying an unbeatable season but, on the verge of winning his first Worlds, imploded in the free skate and finished fourth.

But he learned quickly and began trusting his artistic strengths to carry him when the jumps weren't quite perfect. He received his first perfect 6.0 mark when he was 16, the youngest ever for a man, and by the time the old system was mothballed after the 2003–04 season, Plushenko had amassed 75 perfect 6.0s, including the last four given out to a male competitor at the Worlds (2004, for free skating presentation).

And after a groin injury, and subsequent surgery, kept him out of the 2005 World Championships and Grand Prix final, he blew the field away at the 2006 Olympics, setting new points records in both segments of the competition and taking the gold by an unworldly 27-point margin over rising star Stéphane Lambiel.

While he stopped competing after his Olympic win to rest the knees which had been battered by thousands of powerful takeoffs and landings, Plushenko has often threatened a return to eligible skating, both to quench his competitive thirst and to boost declining Russian fortunes in the men's division.

He is a hero in Russia, largely for his spectacular track record, but also because, like Irina Slutskaya, he did not leave for greener pastures during the country's rudderless period.

"I couldn't," he explained. "Russia is home."

Elvis Stojko

Anyone who had doubted that Elvis Stojko was the toughest skater of his generation, physically and mentally, was converted during the Nagano Olympics.

In February 1998, Stojko tore the adductor muscles

and two double loops to loudly punctuate a victory which was already his.

At a gala exhibition in 2005, he landed a triple-triple-triple-double combination and then went overboard during an exhibition at the Europeans, combining two triple jumps with a string of four double jumps — a dizzying 14 successive rotations.

in his groin so badly that, for the next few weeks, he could barely walk. He was also battling a serious flu, but he hid his debilitated condition from fans and the media until after the men's free skate at the Olympic Games.

"He didn't want to whine or look like he was making excuses," explained his longtime coach Doug Leigh.

So, Stojko's ultra-disciplined mind willed his broken body through four-and-a-half excruciating minutes to win his second successive Olympic silver medal behind Ilia Kulik's sublime skate. The Canadian had somehow managed to land six triple jumps while having the full use of only one leg.

"Considering the conditions, that was the best performance I've ever done," recalls the man who radically altered skating's landscape, moving the quadruple jump from the rare to the everyday.

The intrepid display in Nagano was not the first time Stojko had ignored an injury that would have taken most athletes out of commission. In 1995, severely torn ankle ligaments forced him to withdraw in the middle of the Canadian Championships, but just two months later, despite searing pain in his ankle, he won his second global title with a muscular free skate, which included a riskily timed triple-triple combination only seconds from the end.

Few skaters have ever maximized their talent as Stojko did during his luminous, if unlikely, career. On the plus side, his short, thick body, crammed with fast-twitch muscles, gave him great speed and the power to quickly launch himself into high jumps and maintain tight rotation. But on the other hand, lacking the natural classic body lines of so many of his peers, Stojko always had to struggle to convince some judges that his kinetic "masculine" programs were just a different, not lesser, kind of artistry.

It was a battle in which the opposition never fully conceded, so Stojko had to be significantly better than the rest of the field in order to win. And he usually was. He won three world championships, matching his domestic rival Kurt Browning for most titles by a man in the 1990s, and took another two world silver medals, as well as a bronze and two fourth-place finishes. He won silver medals at the 1994 and 1998 Olympics and had judging not been so political, Stojko probably would have medaled at

Elvis Stojko skating his Merlin free skate at the 1999 World Championships in Helsinki where he placed fourth.

the 1992 Olympics too. He competed in 11 world championships, the most ever by a North American man, a constant and threatening presence that affected every competitor in the field.

Stojko, whose parents were Elvis Presley fans, was named after The King of Rock and Roll. His father enrolled his undersized seven-year-old in karate lessons to learn how to defend himself, and Stojko immediately took to the combat skills and, more enduringly, to the mental discipline and spiritual approach of the martial arts. By 16, he was a black belt. As he matured as a skater, he often incorporated martial arts moves into his programs. And when he settled upon movie themes as the perfect choreographic vehicles to counter the continued criticism of his artistic quotient, his 1994 breakthrough program was skated to the soundtrack of *Dragon: The Bruce Lee Story*.

"I want to showcase and celebrate masculine skating," he said famously. "I don't really have a feminine side."

Stojko at the 1994 Lillehammer Olympics. He placed second behind Alexei Urmanov; Stojko would again finish second at the 1998 Nagano Games.

Eventually, Stojko took up kung fu and credits its mental and spiritual rigor with helping him deal with major snubbings, such as losing a 5–4 split to Alexei Urmanov at the 1994 Olympics, partly because, as some judges admitted, they "liked his [Urmanov's] lines better." And when he was ranked fourth at the 1997 Worlds, despite a brilliant short program, he prepared for his free skate with a determined, almost toxic, focus — winning his third title in four years,

Already displaying that perfect sense of balance that would help him win championships in skating, martial arts and dirt biking, Stojko moved from Ellen Burka to Doug Leigh's Mariposa School when he was 13, where new clubmate Brian Orser was reaping world medals. As Orser had taken Vern Taylor's first triple

Axel and made it his own, so Stojko appropriated the quadruple toe loop, first landed by Browning.

Stojko performed the world's first quadruple combination, tacking a double toe loop onto the end of the monster jump at the 1991 World Championships, where he finished sixth. The next year, he was the surprise and talking point of the Albertville Olympics, as the only top male skater to deliver two clean programs in what was otherwise the most poorly skated men's Olympic competition of all time. But, ridiculously, judges doled out too many high marks early in the free skate competition, which meant, under the old 6.0 system, that there were no top marks remaining for Stojko, the last skater of the event. The only marks remaining would place him first, or seventh. So, Stojko dropped from sixth after the short program to seventh overall despite a clean, inspiring performance. A month later, though, he won his first world medal, a bronze.

In 1993, he inched up to silver behind Browning, only the second time Canadians had finished 1–2 in any discipline at the Worlds. Stojko really became a world star in 1994, finally beating Browning for the first of his seven national titles, narrowly missing the Olympic gold and winning his first world championship.

Through it all he resolutely refused to alter his style or his beliefs, despite an overt prejudice in many quarters against his body shape, his choreographic choices and even his costuming.

He loved to compete so much that he worked his way back from the 1998 injury to take a silver medal at the 2000 Worlds. He finished eighth at Salt Lake (2002), his fourth Games, retired from amateur skating, then unretired, then quickly retired again.

Stojko toured until 2006, but the adrenalin of competition was lacking and he cut his professional career short to devote time to a myriad of other eclectic interests: In 2005, he represented Canada in a second sport, taking a silver medal in the World Karate Association Amateur World Championships; in 2008 he reached into acting and singing, recording his first CD. He also began coaching some skaters in Mexico.

"I'm always the one who's done things differently," he says. "But I'm glad I did it my way. I've learned that there is drive and there is a passion. You cannot

teach talent and you cannot teach drive. And those two things together can make you a champion. You have to be obsessed to be a champion."

Four-time world champion Alexei Yagudin is all smiles after claiming gold at the 2002 Salt Lake Olympics — his only Olympic podium finish.

Alexei Yagudin

When the economy and political structure of the Soviet Union fell apart in the early 1990s, it was assumed that its assembly line of great skaters would also screech to a dead stop.

But somebody forgot to inform the Russian skaters, particularly the men.

In what at first seemed like a paradox, after the abrupt demise of its rich, state-financed athlete development system, skaters from the former Soviet Union won the next five men's Olympic championships. Viktor Petrenko, a Ukrainian raised and trained in the USSR, won the 1992 Games and World Championships representing the generic

United Federation, and the next four Olympic winners were all Russians: Alexei Urmanov, Ilia Kulik, Alexei Yagudin and Evgeny Plushenko. Prior to that, despite plenty of raw talent and training resources, Soviet men had never won an Olympic gold medal.

There are various theories for this historic, and apparently contradictory, turnaround: The training residue from the former system still carrying the skaters (certainly true in Petrenko's case); the massive potential talent pool in a gigantic frozen nation; financial deprivation acting as motivation and catalyst in a skating world that offered huge economic rewards to winners; the new freedom to emigrate to North America to train; and the influence of master coaches — Tatiana Tarasova, who relocated to the

U.S., and Alexei Mishin, who did not.

Alexei Yagudin embodied all of these elements, but the primary reasons he became Russia's first internationally dominant male skater are less complex: he is a magnificent athlete and has the strongest competitive backbone of any male skater in Russian history.

Like Elvis Stojko, Yagudin was at his best when seriously challenged: by injury, by feeling rejected by his own federation, by an intense rivalry with Plushenko.

Yagudin had originally been left off Russia's 1998 world team, despite finishing a respectable fifth at the Olympics. He was reinstated on the team just two weeks before the Worlds, but then was stricken with food poisoning. He rose to the occasion, and two weeks after his 18th birthday became the youngest men's world champion in history.

Twelve days before the 2000 Europeans, Yagudin snapped a small bone in his right hand during a training mishap. Skating with his hand in a soft cast, which can affect jumping balance, he won a silver medal. A month later, he became the only singles skater since compulsory figures had been abolished to win three straight world championships.

But it was the one world championship he didn't win in a five-year period that most endeared the spunky Yagudin to a growing legion of North American fans. Just before the 2001 Worlds, Yagudin badly injured his foot during a fitness run and was advised to skip the competition. Hobbled by severe pain, he hesitated and nearly left the ice during the qualifying round, in which he finished a distant fifth. But he persevered, landed quad-triple combinations in both the short program and free skate and pulled up to second behind Plushenko, earning standing ovations from the Vancouver crowd. A reputation that had been tarnished with his well-publicized expulsion from the 1999 post-Worlds tour for behavioral problems was fully restored.

"I wanted to prove that I'm fighter and a good skater," he said.

Despite the moral victory, the 2001 Worlds completed a pre-Olympic season in which Yagudin lost every time he faced Plushenko.

"The shock was complete," he recalled in an online Russian interview. "I performed as if I played roulette: would I be lucky or not?"

So he dedicated himself to a spartan training regime, which resulted in a near-perfect 2001–02 season during which he swept the European, Grand Prix Final, World and Olympic Championships. Throughout, Yagudin was driven by a desire to outdo Plushenko, whom he always felt was more favored and promoted by the Russian federation.

"It didn't matter if it would be for first place or sixth place, as long as he beat Plushenko," says Nikolai Morozov who assisted coach Tatiana Tarasova with Yagudin in the 2002 Olympic season. "He worked so hard and long at everything that year, every single finger movement was absolutely perfect."

At the 2002 Worlds, he received a stunning five perfect 6.0s for presentation in the short program, the most ever by a singles skater. He also became the first man since Scott Hamilton, and just the second since 1960, to win four world titles and the Olympic gold medal. And he is the only Russian man ever to hold the world and Olympic titles simultaneously.

Yet, for all his international pioneering, Yagudin never won the Russian Nationals, which stoked his suspicions about the federation's favoritism regarding the younger Plushenko.

"And the federation can only support [politically] one Russian skater," Yagudin said.

Back in 1996, Yagudin had won the World Junior Championships and in 1998 won his first major senior crown, leading Plushenko and Alexander Abt to a sweep of the European podium. At the time, Yagudin and Plushenko were clubmates, studying under Alexei Mishin, but Yagudin didn't like Mishin's controlling style and felt that the coach strongly favored Plushenko.

After winning the 1998 Worlds, Yagudin left Mishin for Tarasova, who had relocated to Connecticut. She provided a warmer atmosphere, added a softer touch to his skating and gently nurtured Yagudin's latent, but fulsome, artistry. He became that elusive "complete package" which was rare in men's skating at the turn of the 21st century.

After he won the Salt Lake Olympics in 2002, Yagudin had intended to continue his eligible career, but pain in his right hip forced him to withdraw from

Yagudin salutes the crowd as Olympic champion after completing his exhibition performance at the Salt Lake Games.

the Grand Prix circuit the next fall, and he became a headliner with Stars on Ice and, later, Ice Symphony in Russia.

In 2005, Yaguin returned to live in St. Petersburg after seven years in the U.S., and found that he was more popular in his native country than he had thought. But he never forgot how difficult it was for him as a child in the late 1980s and early 1990s when the entire nation was cast into uncertainty and he, his mother and grandmother shared a small, four-room apartment with another family.

"We were very poor," he said. "Without my family, I would have been no one. So when I was able to buy a flat for my family, I did it right away."

Proving that hard work certainly pays off — the perfect metaphor for his skating career.

FIGURES AND 6.0

They were symbols of stability and suspicion, living side by side for nearly 100 years.

One died, gradually, of old age. The other was abruptly executed.

Compulsory figures and the 6.0 scoring system were the entrenched, if often mistrusted, cornerstones of competitive figure skating well into the late 20th century. But, by the 2006 Olympics, both were museum pieces. Each demise was preceded by judging improprieties and a change in the image which big-league competitive skating wanted to project to the ticket-buying public. And in both cases, the public, through the media, had a strong influence on the changes.

COMPULSORY FIGURES

In 1990, compulsory figures were finally legislated out of existence, ostensibly so that the sport could create champions out of its best free skaters. There was an undertone, though, that the judging of figures was, at best, incomprehensible and, at worst, prearranged.

An entire generation of skaters has now grown up, and retired from competition, without ever having to trace compulsory figures in front of a panel of judges. Among skating's elders, the debate still smolders as to whether ridding the sport of the precise tracings has been, on balance, a benefit or a detriment.

It's often said in North America that by abandoning compulsories, figure skating surrendered the activity that gave the sport its very name. But figure skating is known as that only in English. In most other languages it's recognized more as artistic skating, as in the French "patinage artistique."

Patterns carved into ice, to be appreciated for their own sake, are at the very root of the sport. Early skating — on carved animal bones, and later on iron blades — was for travel, some commerce and for racing. But, possibly by the mid-17th century and certainly by the mid-18th, elite society in the British Isles and Holland began using their skates to scratch various designs onto ice.

Jamie Sale and David Pelletier are awarded a gold medal — alongside pairs gold medalists Elena Berezhnaya and Anton Sikharulidze — at the 2002 Olympics in an attempt to stem criticism over a French judging controversy.

Although the finished product was the ultimate goal, especially in North America where results tend to mean more than style, in certain self-described "refined" circles, such as the burgeoning skating clubs of England, the elegant manner in which that result was achieved was also important. This was an early signpost of the result-performance duality inherent in skating, and also of the conflict between European and North American cultural and political sensibilities, which would ride shotgun to the sport throughout most of the 20th century.

While letters, numbers, serpentine variations and geometric forms were all being traced, the most prevalent etchings were forms of the figure eight.

Before 1860 the basic three-turn (which looks like the number, and requires a change in blade edge), was the main figure being skated. In the latter part of the century, the three-turn was joined by the counter (which looks like the letter "C" sitting on top of another "C" that opens in the other direction), the rocker (which looks like a counter, but with the transition point between the two "C"s' facing the

opposite direction), and the bracket (which looks like a three-turn, except the turning point — the middle of the "three" — is rotated in the opposite direction, making it look like a parenthesis) and all their variations, as the core of compulsory figures.

There were 23 different figures skated at the first major international meet in 1882. The influence of master skater Jackson Haines, who had died seven years earlier, was still evident both in that the event was organized by the Viennese, who were most affected by the flamboyant American, and also that there was a four-minute free skate. ("Free" meaning not burdened by figures.) By 1892, when the *Internationale Eislauf Vereinigung* (now known as the International Skating Union) was formed, the number of official figures had climbed to 80.

After the first rules of competition were formalized in 1897, a skater was required to do three tracings of 12 figures (six different figures, on each foot). That portion of the competition accounted for 67 percent of the final mark, and the lowly regarded free skating accorded only one-third of the total.

Over the next 70 years that heavy weighting in favor of figures dropped only slightly, to 60 percent. But with the advent of professional ice shows and the populist appeal of Sonja Henie in the 1930s and 1940s, free skating gradually took over as the public face of the sport.

When the World Championships resumed after World War II, there were so many entrants that the competition became unwieldy and figures took far too long to judge. So while figures retained their 60 percent value, in 1948 the required number was reduced from 12 to 6.

That format continued for another 20 years, but a rising new social force was threatening the status quo. With North Americans Dick Button, Barbara Ann Scott, the Jenkins brothers and Carol Heiss dominating singles skating, North America became more interested in skating, and so did its TV

Dick Button tracing figures in world competition.

OPPOSITE: Barbara Ann Scott traces figures at the 1948 St. Moritz Olympics. Scott placed first in compulsory figures and in the free skate to win the gold.

networks. Broadcasts began in the early 1960s.

The lifeless compulsory figures, which seemed like another language, made lousy TV and weren't broadcast, except for the occasional recap. New fans then didn't understand, or accept, why the best skaters they'd seen perform their free skate routines on TV often didn't win because they'd been too far behind after the compulsory figures. That led to public scorn for the figures and some suspicion that figure skating was rigged.

In 1968 the value of figures was reduced to 50 percent of the final mark, giving free skating equal weight. Then Beatrix Schuba arrived. The pleasant Austrian was perhaps the greatest practitioner of figures in history, and by building up huge leads in the compulsories she was second at the World Championships of 1969 and 1970, won the Worlds in 1971 and 1972 and took the 1972 Olympic gold. Brilliant free skaters Janet Lynn and Karen Magnussen were always too far back to catch up, and TV interests howled loudly.

In response, the short program was introduced for the 1973 season. It had six required elements (later increased to seven, then eight) but was essentially free skating. The short program accounted for 20 percent of the final mark, while traditional free skating was reduced from 50 percent of the final score to 40 percent. The two "free" skating portions (the short program and free skating) added up to 60 percent of the final mark; figures were pared to 40 percent, and the number of figures was slashed from six to three.

Three years later, the figures lost another 10 percent, as free skating was hiked to 50 percent and in 1989, the figures' value was reduced to just 20 percent of the total mark.

In reality, the influence of figures had declined more than just mathematically, except in a few glaring cases. The figures' competition tended to serve as a hierarchal tool, seeding skaters as they worked their way up the pecking order. Only in cases of exceptional skill did skaters hit the international scene with a good result in figures, and while, with time, international skaters did tend to improve their figures and competitive nerve, it was amazing how during the final decade of figures' existence a skater often scored much better in figures the year after making a huge

smash as a free skater.

But because of that seeding process, there was always suspicion that interest groups could form judging blocs to promote one skater over another by keeping one too far behind in compulsories to catch up in free skating.

That was the accusation in the 1980 Olympics, when it appeared reigning world champion Linda Fratianne of the U.S. was the victim of some agreement between judges of the then-divided Germany in the compulsory figures. Too far behind after figures, Fratianne finished second overall to East German Anett Pötzsch, with West Germany's Dagmar Lurz third.

"I thought 1980 smelled," Frank Carroll, Fratianne's coach, said after the figures had been abolished. "As a teacher, I think it's bad, but as a coach trying to get a fair shake for his skater, I'm glad they're gone."

Finally, the ISU declared that the World Championships at Halifax in March 1990 would be the last to include compulsory figures.

The last man to skate a compulsory figure at the Worlds was David Liu, who was raised in the U.S., but represented skating lightweight Taipei (Taiwan), where he was born.

"It's very ironic, because I really, really, dislike figures," said Liu, an expressive free skater who got marks of only 2.1 to 2.6 which, with the nostalgia factor, were still probably higher than he deserved.

Two days later, the final figure overall was traced by Željka Čižmešija of what was then Yugoslavia. Tellingly, she finished fifth in compulsories, but only 18th overall.

Surprisingly — considering that figures had probably cost Donald Jackson one world championship, Toller Cranston two and Brian Orser the 1984 Olympic gold and two world titles — Canada was not in favor of the mostly European initiative to curtail figures. The U.S. also was against it.

The North Americans had massive skating infrastructures partially supported by the income derived from ice rental and teaching fees for figures, which required at least three hours of practice per day for elite skaters.

"It's a dark day for skating," said David Dore, who became vice president of the ISU, but was then the director-general of the Canadian Figure Skating Association.

Many experts felt that figures developed the proper balance, feel for the ice, poise and use of edges necessary for proper free skating techniques, especially in footwork and entry to jumps.

And two-time Olympic champion Katarina Witt, more a free skater than figures competitor, said working their way up the figures ladder bought younger skaters time to develop the mental strength to deal with the pressure of contending.

Witt and many others were worried that women's champions would be less mature, because ballistics and muscle-to-body ratio favored younger female free skaters who, without the rein of figures, could now vault to the top on the strength of their jumps. Immediately after figures were abolished, three of the next four women's Olympic champions — Oksana Baiul (16 years old in 1994), Tara Lipinski (15 in 1998) and Sarah Hughes (16 in 2002) — were the youngest since Sonja Henie. That said, 2006 women's Olympic champion Shizuka Arakawa, at 24, was also the oldest since Henie.

Even though it took 30 years, television was destined to kill figures, especially as more and more competitions were broadcast live. Already under suspicion by the general public because it is a judged sport, skating could no longer afford compulsory figures' lack of transparency.

6.0 JUDGING SYSTEM

The death of figures did not solve skating's perception problems. Not even close.

Interest in the sport increased dramatically, with the emancipation from figures adding to the three other major growth factors: the Battle of the Brians at the 1988 Olympics; the staging of three Winter Olympics within six years — Calgary (1988),

Great Britain's Jayne Torvill and Christopher Dean score perfect 6.0's for artistic impression on the Bolero at the Sarajevo Olympics in 1984.

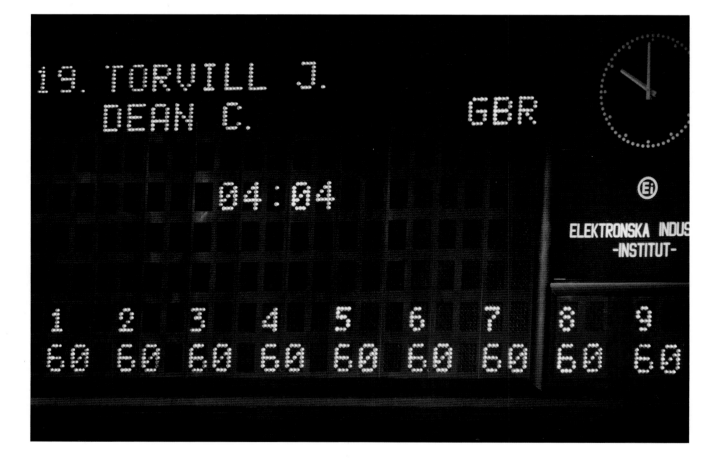

Albertville (1992), Lillehammer (1994) — and the assault on Nancy Kerrigan by associates of her national and world rival Tonya Harding in 1994.

But attention was a double-edged sword: with that unprecedented surge in interest came an increased public focus on judging irregularities, assumed and real. Fans and media new to the sport weren't going to buy into figure skating's vague explanations of questionable results.

There was a mild controversy during the 1992 Olympic men's championship, one of the most poorly skated events of all time. Emerging Elvis Stojko was technically superior to almost every skater, and was one of the few to actually make it through the free skate without falling. But instead of vaulting toward the podium, Stojko astoundingly dropped from sixth to seventh. The reality was that judges had started awarding high marks of 5.4 and 5.5 too early in the evening, and by the time Stojko, the final skater, performed, virtually all the possible marks had been taken except for those that would give him first place, or seventh.

Then, with all the media at the Lillehammer Games to watch Americans Harding and Kerrigan in 1994, Ukrainian Oksana Baiul's narrow win over Kerrigan caused a louder uproar than usual about the possibility of bloc voting.

Those suspicions were borne out after the 1998 Nagano Olympics when it was revealed that a Canadian judge had taped a Ukrainian judge telling her by phone, well before the event, exactly what the final result of the ice dancing competition would be. Somehow *both* judges were suspended and the Ukrainian made it back to a world championship judging panel before the Canadian did.

But all those situations were just the warm-up act for the main event, four years later.

A few hours after the pairs free skate at the 2002 Winter Olympics in Salt Lake City, French judge Marie-Reine Le Gougne tearfully confessed that she had been pressured by Didier Gailhaguet, head of the French federation, to place Russian pair Elena Berezhnaya and Anton Sikharulidze first. In return, she intimated, France would get Russia's vote in the ice dance competition. Le Gougne's vote gave a 5–4 split to the Russian pair over Canadians Jamie

Sale and David Pelletier, who had clearly been the better skaters. The other four votes for the Russian pair were part of a fairly predictable pattern: the Russian, Ukrainian and Polish judges voted as part of a continuation of the old eastern bloc, while the Chinese joined, arguably, because the Canadians posed a greater threat to the Chinese pair of Xue Shen and Hongbo Zhao. The ensuing furor, fanned by the massive American media, completely took over the first half of the Games, and led to the International Olympic Committee ordering the ISU to clean up its act. At the IOC's suggestion, a second medal ceremony was held with both pairs presented with gold medals.

It also accelerated, by three years at least, the ISU's plan to implement a radical new scoring system. By the 2004 World Championships in Dortmund, Germany, the 6.0 scoring standard had been buried, mourned by a tight group of loyalists but likely to be virtually forgotten within a half-generation of skaters.

When international competitive rules were first formalized by the ISU in 1897, the scoring ceiling was not 6.0, but 5.0. Reasons for that choice are unclear, but eminent skating historian Benjamin Wright suggests it might have been a number that continental Europeans could understand and accept. (It is half the metric base of 10.) Five was also the minimum number of judges required for a major competition.

In 1901, the scale of marks was extended from 0 to an upper limit of 6, with the highest reserved for "faultless" performances. Wright explains that 6.0 was a simple multiple of the three times each figure was traced. The decimal points allowed for minor deductions to be made for each mistake.

From the beginning, judges were identified and connected to the marks they posted. Originally, the arbiters were appointed not by country but by skating clubs, which led to one of the earliest major marking controversies and the ensuing rule changes.

At the 1927 World Championships in Oslo, the five-judge panel consisted of one German, one Austrian and three Norwegians (all from different clubs). With the King and Queen of Norway in attendance at Frogner Stadium, all the Norwegians voted for 14-year-old Norwegian Sonja Henie over five-time defending world champion Herma Jaross-

THE BIG SHOCK

UNFORTUNATELY, for Nancy Kerrigan, who came within a tie-breaker of winning an Olympic championship, her name will always be associated with a far more nefarious one — Tonya Harding. The two were involved in the most shocking incident in figure skating history, one that catapulted the sport into an unsought limelight and showed just how ruthless competitive skating can be.

"We will be talking about it for as long as we live," said Claire Ferguson, then president of the United States Figure Skating Association.

Kerrigan (the more artistic and cut from classic skating cloth) and Harding (the more athletic and a rough-edged outsider) were relatively equal rivals for the 1994 U.S. women's title and, by extension, the World and Olympic Championships. Each had won a silver medal at the Worlds and each had won a national championship.

Just after a practice at Detroit's Cobo Hall during the 1994 Nationals and Olympic trials, Kerrigan was viciously struck across the right knee with a pipe by an unknown assailant, badly injuring the knee. Harding won the National title in Kerrigan's absence, but six days later three of Harding's associates, Derrick Smith, Shawn Eckardt and Shane Stant were arrested by the FBI and charged in connection with the assault. Five days after that, Harding's then-husband Jeff Gillooly was charged with hiring the attacker (Stant wielded the pipe) and later admitted Harding knew of the plans.

The sordid affair attracted worldwide attention and triggered a media feeding frenzy. Harding sued to prevent the United States Figure Skating Association from barring her from the 1994 Olympics in Lillehammer and was allowed to compete in return for dropping the suit. The first time the two American women stepped on the Olympic practice ice together, so many cameras flashed it looked like lightning had struck the arena.

Kerrigan, who had undergone intense physical therapy just to reach Lillehammer, admirably shook off the serious psychological and emotional repercussions to win the short program, but narrowly lost the free skate — and gold — to Oksana Baiul's delicate performance. She did, however, sign a $10 million contract with Disney and went on to a solid professional career.

Harding flubbed the Olympic short program, famously requested a re-skate in the long program after she broke a skate lace and finished eighth overall; was stripped of her 1994 U.S. title; was banned from amateur skating for life; and avoided prison through plea bargaining.

"It was almost good against evil, wasn't it?" marveled Hall of Famer Christopher Dean. Millions of people tuned in to skating out of prurient interest, but a large number of them then discovered the more constant beauties of the sport and stuck with it.

"It is very sad to think that to make skating popular," lamented famed coach Carlo Fassi, "we needed some skater to beat up another."

Szabo of Austria. The 3–2 decision gave Henie, who had been second the year before, her first of 10 consecutive world titles.

This was not the only time Henie won when many thought she shouldn't have, but it was the last time under those circumstances. A new rule, which still exists today, was instituted whereby no country is permitted to have more than one judge in a discipline.

Didier Gailhaguet, head of the French skating federation, defends French judge Marie-Reine Le Gougne after accusations of voting impropriety during the Olympic pairs final.

Disputes, controversy and outright scandal have plagued figure skating judging for more than a century.

Because there were few formal guidelines, except certain ranges suggested for "good," "average" and "poor," and few mandatory deductions for mistakes, judging naturally became very subjective. That was particularly true in free skating. There were two sets of marks, with each having several different names over the years, but generally they were separated into "technical" and "artistry."

Even with numerous, well-intentioned attempts at "quality control" through increasingly specific guidelines, widespread training to help the poorer skating nations, regular seminars and testing, and oversight and event-review by a referee and assistant referee, judging panels had a huge amount of latitude. In the artistic (or presentation) mark, particularly, a judge could almost always successfully offer a defense, which could be essentially reduced to, "I liked that one better."

More often than not, the right skaters won the right medals, but there were many dubious decisions throughout the 20th century, on the podium and lower down in the rankings.

There were many reasons for bad judging, including individual incompetence, but usually it fell under some form of national bias. The practice of countries appointing judges for international competitions made the judges beholden as much to their national associations as to the ISU, for which they were allegedly working during a competition. There have been repeated calls for the ISU to employ the judges independently. But, so far, it has been deemed too expensive and, more so, deeply offensive to the national associations which pay for the recruitment and training of judges.

Long before Le Gougne made "French Figure Skating Judge" a common pejorative in North America, a humorous catchphrase for praise or criticism not related to what actually happened was "And a five-point-nine (or, four-point-eight) from the East German judge." The common belief — much of it eventually borne out — was that the Soviet Union (later Russia) had power over its satellites and allies to command certain desired results. Austria was said to have had similar skating political power right through the 1950s, but in the 1970s and 1980s, that influence had swung to the USSR because of its political and economic control of Iron Curtain countries.

That's not to suggest that such luminaries as Irina Rodnina, the Protopopovs and Liudmila Pakhomova and Alexandr Gorshkov were not true champions. But there were so many other results that cast a shadow over all of figure skating.

Sergei Chetverukhin's silver medal in the 1973 Worlds was long thought to be a trade-off with the East Germans in exchange for Soviet support of East Germans Manuela Gross and Uwe Kagelmann for the pairs bronze.

With his gold medal Olympics only a few weeks away, Britain's John Curry was advised by his coach Carlo Fassi to withdraw from the 1976 European Championships, because five of the nine judges were from Iron Curtain countries. It was expected that they would all vote for the Soviet Union's Vladimir Kovalev, and Curry would have the psychological and political disadvantage of heading into the Olympics off a loss. But Curry skated, was clearly the best, and a Czech judge broke ranks to give him the victory. That judge was said to have suffered sanctions within his own country.

It got so bad that by 1978, at the suggestion of technical chairperson Sonia Bianchetti, the Soviet Union was barred from providing international judges for an entire season.

Canadians and Americans, among many others, also were convicted and suspended for national bias. In fact, the biennial North American Championships were finally killed in 1971 because in 1954 the event was forced to go from an even number of judges from Canada and the United States to an odd number of judges (dictated by ISU rules), the extra judge being from the host country. There were regular accusations of national bias, and many skaters refused to take part.

The gradual devaluation of compulsory figures was a forward step in limiting the opportunities judges had to influence results and that skaters had to run away with a victory, as was the introduction in 1973 of the short (sometimes called technical) program, and its mandatory deductions for mistakes or omissions. In the early 1980s, another radical change was instituted so that a skater could not run

away with the competition early. Instead of points results carrying over from segment to segment, only a skater's finishing order counted. So even if a skater won figures, or the short program or the free skate by a country mile, he or she would receive only a "1" and the runner-up a "2," the third place finisher a "3" and so on, the same as if the victory had been by only the narrowest of margins. The finishing ordinal would be multiplied by the value of that particular segment and factored into the final score.

That weighting system stood until the 2003–04 season and helped many skaters remain in contention through early missteps. For example, Brian Orser climbed from a seventh-place finish in compulsory figures to the 1984 Olympic silver medal by winning the short and free skate programs. But while it meant some vertical movement, the system often meant a skater who'd had a bad segment couldn't catch the leader, as results were based on relative standings: a skater too far behind the leader couldn't catch the leader without other skaters also beating the leader.

Meanwhile, the pool of talent was deepening, particularly in the men's and ice dance disciplines. So the 6.0 grading system was proving inadequate, especially since judges were reluctant to give marks below 5.0 because of adverse crowd reaction. There simply weren't enough positions available without slotting skaters into a certain "range" where they might finish. Any surprises, positive or negative, threw the whole grid into disarray — even when the marking was totally honest. That happened to Elvis Stojko in the 1992 Olympics when there was simply no "room" left for him near the top, when he skated last in the free skate.

One suggestion to alleviate this problem was to add a second decimal place (for example, 5.95) to create a far wider range of marks, but that idea was never given a shot after the mega-decibel resonance of the 2002 pairs scandal.

ISU president Ottavio Cinquanta, whose competitive background was speed skating with its time trials and finish lines, had already commissioned research into systems that would lessen figure skating's subjectivity of judging. Shepherded by Canada's Ted Barton, the International Judging System (IJS) was developed and tested in time for approval at the 2004

ISU congress and instituted for all ISU championships the next season.

To the sport's everlasting shame, skating officials admit that a critical component of the new system is that the judges will no longer be linked to the scores they give, so that their own national federations will not be able to influence them. For the same reason, a computer randomly selects a predetermined number of judges whose scores will "count."

The new system is based on cumulative points, and almost every second of a skater's program is marked for its technical content. Technical specialists identify each element and its level of difficulty, as it is performed by the skater. Judges immediately mark the quality of the element on a scale of −3 to +3, which is added to the base value of the element. There is video replay available, should judges require it.

As well as the technical elements, judges are required to assess the overall presentation, similar to the old "artistic" mark, using five components: skating skills; footwork and movement; performance; composition; and interpretation.

There are definitions of "well-balanced" programs, which include restrictions on the number of jumps, spins and footwork sequences.

All of the scores are added up, and points in the short program carry over to the free skate so, in theory, and usually in practice, a skater is able to overcome a poor start with a great finish. There are several examples of skaters rising from as low as ninth after the short program to win an event.

The idea is to strip judges of the need for, and power of, comparing skaters. In theory, judges are only marking what they see, precisely when they see it.

Under the old system, scoring was comparative, so a 6.0 in one event might not mean the same as it did in another. Under the IJS, a mark given for an element at one competition should be the same for the element performed at the same level in another competition.

This has led to the beginning of statistics and records which approach those of other sports. And it

has reduced the number of repeat winners from event to event.

There are many complaints about the new system, one of which is that anonymity of judges breeds suspicion that the sport is still not transparent, even if there are internal checks and balances. Its unfamiliar points totals are unwieldy and foreign to generations raised on 6.0. There is also still room for subjectivity — and bias — in the marks given for components in the program, although random selection does neutralize this somewhat. But with random selection, an event could have one set of results when certain judges are chosen, and another set had other judges been selected, suggesting a lottery effect.

One of the biggest objections is that because so many elements, at a high level, are required, many programs are starting to look the same. And because certain elements — such as quadruple and potentially quintuple jumps — aren't scored high enough, skaters will stop pushing the technical envelope. That was a big concern in the men's world championships of both 2008 and 2009, when neither the gold nor silver medalists even attempted a quad. Additionally, with programs jammed to the hilt with points-producing elements and movements, there is little room left for most skaters to highlight their personal calling card, as Michelle Kwan did, for example, with the extended time she accorded to her famous spiral.

All scoring systems are designed to produce the kind of athlete that organizers of that particular sport want to see thrive. Through the 1980s and 1990s, rules were adopted to increase athleticism, then artistry, then athleticism again. In the 21st century, the ISU has decided it wants all-round ability. And it wants to make sure that the best skater on a particular night, and that night only, wins.

That may actually reduce the number of "legends" that skating produces, because legendary status often results from pushing the technical envelope, or from having a distinct style or a few signature moves, or from dominating competition after competition. In short, separating oneself from everyone else.

But perhaps the new scoring system will mean only that skating legends will be created mostly in the same way they are in many other sports: by the enormity of their statistical records.

Ted Barton explains the International Judging System (IJS), an anonymous, computer-based cumulative points system, to reporters before the start of skating events at the Turin Olympics.

THE WOMEN

Although the first few formal major championships were intended for men only, figure skating has come to be regarded as a "women's sport." After Madge Syers challenged the male figure skating establishment by entering the 1902 World Championships and winning the silver medal (which led to the creation of a separate women's division in 1906) figure skating eventually became the sport which has provided the greatest, and most far-ranging opportunities for female athletes: as competitors, coaches and choreographers; as officials; as high-wage performers; as national association executives; as international power brokers.

And as legends.

It was a female competitor, Lily Kronberger, who began holding musical accompaniment, and therefore choreography, to a higher standard during the early 20th century. That evolution continues to this day. And, arguably, Sonja Henie is the most important figure in modern skating history. By shortening the skating costume and changing the color of her skates, Henie began emphasizing "lines," as well as the human female body form and the athleticism and footwork that was obscured by traditional long skirts. It was a revolution in the sport. Her arrival in North America in 1930 launched a continent's love affair with skating and created the popular template of the "ideal" women's champion. At least three North American women — Barbara Ann Scott, Peggy Fleming and Dorothy Hamill — have since transcended figure skating to become, and remain, icons of North American pop culture.

While the average fan may think primarily of the grace and beauty of women's skating, the "ladies" division has also produced tough competitors, like Nancy Kerrigan, Irina Slutskaya, and, perhaps the greatest mentally-tough competitor in the sport's history, Katarina Witt. And the current revolutions — the biggest technical advances in modern skating — being made by skaters such as Mao Asada and Miki Ando, began decades earlier with jumping pioneers like Petra Burka and Midori Ito.

All of these women have left skating a legacy to be proud of.

Carol Heiss, who in four years' time would be known as The First Lady of American Figure Skating after winning the Squaw Valley Olympics, leaps in Paris in 1956.

PIONEERS AND TRENDSETTERS — *Skaters through to the 1950s*

Tenley Albright

Not only did Tenley Albright set towering standards for herself while blazing a path for other American women, she did it in two demanding disciplines: figure skating and medicine. Her oft-quoted mantra about both specialties is "If you don't fall down, you aren't trying hard enough," and it's clear she has lived her life according to that principle.

Albright was the first female skater from the U.S.A. to win a world championship (1953), and the first American woman to win an Olympic title in figure skating (1956).

And when, in 1957, she ignored the siren call of professional skating to enter Harvard Medical School, she was one of just five women in a class of 135. She had become interested in medicine at a young age (Albright's father, Hollis, was a prominent Boston surgeon), but she had assumed she would be a pediatric physician, not the celebrated surgeon and researcher she eventually became.

She got her first pair of skates from her grandmother when she was nine. Her father built a backyard rink for Albright and her brother Niles, who became an accomplished speed skater. Although at the time she considered skating a diversion to her studies, she showed some talent and loved the sense of freedom on skates.

"What attracted me to skating was that I wanted to fly," she told *Sports Illustrated*. "I broke umbrellas trying to jump off the roof when I was little."

When Albright was 10, her coach Maribel Vinson gave her and other young skating students a strong lecture about not shirking on compulsory figures, and Albright took this advice to heart. She still loved free skating more than the arduous tracings but came to regard figures as a fascinating challenge, and she excelled at them.

But when she was 11, Albright was hospitalized with a frightening attack of non-paralytic poliomyelitis, and lost the use of her legs, back and neck. Some doctors thought she might never walk again, but after a few weeks she began moving her toes — and her recovery began.

Doctors urged her to return to skating. It was something familiar from her pre-polio life, and would also help her regain her strength. Albright recalls hanging onto the boards for support and feeling that the rink seemed so big after the confining hospital room.

"Maybe when I was diagnosed with polio, getting through that, being one of the lucky ones who did get through it, was what changed it [life] for me and made me appreciate things," Albright recalled many years later.

Stunningly, just four months after being released from hospital in 1946, Albright won her first sectional skating championship. When she was 13, she won the national novice championship and, in 1950, she won the junior crown, prompting a member of the judging panel to say of her jumps, "She looks like a colt let out to pasture on the first day of spring, kicking up his heels for joy."

Tall and leggy, Albright carried the graceful moves of dancing onto the ice and enhanced them with power and speed. She insisted on designing her own programs, but given her reserved and studious nature, sometimes she had to be reminded to smile more when she was competing.

"As a pupil she was serious, receptive and diligent, and displayed enormous powers of concentration," Vinson once wrote.

In 1951, Albright finished second to Sonya Klopfer at the U.S. Senior Nationals to qualify for her first world championships, where she finished sixth. In 1952, she won the U.S. title and, although not predicted to medal, finished second to Britain's Jeannette Altwegg at the Winter Olympics in Oslo. It was the highest Olympic skating finish by an American woman since Beatrix Loughran who had won silver in 1924.

Tenley Albright in warm-up at the 1956 Olympics in Cortina d'Ampezzo, Italy. Note the bandages covering a nasty training-session gash.

Albright was forced to skip the 1952 world championships with a bronchial infection, but in 1953 she made history at Davos, Switzerland, by beating Germany's Gundi Busch to become, at age 17, the first women's world champion from the U.S.A.

At the 1954 Worlds, she led Busch by 21.8 points after compulsory figures, but inexplicably fell on an Axel-double loop combination and could not recover, dropping her to second place.

"I had to go off by myself and do that jump again and again to prove I could do it without falling," the determined Albright told reporters.

Albright beat her emerging American rival Carol Heiss for the 1955 title to become the first woman ever to lose a world championship and then reclaim it, making her the favorite for the 1956 Olympics.

Two weeks before those Games, taking place in Cortina, Italy, Albright fell when she hit a rut during practice in Europe. Her left skate sliced into her right ankle and scraped her bone. Her father arrived two days later, patched up the injury and took charge of her recovery, but it was only the day before the competition that she could confidently land all her jumps. She went on to win first place marks from 10 of the 11 judges

Albright chats with soldiers at the Cortina d'Ampezzo Games where she would later become the first American woman to win Olympic skating gold.

and the first Olympic gold medal in figure skating by an American woman.

About 90 seconds from the end of her program, the Italian audience began to sing along to her music, "Barcarolle" from *The Tales of Hoffman.*

"Their voices just thrilled me," she told reporters. "Chills were going up and down my spine. I forgot about the injury and just skated."

After winning Olympic gold, Albright finished second to Heiss at the ensuing World Championships, but won the year's rubber match with a victory at the U.S. Nationals.

Through it all, Albright was preparing for medical school. She had taken a semester off her pre-med studies in the fall of 1955, but had already made up the time at summer school.

For most of her championship years, Albright got up at 4 a.m. to hit the ice for several hours, spend a full day in classes at Radcliffe College and then return to the ice for a daily total of seven hours of training. She could be seen doing homework and studying while waiting to skate at her competitions.

Although she had an offer to skate professionally with the Ice Capades, Albright retired in January of 1957 when she was accepted into Harvard Medical School.

During the following years, Dr. Tenley Albright's many medical interests included speeding up the early detection of diseases, cancer and cholesterol research, fundraising for human-genome research and a posting with the World Health Organization to work on initiatives in the eradication of polio.

"Again and again I am reminded," she said in an insightful interview, "that we can do more than we think we can do."

Carol Heiss

Had American television discovered figure skating near the beginning of Carol Heiss' extraordinary championship run, rather than near the end, she would have dwarfed the description "superstar."

As it was, in 1955 she became the first woman athlete ever featured on the cover of *Sports Illustrated,*

Carol Heiss and her sister, Nancy, use a measuring device called a scribe to ensure Carol's figures are spot-on at a New York City rink in 1955.

in 1960 she was celebrated with a Broadway ticker-tape parade in her native New York City after winning the Squaw Valley Olympics, and in 1976 was inducted as a charter member of the World Figure Skating Hall of Fame on the same day as her husband, Hayes Alan Jenkins, and brother-in-law, David Jenkins.

Although Heiss was the second American woman (after Tenley Albright) to win the world championship and the Olympics, she was American skating's "first" lady: the first American woman to win a world championship on American ice; the first to win a Winter Olympics in the United States; the first to win back-to-back Worlds; the first to win five world titles; and the first woman to master the double Axel.

It was the latter that Heiss calls her greatest impact

on the sport. Well into the 1980s, the double Axel remained a treacherous jump for most women, but Heiss began landing hers with regularity in 1955, when she was just 15 years old.

"It took me two years to get it down," Heiss recalls. "Before that it was cheated [not fully rotated], and so was Tenley's. But I felt that to beat Tenley, I needed it."

After finishing second at four straight U.S. Nationals, the 1955 Worlds and the 1956 Olympics, Heiss finally defeated Albright at the 1956 Worlds, largely because she landed two double Axels. And she did them just seconds from the end of her program, rendering the then-rare jump immeasurably more difficult.

Heiss' natural athleticism was evident early. She began skating at the age of four and started taking lessons from coach Pierre Brunet in New York when she was just seven. Two years later, she won a speed skating competition at Madison Square Garden in which she wore figure skates and her older opposition wore the more appropriate speed skates.

She was renowned for her ability to jump in both directions. A natural counter-clockwise spinner and clockwise jumper, Heiss took lessons from another coach in Brunet's absence one summer and he insisted that she practice jumping counter-clockwise.

"I got all the way up to double flip," Heiss says. "When Pierre came back, he said I should stop doing them, and tears welled up in my eyes because I thought I'd just wasted a summer."

So, instead, Brunet made the versatility her signature move. She'd do one single Axel in each direction going down the ice, and do the same thing on a return pass, igniting the audience.

"I was always described as a happy athletic skater, with a lot of energy," she says. "I was always smiling."

Heiss won the 1951 U.S. novice title and was junior champion in 1952. In 1953, at the age of 13, she finished second to Albright at the Senior Nationals, qualifying for her first Worlds, where she debuted in fourth place. Two years later, she was second at the Worlds, and lost the Nationals to Albright a few weeks later. But after that, Heiss never lost another event.

"Carol was extremely competent in figures, very consistent," recalls Hayes Alan Jenkins, the 1956 Olympic champion who became Heiss' husband

two months after she won the 1960 Olympics. "And as a free skater, she had tremendous vitality and exuberance on the ice. She combined athleticism with being very effervescent."

Heiss was offered $75,000 — eight times what her father was making — to headline the Ice Capades in 1956. "But my mother was dying of cancer, and I wanted to stay on and win the Olympics." So she extended her world championship streak, with victories at Colorado Springs in 1957 and 1959, Paris in 1958 and Vancouver in 1960, and won all nine judges with a dominant Olympic performance at Squaw Valley. Until Michelle Kwan matched her record in 2003, Heiss was the only American woman to win five world titles. It's the second-highest total of all time behind Sonja Henie's unreachable 10.

"Stepping down from the podium in Squaw Valley, I realized how wonderful it is to have a dream, and then have that dream come true," she said.

This time, she was offered more than $100,000 to go on tour, but turned it down because she was about to get married and wanted to start a family. She got the same fee, with less time commitment, from the movie *Snow White and the Three Stooges*, in which she played the lead role. That led to other movie offers, "but I knew that was a whole new full career and I'd just finished with a full career in skating."

She and Jenkins moved to Akron, Ohio, raised three children and in 1978 she returned to the sport as a coach, eventually guiding the careers of, among others, world competitors Tim Goebel, Tonia Kwiatkowski and Miki Ando.

Heiss, husband Hayes Jenkins and brother-in-law David Jenkins combined to win 12 world championships, plus three Olympic gold medals, a silver and a bronze. "When we get together, we don't dwell on it, but it's fun. We never take it for granted. It's been big part of our lives, but not our whole lives."

Although she should be even more of an icon than she is, Heiss is more celebrated than either of the Jenkins' boys, which, she agrees, reflects the general

Heiss has legendary coach (and former skater) Pierre Brunet check her edges as she practices at the Squaw Valley Olympic facilities in preparation for the Games.

American attitude toward figure skating.

"I think the women [figure skaters] in the U.S. do get much more publicity than the men," she says. "And it embodies everything that the general public likes women to be: you can be mentally tough and still you can be graceful, feminine, maybe a bit fragile. There are so many male sports, and this is a place where women really shine.

"Women needed another sport."

And Heiss was instrumental in giving them one.

Sonja Henie

Right from that rainy afternoon in 1924, figure skating insiders must have suspected that their sport would never be the same again.

Sonja Henie had arrived, and apart from Jackson Haines, nobody before or since has influenced figure skating as permanently as the petite Norwegian.

Henie, from a wealthy, athletic family, was just 11 years old, but had already won two Norwegian championships when she arrived in Chamonix, France, in late January 1924 for the first Winter Olympics.

The weather had turned rainy, and the main outdoor rink was rendered useless. So every Olympic athlete competing on ice — figure skaters, hockey players, speed skaters — jammed onto a small curling rink battling for practice space. Henie barged through the mob of bigger, older athletes and immediately launched herself into a jump, then a sit-spin, and nobody could ignore her.

That moment was a fitting metaphor for a striking career which, in its entirety, validated women's skating as an Olympic sport, ignited massive skating interest across the New World, created the American perception of the "ideal" female champion, advanced the evolution of choreography, stimulated the era of touring shows and provided hard evidence that figure skating had the capacity to become the sport which empowered women, financially and societally.

Henie was the figure skater who first delivered the sport to the masses, somewhat of a paradox, given

that she was an aristocrat and prone to aloofness.

From her early childhood, she wanted to be an actress and after a extraordinary competitive career, capturing a record three Olympic titles and 10 world championships, Henie captured Hollywood, eventually starring in 15 films.

Those movies popularized figure skating across North America more than any gold medals could have, and the success of the films attracted larger audiences to her lavish skating tour, Sonja Henie's Hollywood Ice Revue.

Henie was a powerful, natural athlete with a muscular build. As a child, she excelled at equestrian sports and running, and became the third-ranked tennis player in Norway. Her parents each came from wealthy families, and her father, Wilhelm, a champion cyclist, had established a lucrative business as a furrier. He and his wife Selma began devoting most of their time to their daughter's career when Sonja was just nine, and the Norwegian junior champion.

Henie studied ballet and was smitten with the great ballerina Anna Pavlova after seeing her perform. The ballet influence on her skating was obvious in her spins and body movements and, most radically, in the flowing connecting steps she began introducing at the 1928 Olympics, planting the seeds of true choreography in the sport.

At the 1924 Winter Olympics at Chamonix, Henie finished eighth and last, trailing champion Herma Szabo from Austria by a whopping 95 points. One American correspondent wrote that Henie "executed her sitting and standing spins as well as the best" and praised her spread eagle, but complained about her weak connecting steps.

Just two years later she returned to the international stage, two months short of her 14th birthday, and finished second to Szabo at the World Championships. The next year, at the Worlds, she defeated Szabo, the win slightly tainted since three of the five judges were Norwegian. With her title, Henie established a record as the youngest female to win the world championship, a record that would stand for 70 years until Tara Lipinski, also 15 but a few weeks younger, won the 1997 Worlds.

Because she was a girl among women, Henie was permitted to wear mid-thigh-length skirts rather than

Sonja Henie at the 1928 St. Moritz Olympics; her first of three Olympic gold medals.

the heavy and rather clumsy skirts of the era. In the interest of modesty, the other women were sacrificing freedom of movement while Henie, suffering no such restrictions, could perform far more athletic elements.

Henie also moved away from the traditional black to beige skates which, combined with the beige bloomers she wore under her skirt, extended the lines of her legs. When others began to wear beige, she switched to white.

And instead of graduating to longer outfits as she matured, Henie went in the opposite direction, making them shorter. By 1927, her mother was designing her outfits to be closer-fitting through the torso, and Henie virtually defined the women's skating skirt. Social historian Ellyn Kestnbaum argues in her study *Culture on Ice: Figure Skating & Cultural Meaning* that, with the shorter and form-fitting outfits, Henie single-handedly made the female body more visible than the male for the first time in skating history. This mode of fashion continues to this day and distinguishes skating from all other sports.

In her second Olympics (St. Moritz, 1928), Henie captured her first gold, and brought balletic movements to the connecting steps, a revolutionary development which would expand over time, and which earned her the nickname "Pavlova of the Ice."

In 1930 Henie made the trans-Atlantic crossing that proved as history-altering as the trip Jackson Haines had made in the other direction 71 years earlier.

That year the World Championships were held in New York, the first time they'd left Europe. Already a star, the 17-year-old Henie arrived in the media and entertainment capital of the U.S. five weeks before the Worlds. In early January, she performed in a sold-out benefit carnival at Madison Square Garden with men's champion Willie Böckl and a number of leading North American skaters. She wore a costume studded with diamonds and gold, and America instantly fell in love.

"It befitted a Norwegian Princess," the *New York Times* wrote.

After conquering the U.S. in 1930, Henie was

Henie, Cesar Romero and Don Ameche (crouching) star in *Happy Landing*, in 1938, Henie's third Hollywood film.

back again two years later to win gold at the Lake Placid Olympics and the Montreal Worlds, further cementing her reputation in North America.

She went on to win her last Olympic gold at the 1936 Games at Garmisch-Partenkirken in Germany. In those Games, she was the final of the 23 competitors and skated dramatically under spotlights, a practice later outlawed in amateur competition. After the Games, she accepted Adolf Hitler's invitation to lunch which, combined with a Nazi salute she had given to the German chancellor two years earlier, fuelled suspicion in her home country that Henie was a Nazi sympathizer.

When she retired after the 1936 season, Henie had won three Olympic championships, a record matched only by Gillis Grafström and pairs skater Irina Rodnina, and 10 straight Worlds, twice as many as any other women's singles skater, and the only such uninterrupted string, in any discipline.

When her amateur career ended, Henie and her

father headed to California, rented a rink and staged a show, attended by such celebrities as Ginger Rogers, Bette Davis, Gary Cooper and John Barrymore. That heightened her star status, and the Henies eventually persuaded producer Darryl F. Zanuck to give her a small part, and later to make elaborately-scened movies around her and her skating talent. Additionally, Chicago impresario Arthur Wirtz mounted the touring shows that would inspire the growth of other spectacular skating touring productions and trigger a massive North American skating boom. Her peers often saw her as self-centered, but she remained a national icon in the U.S., her name becoming almost synonymous with skating.

Henie retired from touring in 1960, and soon thereafter was diagnosed with leukemia, which took her life in 1969.

The sport she left behind had changed dramatically from the sport she started in: more women were involved in skating, and more and more, younger women were taking control; professional touring shows had gained star power and legitimacy, and Americans had come to view the women's champion as the Ice Princess.

No one has ever had a greater impact on the sport.

Lily Kronberger

Jackson Haines, the father of modern figure skating, would have been proud.

At the 1911 World Figure Skating Championships in Vienna, the city where Haines had popularized the International Style, Lily Kronberger amplified one of the most important components of his revolution — the music.

At just 20, Kronberger was already a three-time world champion, succeeding inaugural title-holder Madge Syers from England, in a division that was still searching for acceptance — and competitors.

Kronberger, from a wealthy and aristocratic Budapest family, arrived in Vienna with a small, but polished and skilled, brass band which set up at rinkside to perform "Pas des Patineurs," the accompanying music to her free skate program.

She explained that she had wearied of her skating being framed by the "indifferent and under-rehearsed musicians" that organizers usually hired for competitions.

This audacious and expensive action captivated the music-centric Viennese, who also appreciated Kronberger's gesture of providing the band's services to the runner-up, fellow Hungarian Opika von Horváth. As a result, publicly chastised skating officials began making sure that major events were staffed by trained musicians who had time to practice with every competitor.

Kronberger was a colorful figure, arguably the first female star in figure skating, who spent large sums on her lavish, highly colored, long-skirted costumes.

But providing her own band wasn't just a display of wealth. Primarily, it addressed Kronberger's concern that skating wasn't maximizing its artistic possibilities.

Since Haines had introduced the concept a half-century earlier, music had become more and more important to competitive skating, but the evolution had been slow and music was still being used more as a pleasant backdrop to free skating, rather than as an integral part of the program.

Kronberger was the first competitive skater to recognize that choosing appropriate music, and then connecting to it physically and emotionally, would enhance the impact of the program. And, because the proper interpretation of music can help even an outsider grasp what's happening on the ice, the sport would become more attractive to a broader audience.

"It is necessary to first hear the music internally and then interpret," she said, and coaches have been preaching various forms of that mantra since then.

That symbiotic link between music and skater has become such a critical attribute of modern skating that it's easy to forget that the link was rarely made before Kronberger and, in later years, Karl Schäfer.

Kronberger had been on the scene since the inaugural women's world championships in 1906. In the first two championships, she finished third behind Syers and silver medalist Jenny Herz of Austria.

With Syers retiring after winning the 1908 Olympics (in which neither Kronberger nor Herz competed), Kronberger won her first world championship title later that season in Hungary.

Kronberger was a splendid skater, but faced few opponents. Runner-up Elsa Rendschmidt from

Germany was the only other skater in the field at the 1908 Worlds. The next year, at the 1909 Worlds, not even Rendschmidt was present in Kronberger's hometown of Budapest, and Kronberger was the sole competitor. In 1910 in Davos, it was just she and Rendschmidt again.

Interest began picking up in 1911, with three women entrants at the Worlds, which were Kronberger's last. With no opponents left to defeat, no figure skating scheduled for the 1912 Summer Olympics, and the concept of a European women's championship still nearly two decades away, Kronberger stepped away from international competition.

After four world championships fellow Hungarian Opika von Horváth succeeded Kronberger, and their combined seven world titles are the only seven World gold medals Hungary has ever won in singles figure skating.

Barbara Ann Scott

It was eerily appropriate that Barbara Ann Scott received her Olympic gold medal during a driving snowstorm, just before a hockey game. For nothing captures the essence of Canada like snow, hockey and the woman who, in 1948, was referred to as "Canada's Sweetheart." She enchanted her country like no athlete before or since.

Although Canada has since won two other Olympic skating championships, and 24 other world championships, Scott remains the uncontested symbol of Canadian figure skating. She was first, and she has lasted.

In the late 1940s, Canada, like the rest of the world, was mired in post-war doldrums, when a superb young athlete from Ottawa began receiving front page headlines in a sport that had usually been limited to the society pages.

Scott attracted attention as early as 1940, when she won the Canadian junior title at the age of 11. The previous year, she had become the youngest

person to successfully pass all of Canada's basic school figures tests.

At the age of nine she began training seven hours a day, regular school having been replaced by a tutor. She mastered compulsory figures, likening them to the finger exercises she did on the piano and estimated that she skated 11 miles of figures per day during practice. She was an elegant free skater with rapid spins, and she became the first woman to land a double Lutz in competition (at the age of 13). At 15 she won her first of four Canadian senior titles and in 1946, at 18, she became the youngest-ever winner of the North American Championships, then considered a premier competition. There had never been anything in Canadian sport like the 13 months from early 1947 to early 1948, when Scott conquered two continents and made figure skating a national passion that still burns. In today's skating jargon she would be "The Whole Package."

When the European and World Championships resumed in 1947 after a seven-year hiatus because of World War II, 18-year-old Scott — with the help of funds raised by family and friends in Ottawa — crossed the Atlantic and won both titles. The Worlds were held outdoors in Stockholm on an ice surface turned rock hard by the 20 degree (Fahrenheit) temperatures, and although Scott had rarely competed outdoors, she had developed the focus and iron will to prevail both over the conditions and 18 other competitors.

It was the first time that a World or European title, in any discipline, had been won by a skater from North America, and when the news was telegraphed home to Canada, the country went wild. Barbara Ann Scott became a household name and, she complained at times, an Ottawa tourism attraction.

The City of Ottawa celebrated Scott's triumph with a parade and wanted to present her with a new yellow Buick to recognize the ground-breaking championship. But International Olympic Committee chairman Avery Brundage warned Scott that she would forfeit her Olympic eligibility if she accepted, so she turned the gift down, and Brundage has remained an ogre in Canadian sports history ever since.

The 1947 hysteria for Scott paled beside the reaction Canadians would have in 1948, when Scott defended

Barbara Ann Scott is surrounded by photographers during a training session prior to the 1948 St. Moritz Olympics.

Canada's Sweetheart, Scott, bundled up for an outdoor practice in 1948.

"When they presented the medals before the hockey game, it was a blinding snowstorm and I'll never forget seeing the flag go up, with the snow falling and hearing 'O Canada' so far away from home."

A photo of two forwards from the Canadian hockey team hoisting Scott upon their shoulders appeared in most major newspapers across the country, and came to symbolize joyful Canadian athletic achievement.

Scott stayed in Europe to win her second Worlds, at Prague, ignoring the shadow of a helicopter hovering overhead and spectators taking flash pictures during her figures.

She returned home to find she was even more of a national icon than she'd been the previous year. Prime Minister Mackenzie King congratulated her and theorized that her triumph had lightened Canada's post-war gloom.

That spring, Scott decided to turn professional, accepted the canary-yellow convertible from the city, agreed to replace Sonja Henie in The Hollywood Ice Revue and signed numerous endorsement deals. Her name or likeness was soon on a wide variety of products, including sweaters and soft drinks and, most famously, the Barbara Ann Scott doll, which became the country's favorite Christmas and birthday gift that year.

her European title and on February 6 became the first female skater from North America to win an Olympic title. (Only Sonja Henie had been a younger Olympic winner than the 19-year-old Canadian.)

At the Olympics, the first held since 1936 as a result of World War II, Scott was by far the best of 39 skaters on the soft and potholed outdoor ice in St. Moritz, Switzerland. "I remember so well the day of the free skating," she recalled on the 60th anniversary of her Olympic victory. "They played two hockey games that morning, and my coach Sheldon Galbraith and I were out there to check the ruts in the ice, so I wouldn't do any jumps near them.

The financial success was a dramatic change for Scott. Her father had been disabled fighting in World War I, but had inspired his daughter to golf, study piano and, when she was seven, take up figure skating. Colonel Clyde Scott did not live to see his daughter's major skating accomplishments, but before he died in 1941, when Scott was 12, she finished second in her first year of Canadian senior competition.

After her father passed away, Scott and her mother Mary were living on his pension. There was little extra money, so Minto Club members, family friends, and Ottawa citizens raised the funds to send her to competitions, including the $10,000 required for her first triumphant trip to Europe in 1947.

Scott skated professionally for only five years, retiring at 25. In 1955, she married businessman Tom King, who had done public relations for the Hollywood Ice Revue, and they settled into a busy life in Chicago and later, Florida. Scott ran a beauty salon, did commercials, wrote two books, donated her time and image to numerous charitable causes, and became involved in equestrian competition, winning several medals showing and training horses.

And, although she lived in the U.S., Canada never forgot her. She is still the only Canadian to win an Olympic singles skating title and, since her victories, only two other women — Petra Burka and Karen Magnussen — have won the world championship.

For decades, Scott has been a regular and celebrated guest at domestic and international competitions. Her smiling, regal presence is a living reminder that the westward shift, from Europe to North America, in figure skating power began with a charming, but iron-willed Canadian.

Madge Syers

A sport that owes so much to its women, and to which women owe so much, should give daily thanks to Madge Syers

But only in passing is Syers given her proper due as a preeminent figure skating pioneer, perhaps second in historical importance only to Jackson Haines.

In 1902, as the British women's suffrage movement was gathering momentum, and colonial Australia had just granted the vote to women, Syers took on the male-oriented world of international figure skating.

At the urging of her coach-teammate-husband Edgar Morris Wood Syers, Madge Syers (already a well-known member of the Prince's Skating Club), entered the 1902 World Championships in London.

Officials were flummoxed but soon found, as the Syerses had already discovered in their research, that there were no specific rules denying women access to international competition. It was only assumed that they should not take part because competitive skating was, after all, more suited to male aggressiveness.

Madge Syers participating at the 1908 London Summer Games, the first Games to include figure skating. Syers took the gold.

While insider sentiment ran against Syers's inclusion, there was also a timely political issue at play. The Syerses were influential members of the National Skating Association, the hosts of the World Championship competition. So Syers's registration was reluctantly accepted.

Stylishly outfitted in a full-length skirt, satin blouse, a pearl necklace, hat and expensive soft-leather gloves, Syers took on three men and finished behind only the great Ulrich Salchow, who won his second of 10 world titles.

It was reported locally that many thought Syers had outskated Salchow. This may have given rise to the unsubstantiated legend of Salchow presenting Syers with his championship medal.

Within a year, the International Skating Union was vigorously debating the issue of women as competitors, and it decided that women could not enter existing competitions for three major reasons, the most important being — to the men making the decision — that judges could not get the necessary view of the women's skates because of the dresses. Other references were made to the difficulty of comparing men to women and the possible problem of a judge being romantically involved with a female competitor. Hardly convincing stuff.

Britain's national federation protested against the ruling and also lobbied heavily for a separate women's championship, which was finally approved in 1905, and instituted in 1906 at Davos, Switzerland. The "official" World Championship was reserved for men, and the new event was known, for the time being, as just an ISU championship, later becoming the "Ladies" World Championship. And until 1930, the men's and women's events were held in the same city only four times.

Meanwhile, Syers continued her pioneering ways. The newly-founded British Championships were open to both sexes right into the 1930s, and Syers won the inaugural 1903 and 1904 titles, beating her husband in the first one.

To answer her critics, she wore mid-calf dresses to show her skates fully, establishing a new skating fashion trend. She then won the first two women's world championships, beating four skaters from three other countries, including Lily Kronberger, who would go on to establish new standards with her concentration on music, costuming and artistic presentation.

When, because of advanced British refrigeration technology, figure skating was included in the 1908 Summer Olympics in London, Syers became the first women's gold medalist. She and her husband finished third in pairs, making Syers the only woman figure skater ever to medal twice in the same Olympics.

It was Edgar who had recognized the potential of the former Florence Madeleine (Madge) Cave, one of 15 children in a Kensington family. A man of "independent means," and a superb skater himself, he met the athletic 18-year-old in 1899 and convinced her to drop the strict English style of her skating and switch to the more physical, flamboyant International Style.

They eventually married, gave much of their time to skating, and wrote three books together,

the most influential being 1913's *The Art of Skating (International Style)*.

After helping skating to become one of the first Olympic sports open to women, Madge Syers was forced to retire from competition because of heart issues.

When she died of influenza in 1917, she was just 35, but she had made a contribution to figure skating far out of scale with the length of her life. She was figure skating's first feminist and should be celebrated that way.

Herma Szabo

Because of varied translations, and because she was married four times, history books refer to her by several different surnames: Szabó, Szabó Planck, Planck-Szabo, Jarosz-Szabo and Jaross-Szabo. But it is all the same person: Austrian Herma Szabo, the first women's champion of the Winter Olympics.

Szabo was the daughter of Christine Szabo, a pairs skater who once performed on the royal rink in St. Petersburg in front of Czar Nicholas II, and Eduard Engelmann Jr., the European men's champion in 1892, 1893 and 1894. An engineer, Engelmann built an artificial ice rink in a Vienna suburb in 1909, when his daughter was seven, and she honed her skills on that historic surface.

Those skills were considerable, and when the World Championships resumed after a seven-year hiatus caused by World War I, Szabo became the undisputed leader of the women's division. She won five straight world titles, a string equaled by only Sonja Henie and Carol Heiss. Michelle Kwan is the only other woman to win five Worlds, but hers came over an eight-year stretch.

Szabo was celebrated for being as proficient at compulsory figures as any man in the world, and her free skate included the best spins of the time, a memorable spread eagle and excellent dance steps. She skated with great speed and ease but, wrote American skater Nathaniel Niles, "her form is possibly a little too masculine."

When the first separate Winter Olympics were held in 1924 at Chamonix, Szabo was the favorite, but she had deep concerns heading into the historic event. Germany had not been invited to the Olympics because of its role in The Great War, and with Austria so closely associated with Germany, Szabo feared a backlash against her and the other three members of the Austrian team. Also, she had never seen British or American women skate. When the likes of Beatrix Loughran and Theresa Weld Blanchard arrived in France, their beauty and "modern style" overwhelmed Szabo.

However, she needn't have worried. The Austrians were cheered wildly during the opening parade, and Szabo won both the figures and free skate by a healthy margin over runner-up Loughran. But she left the rink thinking she had lost, and her father had to retrieve her from her hotel as they were playing the Austrian anthem.

On the day of Szabo's Olympic triumph her father, a wealthy import-export businessman, predicted that Henie would eventually become the world champion. His words were prophetic but neither he nor his daughter enjoyed the manner in which they came true.

Henie was runner-up to Szabo at the 1926 World Championships, but when Szabo arrived in Oslo, Henie's hometown, for the Worlds the next spring, she found that there were posters all over the city proclaiming Henie as the new champion. The judging panel was made up of three judges from the home country and one each from Germany and Austria.

"No matter what I did, I could not win," she recalled. And she did not, as the judges voted along strict national and language lines to place Henie first and Szabo second.

That week, Szabo won the world pairs title with Ludwig Werde, as she

had done in 1925, when she became the first woman to double-medal at the Worlds.

But that could not quell her anger at the perceived judging bias, and she retired from skating. Austria would not win another women's world title for 45 years.

Forsaking her first sport, Szabo demonstrated just how athletic she was by switching to skiing, and she spent another 10 years as a member of the Austrian alpine team.

For all her athletic celebrity and social status, Szabo remained an approachable athlete. She explained in 1926 that "the finest moments are the ones when total strangers come to me before a competition with their advice and help." Not many skaters of any era have ever said that, or anything like it.

Herma Szabo performing in Chamonix, France, in 1924 at the first-ever Winter Olympic Games. Szabo won the ladies' gold.

AGENTS OF CHANGE — *Skaters from the 1960s through the 1970s*

Petra Burka

In Canada's greatest international skating year, even the domestic events produced world records. At the 1962 Canadian national championships in Toronto, 15-year-old Petra Burka became the first female in history to land a triple jump in competition when her Salchow came down safely and propelled her to the silver medal.

But the new silver medalist was even further advanced than the rest of the skating world knew.

"I was landing triple Lutzes in practice," Burka recalls of a jump that would not be performed by a female skater in competition (Denise Biellmann of Switzerland) for another 16 years.

Burka's enormous contributions to world and Canadian skating were far out of proportion to the mere four years she spent as a senior skater. Besides introducing the soon-necessary triple, in 1965 she became Canada's first women's world champion in 17 years and the second of just three (the others were Barbara Ann Scott and Karen Magnussen) ever. She also won world bronze medals in 1964 and 1966.

"I am a bit surprised there haven't been more [female Canadian world champions]," Burka says. "We do have a lot of good talent, but you need killer instinct. I thrived under pressure. I wanted to be better than everyone. If someone jumped a foot high, I wanted to jump two feet. That's probably one of the reasons I did the triple Salchow."

The other was to get noticed by the judges.

"When I skated, you could free skate your heart out and not get the marks. I used it as ammunition. Doing triples in those days was considered very unladylike."

Burka is the daughter of one of the world's most accomplished coaches. Ellen Burka is a Holocaust survivor, who met Petra's father in a concentration camp. In 1946, she won the Dutch national championship and the following year, Petra was born. The family moved to Canada where Petra started skating at age six.

Because of club rules, Ellen Burka was not permitted to teach her daughter at the Toronto club where she was a professional, so Petra trained on her own with coach Osborne Coulson, who recognized her emerging talent.

At age 11, Burka's attitude about skating was permanently altered when she saw Carol Heiss perform an exhibition skate.

"I came back to the rink and said, 'I want to be like her.' Before that I was just fooling around."

Eventually Conn Smythe, the owner of the Toronto Maple Leafs hockey team, provided mother and daughter with free ice time from 7 to 10 a.m. at Maple Leaf Gardens. Sometimes the Leafs would watch and Petra would challenge them to races, winning every time.

After landing the triple Salchow at the Nationals in 1962, Burka finished fourth at the Worlds. She dipped to fifth in 1963, but in 1964 beat incumbent Wendy Griner for her first Canadian championship, and went on to win the bronze medal at the Worlds and at the Innisbruck Olympics.

In 1965, she won the triple crown: the Canadian, North American and World Championships. She returned home to a parade in downtown Toronto and was named Canada's Athlete of the Year.

But in 1966, she ran into emerging political realities, as she discovered that in a judged sport, preconceptions and rumor can become truth. Burka was told by a Canadian official that she was too heavy, and shortly after she lost 25 pounds. But when she arrived at the Worlds amid rumors, perhaps planted by competing federations, that she was vastly *underweight*, she found that American star Peggy Fleming had gained judging favor.

"I knew before I competed that I wasn't going to win," says Burka. "Another coach came up to my mom at a party and told her. That's how it was in those days." Burka did not skate well, and finished third.

Burka, just 19, then turned pro with Holiday on

Petra Burka leaping in 1965, her most decorated year, as she won the Canadian, North American and World Championships.

Ice. The situation at the 1966 Worlds was a factor, but the decision was primarily a financial one.

"We were a single-parent family and it was expensive," she says. "Today, I would have stayed in. But there was no financial assistance, and you couldn't make more than $25 for an exhibition. So a lot of us had to jump [turn pro] when we were young."

After returning from touring in 1969, Burka worked as an ambassador for Canadian skating, produced TV commercials and, after a long career coaching, was named a national coaching consultant for Skate Canada in 1999. Many of the young skaters she works with today may not know about that first triple jump, so many years ago.

"It probably did have an impact historically by lifting the bar," she modestly understates. "Other women saw that you could do it."

Sjoukje Dijkstra

Although the patron saint of skating, Lidwina, was from Holland, and bladed skates first appeared on the Dutch canal network before migrating around the world, the Netherlands had never had an international figure skating champion. That is, until Sjoukje Dijkstra opened the 1960s with a string of world titles and Olympic medals.

From its earliest days, skating has been marked by struggles between cultural values, and in Holland, those battles had always been dominated by speed skating rather than figure skating.

But in the mid-1950s, Dijkstra and her friend Joan Haanappel began to revive Dutch figure skating.

Haanappel, who was 14 months older than Dijkstra, was more elegant and stylish, and early on had far superior results, winning four consecutive national titles beginning in 1955, and capturing bronze medals at the 1958, 1959 and 1960 European Championships. But her confidence was fragile and she could not medal at the Worlds or Olympics.

Dijkstra was more muscular and powerful, with a sturdy frame that enabled her to move steadily over her compulsory figures (at which she excelled), and which lent an overriding athleticism to her free skating.

Dijkstra also had a steely competitive mindset, perhaps the result of a family heritage of speed skating.

Her father, a doctor, was a speed skater who had represented the Netherlands at four different distances in the 1936 Winter Olympics when he was just 16.

By the age of 10, Dijkstra was training in London under the celebrated but demanding Arnold Gerschwiler, who had already coached his nephew Hans Gerschwiler to gold at the 1947 World Championships and Czech Alena Vrzanova to the 1949 and 1950 women's world titles.

Illustrating just how shallow the pool of Dutch figure skating was, Dijkstra finished fourth in the 1953 Senior Nationals, just before her 11th birthday. The following year, she debuted at the European Championships and finished 14th.

Over the next four years, it appeared that Dijkstra's career had reached a plateau. Through 1958, she never climbed higher than sixth at the Europeans, and finished 21st, 12th and 16th (twice) at the Worlds, with no indication that she would soon become the most-decorated Dutch skater of all time.

But in 1959, a maturing Dijkstra made a major breakthrough, hurdling several skaters who had regularly defeated her, including Haanappel, to win the silver medal at the European Championships in Davos, Switzerland. Finishing third at the Worlds behind the U.S.'s Carol Heiss and Austria's Hanna Walter a few weeks later, Dijkstra had suddenly vaulted from anonymity to a 1960 Olympic medal contender.

Dijkstra won her first European Championship, the first by a Dutch skater, in 1960, and finished second to Heiss at the Squaw Valley Olympics. Heiss told *TIME* magazine a dozen years later that judges might have preferred her style over the muscular athleticism of Dijkstra. "I was lighter and more balletic," she theorized.

Dijkstra was second again at the 1960 World Championships, the last time she would not stand on top of the podium. With the cancellation of the 1961 Worlds due to the death of the U.S. team in the crash of Sabena Flight 548, Dijkstra had to wait until 1962 to win the Netherlands' first world title. She won again in 1963 and 1964, the only time a European woman had won three straight World titles since Sonja Henie of Norway completed her incomparable reign in 1936.

Dijkstra was in complete control of the women's figure skating division through 1964, with Austrian

Sjoukje Dijkstra (left) and Joan Haanappel arrive in the United States for the Squaw Valley Olympics. Dijkstra finished second to American Carol Heiss; Haanappel finished fifth.

rival Regine Heitzer being the stymied runner-up in two of Dijkstra's World and four of her European Championships.

After watching Dijkstra lead the field by a whopping 59 points in the compulsory figures at the 1963 Worlds, and then deliver one of the best free skates of her life, skating and broadcasting legend Dick Button told an American magazine, "Fantastic. She has the strength of a man. She is probably the most powerful woman skater who ever existed."

With Queen Juliana of the Netherlands in the audience at the 1964 Innsbruck Games, Dijkstra won the first Winter Olympics gold medal for the Netherlands. No Dutch Olympic athlete had won a gold medal since Fanny Blankers-Koen took four track and field golds in 1948 Summer Olympics.

When Dijkstra turned professional in 1964, for an eight-year tour with Holiday on Ice, she had won both the 1964 Worlds and the Olympic title. She

also claimed an Olympic silver medal, two additional world titles, and world silver and bronze medals.

Since her retirement, the Netherlands has not won an Olympic figure skating gold medal, and its major medals have come from American-born Dianne de Leeuw, who won the 1976 Olympic silver medal and the 1975 World gold, which was bookended by a pair of World bronzes in 1974 and 1976.

After her pro career, Dijkstra did TV commentary and served as adviser to the Dutch national federation and more than half a century after they first competed against each other, she and Haanappel were judges in the Dutch version of the popular *Dancing On Ice* TV series.

Peggy Fleming

For more than four decades, Peggy Fleming has been the reference point, the face, the voice and the conscience of American women's skating.

Fleming has proven so durable, as the most iconic figure skater in the western world, it mocks the descriptions applied to her by the European press during the 1968 Winter Olympics: "fragile," "leggy wisp" and "America's shy Bambi."

True, Fleming skated with a delicate airiness that harkened back to her first experience on skates in California's Bay Area at the age of nine, which she recalls as "quiet and effortless." But, inside, she was anything but frail, and despite the brilliance of her artistry, Fleming's skating was even more substance than style.

"With a lot of skaters there is a lot of furs and feathers but nothing is happening; with Peggy there's no furs and feathers, and a great deal is happening," Dick Button once said.

As a junior, Fleming didn't seem destined for such iconic status, although Carol Heiss Jenkins did predict, after Fleming was third behind Tina Noyes in the 1963 Junior Nationals, that Fleming had the power and ability to win the 1968 Olympics.

The next year, Fleming beat Noyes for her first of five consecutive U.S. senior titles, made a seventh-place debut at the Worlds, and was sixth in the 1964 Olympics at Innsbruck. That U.S. Olympic skating delegation was a living reminder of the 1961 plane crash that claimed the lives of the entire U.S. figure skating team, including Billy Kipp, coach of the then 12-year-old Fleming. As a result of that tragedy, at 15, Fleming was one of five team members who hadn't yet reached their 16th birthday.

She and Carlo Fassi, one of several European coaches brought to the U.S. after the plane crash, represented an Old-World-polishes-America theme that continues to this day. With her beauty, balletic style and an effortless glamour, Fleming reconnected Americans to an earlier fascination with the likes of Charlotte Oelschlagel and Sonja Henie. And since then, the women's division has been by far the most important in U.S. skating.

When Fleming won bronze at the 1965 Worlds, behind Petra Burka and Austrian Regine Heitzer, her medal snapped a three-year world podium drought, the longest that American women skaters had endured since 1938.

Fleming followed her bronze performance with three straight world championship gold medals (1966–1968). Her victories were preceded by a four-year period when no American woman won in the Worlds, and were followed by another seven shutout years, the two longest world gold-medal famines for U.S. women skaters since 1953.

The 1968 Grenoble Games in France were the first to be televised live and in colour, and Fleming stole the show. So commanding was Fleming's on-ice presence that decades later, fans still remember her chartreuse skating dress, one of six her mother stitched that Olympic week.

Although her mistake-plagued free skate was the weakest of her international career and sent her off the ice in tears, the errors were forgotten in the wake of her refined, concentrated artistry. And although she is often remembered for her elegant free skating, which included one of the sport's most creative signature moves — a spread eagle right into a double Axel and back into a spread eagle — it was her mastery at compulsory figures, a function of dedicated and gritty hard work, that gave her a commanding lead over Gabriele Seyfert and allowed her to capture the gold despite her poor free skate.

Fleming was the first true star of skating's television age and, six months after her Olympic victory, she headlined the first TV skating special, which won two Emmys and set the template for a wave of such shows that would appear 20 years later. Her television success forced the industry to recognize the marketing magnetism of figure skating. Her fourth TV special, in 1973, was the first joint U.S.–Soviet TV venture, filmed entirely in the USSR, at a time when the two countries were still Cold War enemies.

Fleming's professional career started with Ice Follies, and fellow marquee skater Don Jackson recalls, "She was paid big money, and was the first

---

Peggy Fleming, wearing her now famous chartreuse skating dress, displays her 1968 Grenoble Olympic gold medal.

skater of those times to have a manager, but she was worth it. She brought a lot of people in."

Fittingly, after Fleming stepped off the ice for the last time, she made her way to the broadcast booth where she has proven just as proficient, providing incisive commentary on skating telecasts since 1981.

When she was frighteningly diagnosed with breast cancer only a few days short of the 30th anniversary of the Grenoble win, Fleming chose to share her illness and treatments with the public, recognizing that her fight could buoy thousands of other women battling the disease.

"It's another Olympics," she said. "A life Olympics."

Fleming gives of her time freely, promoting several major causes including cancer prevention detection. Proceeds from the sales of Victories Rosé, a wine produced by the Fleming Jenkins Vineyards & Winery — owned by Fleming and her husband Greg Jenkins — go toward cancer research.

Fleming's world championship and Olympic victories, amplified by television, created a new American skating boom. Thousands of young skaters, born well after Fleming retired, still cite her career and dignified style as inspirations.

Peggy Fleming was, as American skating journalist Phil Hersch wryly wrote, "the face which launched a thousand Zambonis."

Linda Fratianne

Linda Fratianne was the human bridge between an American era of entrenched, world-renowned artistry, represented by the likes of Dorothy Hamill, Janet Lynn and Peggy Fleming, and a volatile period of dynamic athleticism, led by Elaine Zayak, Rosalynn Sumners and Debi Thomas.

Fratianne won two world championship gold medals, a silver and a bronze, plus an Olympic silver medal and four consecutive American titles. After finishing second to Dorothy Hamill's third national title in 1976, Fratianne graduated to the top of the domestic podium in 1977.

She held the U.S. title until she turned professional in the spring of 1980, completing a remarkable 17-year stretch during which only she, Hamill, Lynn and Fleming possessed the U.S. title. In the 17 years

immediately following Fratianne's retirement, 11 different women won the American championship.

One of the reasons for the multiple winners after 1980 was a dramatic increase in the potentially-costly technical requirements, stimulated by Fratianne's reign as the world's premier jumper. As she raised the technical bar, others had to try more demanding technical moves more frequently. More risk meant more chance of falling, and a precipitous drop in ranking.

Another reason was a change in the scoring system. Previously, a skater's score would travel with her from one section of the competition to the next. Thus a skater could compile a commanding lead in compulsory figures and play it safe in the short program. With the new system, only a skater's relative position could carry over from one segment of a competition to another segment. So, it didn't matter by how much a skater won the figures or the short program. Only the placement was important.

This significant amendment was instituted in 1981, a year too late to help Fratianne in her celebrated Olympic battle with rival Anett Pötzsch of East Germany. Pötzsch and Fratianne were born only a month apart in 1960, but Pötzsch, representing a country with much less internal competition, was able to reach the major international stage in 1973, when she was just 11.

Meanwhile, Fratianne didn't get her first pair of figure skates until she was nearly 10. Before that, she had preferred roller skating. She soon began taking lessons in Van Nuys, California, from Frank Carroll, the only coach she had as an amateur. She was just 15 when she landed two triples at the 1976 U.S. Championships, a world's first by a woman. As runner-up to Hamill, she qualified for the Olympics and Worlds, and finished eighth and fifth, respectively.

The following year she upset the heavily favored Pötzsch to win the World Championship. Although she fell on her triple toe loop, her other technical skills and artistry kept her on top.

Pötzsch and Fratianne traded world titles for four years, the German winning in 1978 and 1980 and the American in 1977 and 1979. Fratianne never finished lower than Pötzsch in combined short program and free skating, but usually trailed after figures, sometimes prohibitively.

Fratianne, the reigning world champion, had been expected to win the 1980 Olympics in Lake Placid because of the home ice advantage. But she finished a distressing third in figures, nearly four points back of Pötzsch, too far behind to catch up unless Pötzsch encountered a disaster. Fratianne won the short program, putting her in second place, but when rising Swiss star Denise Biellmann won the free skate, Pötzsch's title was secured.

At the time, there was uproar in the American media about the figures results and Fratianne's coach Frank Carroll remains dismayed and angered. Given there were only two eastern European judges (not enough to create an eastern bloc to favor Pötzsch), plus the fact that Biellmann had won the free skate, the controversy turned out to be not so controversial and faded with time.

What didn't fade was Fratianne's influence on amateur skating. She was the first woman in the world to land two triples (toe loop and Salchow) in the same competitive program. Graceful and surefooted, she made triples look effortless, allowing her to easily incorporate the jumps into her choreography.

Fratianne compelled others to join the triple club, and her leaping legacy was quickly multiplied by her successors.

During Fratianne's tenure, Biellmann landed the first triple Lutz by a woman. Just two years after Fratianne's last amateur skate, Elaine Zayak won the 1982 Worlds by unleashing six triples. By the end of the decade, Midori Ito was going at the triple Axel. But none of them could combine their quick-twitch ability with superior artistry, as Fratianne did.

She complemented that artistry with an acute sense of costuming. It is often mentioned that Fratianne's most enduring contribution to skating was the use of sequins, chiffon and other stylistic embellishments. As the 1970s, and Fratianne's era, drew to a close, women's on-ice attire had begun to resemble outfits worn by disco patrons. And she was never far from elaborate costuming once she turned professional.

Fratianne spent 10 years touring with Disney on Ice before retiring, and eventually establishing a coaching career in Sun Valley, California.

Dorothy Hamill

The greatest figure skaters always manage to make the most difficult tasks appear smooth and routine. Dorothy Hamill has carried that art over into real life.

No American skater has ever had a longer, more public and more productive performing and competitive career. Until she contracted breast cancer in early 2008, Hamill was still touring with Broadway on Ice, and returned to the show after her initial treatments, some 44 years after she first wore oversized skates stuffed with socks to join her sister on a frozen pond near the family's Connecticut home.

It wasn't until 2007, when she published her second autobiography, *A Skating Life: My Story*, that the broader skating world learned that Hamill had suffered depression for years. In the book, she also revealed a family history of depression and alcoholism, and in interviews promoting the book she spoke freely of her dyslexia and lifelong battle for self-esteem.

Hamill was shy and often cited as having a "nervous stomach" during her amateur competitive career, but she was able to hide her larger inner demons from the general public. She decided to speak out, through her book, because she was then on more solid emotional footing and wanted to help others with depression to understand that it is possible to lead a successful life.

And, Hamill said, she didn't want her only legacies to be four Olympic minutes in Innsbruck and a hairstyle that captivated a continent. But Hamill has meant much more than that to United States skating.

Hamill kept the Olympic throne warm in the period between the U.S.A.'s two golden eras of women's skating: the 1950s and 1990s. She rose to the occasion, and did it while battling her legendary competitive jitters. Although the U.S. produced other female world champions and medalists in the time between Peggy Fleming's 1968 landmark victory and Kristi Yamaguchi's 1992 gold, Hamill was the only American woman to win at the Olympics. And, after taking the 1976 Olympics, she won the 1976 World Championship, breaking the only seven-year drought for U.S. women since World War II.

Hamill's Olympic championship, like Fleming's nine

years earlier, was the springboard for a massive increase in figure skating popularity among young American girls, and many stars of the next generation cited her win as the moment that lured them into the sport.

Hamill had always adored Fleming but felt that her own talents lent herself more to the combined athleticism, artistry, power and delicateness of a skater like Janet Lynn. Hamill prided herself on her athletic ability and, although she didn't need triple jumps in competition, often landed them in practice.

She rose through the U.S. ranks quickly, winning the 1969 U.S. novice title at the age of 12. After finishing second in the Junior Nationals the following year, she started studying under master coach Carlo Fassi in Colorado Springs. While she always considered herself more of an athlete than an artist, Hamill can be credited with making a significant contribution to the inventory of visually impressive skating moves: at just 13 years old she pioneered the Hamill Camel, a creative transition from a layback to a sit spin.

In 1974, she succeeded Lynn as national champion, the first of her three U.S. titles. The previous year, she had finished second at the Nationals and an impressive fourth in her world championship debut, behind Karen Magnussen, Lynn and East Germany's Christine Errath. For the next three seasons, Hamill, Errath and Dianne de Leeuw of the Netherlands would engage in fierce competition to be the best skater on the planet.

At the 1974 Worlds in Munich, Hamill was in third place heading into the free skate, and scheduled to perform after Germany's Gerti Schanchet.

"When she went out to skate, the crowd was throwing things on the ice because they were not happy with the German's mark," recalls Bob Paul, her choreographer, who was standing beside Fassi that night. "But Dorothy thought they were unhappy with her and left the ice, crying. She went back out and skated great. She could get very down."

Hamill won that 1974 free skate and finished second to Errath. She was second again in 1975, this time to de Leeuw, setting the stage for a three-way Olympic showdown at Innsbruck in 1976.

Just a few weeks before the Games, Fassi was too busy with his other star, John Curry, to meet Hamill's coaching needs, so her mother angrily drove the 19-year-old all the way from Colorado to Connecticut to ask coach Peter Burrows to mold her into top form.

With her mother waiting in an Innsbruck hotel, too nervous to watch her daughter, Hamill delivered an inspired but relaxed performance to themes from Erroll Flynn movies. She scored 5.9s across the board for artistic merit to triumph over de Leeuw, who finished second, and Errath, who took the bronze.

Her Olympic victory had spawned an unprecedented flood of endorsement offers and commercial opportunities and even resulted in a Dorothy Hamill doll. The hair style she wore during the Olympics touched off a North American fad among young girls. It was Yusuke Suga, the stylist whom she struggled to land an appointment with for two years, who gave her the unique, short, wedge cut for the 1976 Olympics; "But who knew?" she once said of opting for that style. "I had no idea that it would be that popular."

The Ice Capades became Hamill's home for seven years after she turned professional in 1976. There could be lucrative returns for the skater who could transcend the sport and become a household name but there were also unforeseen pressures and externally imposed images to live up to. For example, a hair-product contract dictated the exact length Hamill had to wear her hair.

When she owned the Ice Capades (1993–1995), Hamill did what she could to help other skaters deal with the some of the pressures of professional skating by ending weekly weigh-ins — a draconian part of most lavish production tours since the 1940s — which have been blamed by many skaters for contributing to eating disorders.

Hamill had enormous peaks and valleys in her life after turning professional and it was in the whirlwind after the Olympics and the Worlds that she suspects she had her first encounter with depression. But she kept it under wraps for more than 30 years, until she felt strong enough to write about it.

"Figure skating is my relief and my therapy," she has said. "It's carried me through a lot of tough times."

Dorothy Hamill, sporting her signature haircut, kisses her 1976 Olympic gold medal, the fourth American ladies gold since the U.S.A.'s first in 1956, and its last until 1992.

Janet Lynn

If the rules of a sport are designed to produce the ideal winner, then the International Skating Union has built an enduring monument to Janet Lynn.

Lynn is often given the label that no athlete really wants: the best skater not to win it all. A dynamic and inspiring free skater, the five-time American champion could never quite reach the top step of the world or Olympic podium, usually because she had fallen too far behind in compulsory figures.

By the late 1960s television had become a major influence in figure skating, especially in North America where Lynn had become an icon for her ethereal free skating. Lynn and Canada's Karen Magnussen would often dominate the televised free skating but would not win the title because of poor scores in the earlier, untelevised, figures portion of the event. Audiences were left confused and suspicious when the brilliant figures technician Beatrix Schuba of Austria won the 1972 Olympics and the 1971 and 1972 Worlds, despite her rather pedestrian free skating.

The ISU took note and introduced the short program for 1973, which reduced the relative importance of figures, and introduced another free skating component.

Ironically, in the 1973 World Championships, the first to include the short program, Lynn finished second in compulsory figures, her best result ever, but fell twice in a disastrous short program. She won the free skate, but was runner-up to Magnussen.

That was Lynn's last stab at an amateur world title, and she turned professional with Ice Follies. The three-year, $1.455 million contract with Ice Follies, which reflected her enormous popularity, made her the highest-paid female athlete of her time. Unfortunately, severe allergies forced her to retire after two years. She did, however, get her global title when she won the first World Professional Championship in 1973, an event carried by her enormous drawing power. Her international TV appeal was one of the reasons the pro event was started.

Lynn's impact on figure skating, aided by heavy American TV coverage, transcended her medal count. Following on the heels of Peggy Fleming, Lynn was a role model for countless young females who watched her grow up on TV.

Born Janet Lynn Nowicki, she began using her middle name for ease and recognition because her surname was constantly being mispronounced. At 11, she was the youngest female in U.S. history to pass her eighth test, the highest in a series of difficult on-ice skills proficiency exams. At 13, she landed a still-rare triple Salchow on the way to the national junior title, and two years later, in 1969, she became U.S. champion, the third-youngest ever at the time. At the age of 14, she finished ninth at the 1968 Olympics in Grenoble.

By 1971, Lynn had climbed to fourth in the world, and was addressing her shortfall in compulsories with renowned coach Pierre Brunet. But she finished only fourth in figures at the 1972 Olympics, which ultimately limited her to a bronze medal, a disappointing result considering her great talent.

Lynn was an excellent jumper, with still-rare triples

Janet Lynn performing her bronze-medal free skate performance at the 1972 Olympic Games in Sapporo, Japan.

dotting her repertoire, but it was the delicate beauty of her delivery that set her apart. Toller Cranston once said that the only thing he and John Curry agreed upon was the mystical brilliance of Lynn's free skating.

And that mystique had a major practical impact on skating history — it guaranteed the eventual death of compulsory figures.

Karen Magnussen

Although she was responsible for a number of important firsts, Karen Magnussen was also a significant last.

No Canadian woman has won the world figure skating championship since 1973 when Magnussen swept the compulsory figures, the brand-new short program and the free skate. She joined Barbara Ann Scott and Petra Burka as the only other Canadian to rank as the top female skater in the world. With Magnussen's victory, the first Golden Age of Canadian Skating had ended.

"With the number of good skaters Canada produces and the money that's put into development, I'm surprised no one has done it since then," says Magnussen about her World Championship win. She herself has nurtured several promising skaters as a coach in her hometown of Vancouver.

Magnussen was the perfect blend of athleticism and artistry that the International Skating Union was encouraging when it introduced the short program for the 1973 Worlds, after Beatrix Schuba of Austria, an ace at compulsory figures, had won two world championships and the 1972 Olympics despite forgettable free-skating skills.

Although Schuba wore the world crown, what really defined women's skating in the late 1960s and early 1970s was the last sustained head-to-head rivalry of Canadian and American female skaters. Magnussen faced talented opposition from both Julie Lynn Holmes and Janet Lynn at the North American and World Championships, but it was her ongoing duel with Lynn that took the rivalry into the public consciousness.

Magnussen and Lynn, the two best free skaters on the planet at the time, were directly responsible for the introduction of the short program. After having

gone head-to-head at the 1971 North American Championships, skating fans were ready for a rematch at the World Championships. Television loved the rivalry but by the time the free skating competition aired, the two North Americans did not have a chance to win, as Schuba's lead after compulsory figures was too large. Magnussen was very good at figures — she practiced them between five and six hours every day of the week — but Schuba was arguably the best in history. So, before the 1972–73 season, figures were reduced in value from 50 to 40 percent, and the short program made the two free skating segments worth a combined 60 percent.

Partly because of that rivalry, partly because she was from Canada's then more-isolated west coast sports world, and partly because she wasn't backed by the gigantic media and entertainment industry that American skaters were, history has somewhat short-changed Magnussen.

Few remember that in nine head-to-head meetings with Lynn, Magnussen won eight times, losing only the 1969 North American Championships. She was the only woman to medal in each of the 1971 (bronze), 1972 (silver) and 1973 (gold) Worlds and her sweep of all three segments of the 1973 competition was a world championship rarity.

Magnussen is not celebrated nearly enough for several innovations she brought to the sport. Her spiral sequence so impressed ISU officials that the element was included as a requirement in the short program. She was the first to do a layover camel, which Dorothy Hamill extended into the Hamill Camel. She was the first woman to do splits in both directions, the first to proceed from an Ina Bauer into a double Axel and the first to do a side layback into a back layback.

Linda Brauckmann, Magnussen's coach, encouraged her to be creative because "it was part of the education process and every Friday night at Vancouver's North Shore Winter Club was invention night and we'd play with moves."

Both Magnussen and Lynn were regularly landing triple Salchows, triple loops and triple toes in practice but, she explains, "It wasn't about the jumps then, it was about the whole package. Now we kick ourselves for not doing them in competitions, because we would have been the first women doing two or three triples in the same program."

Magnussen had always been ahead of her class. She burst onto the national scene in 1965, winning the junior championship when she was just 12. She exhibited her strong competitive drive at that level, finishing 20th and 13th in the first two figures but, responding to a stern talk from Brauckmann, she won two of the next three figures.

Junior champions were ineligible to return to the division, so Magnussen was forced to jump to senior. She finished fourth at the 1966 Senior Championships, but was second to world champion Petra Burka in the free skate, and skating insiders knew that in the dynamic 13-year-old they were seeing the future.

"If ever a child has the aura of potential greatness about her, this is the girl," Hall of Fame skating reporter Jim Proudfoot wrote.

Karen Magnussen at the 1972 Olympics after being presented her silver medal, which she earned after fending off rival American Janet Lynn who took the bronze.

Two years later, at Vancouver's Kerrisdale Arena (where Magnussen had taken her first skating lessons), she dominated figures and delivered a stunning free skate to become the first skater from the west coast to win the Canadian national women's title.

Magnussen finished seventh at the 1968 Winter Olympics, won by Peggy Fleming, but was fourth in free skating and received strong reviews for her dynamic delivery. Fleming's coach, Carlo Fassi, said that the 15-year-old Canadian was the skater who had impressed him most.

Just before the 1969 World Championships in Colorado Springs, Magnussen began experiencing pain in both her legs. She thought it was shin splints, but, in hospital, doctors discovered that she had stress fractures and was confined to a wheelchair and forced to miss the Worlds. Her case was cited in the *American Journal of Medicine* as the first known case of a figure skater with stress fractures, attributed mainly to the power of her huge jumps.

"Everyone said I'd never come back to skating, that it would be too tough, et cetera, et cetera," Magnussen recalls with some relish. "So my favorite skating performance of my career was at Worlds the next year in Ljubljana."

Just a few months after breaking both legs, Magnussen finished fourth and received a five-minute standing ovation.

After her bronze at the 1971 Worlds, and silvers in the 1972 Worlds and Olympics, Magnussen went to the 1973 Worlds at Bratislava, then part of Czechoslovakia, for her final duel with Janet Lynn. It wasn't even close, as Magnussen won the figures, the short program (in which Lynn faltered badly) and the free skate.

Magnussen returned home to Canada's biggest sports-related reception since Barbara Ann Scott's 1948 Olympic victory, was feted with a massive parade and was presented with the keys to the City of Vancouver. She then turned professional, signing the richest contract Ice Capades had ever offered a skater.

Her victory had a profound impact on Canadian skating, particularly in the west, and more than three decades later parents were still registering their children in skating because of Magnussen's example.

BREAKING THE LIMITS — *Skaters from the 1980s through the 2000s*

Midori Ito

It took several years for the revolutions launched by Midori Ito to reach fruition.

But there is no doubt that the post-20th Century dominance of women's figure skating by Asian athletes and the accompanying elevation of the technical bar were deeply indebted to the dynamo from Nagoya, Japan.

Ito, the first woman to land triple Axels — in competition (1988), at a world championship (1989), at the Winter Olympics (1992) and in a professional event (1993) — was so far ahead of her time in sheer athletic power, it's astonishing that she won only a single world championship.

When Ito powered her way onto the international scene in 1983, Japanese sport was dominated by sumo wrestling and baseball, with figure skating no more than a polite afterthought. By the time she left the eligible ranks in the mid 1990s, the power base of women's skating was inexorably shifting eastward.

Ito sometimes spoke despairingly of the natural artistic limits of her sturdy, 4-foot-9 physique. "I envied the look of North American and European girls who are tall," she once admitted. "To overcome the advantage in skating beautifully that they have, I must do very difficult things in my program. But I had to learn to be more of an artist, too."

She would never be known as an artist, although her presentation did mature and her contagious zeal for speed and height kept all spectator's eyes on her. And nobody ever packed more difficulty into the short program and free skate than Ito did.

Besides her triple Axel patent (Tonya Harding was the only other female skater to land one in the 15 years after Ito did her first), Ito was also the first woman to land a double loop-triple loop combination, the first to land five, then six, major triple jumps in competition, and the first to land a triple-triple combination, which she did as a junior.

Ito's courage and enthusiasm for skating were evident from the very beginning. She was noticed by

skating coach Machiko Yamada on a local rink when she was just six. She landed her first triple jump at eight and won the All-Japan Junior Championship when she was 11. The bond between coach and student was so strong that after Ito's parents divorced, she eventually moved in with Yamada at the age of 10.

The major constraint on Ito's competitive success was her notorious inability to master compulsory figures. When she made her international debut as a 3-foot-11 12-year-old at the 1981 Junior Worlds, a brilliant free skate was able to bring her up to only

Midori Ito waves to the crowd after winning the silver medal at the 1992 Albertville Olympics, where she performed a triple Axel, the first ever in women's Olympic competition.

Ito at the Albertville Olympics skating her original program. This program left Ito in fourth place going into her silver-medal winning long program.

eighth after she placed 20th in figures.

In her first senior international competition, the 1983 Ennia Cup in The Hague, 14-year-old Ito performed last in the free skate, landed five triples, got a standing ovation and lost by a slim margin to Katarina Witt, the emerging diva who was less than a year from winning an Olympic title.

Ito didn't skate in those 1984 Olympics, but did compete in her first World Championships a month later, finishing a credible seventh. Just prior to the 1985 World Championships in Tokyo, she crashed to the ice while attempting a quadruple jump in practice, and broke her ankle. That injury robbed Japan of a local favorite and also delayed for a couple of years the debut of her groundbreaking triple Axel.

While the 1988 Olympics in Calgary were promoted as a duel between Witt and American Debi Thomas, who were ranked 1–2 and were skating to music from the same opera, their "Battle of the Carmens" was largely overshadowed by Canadian Elizabeth Manley's memorable free skate and Ito's broad-smiled barrage of triple jumps, which elevated her to fifth overall.

At the 1989 World Championships in Paris, Ito opened with a sixth in figures. But she then unleashed two displays for the ages to capture the first world skating championship by any skater from an Asian country. Her short program was memorably described by a veteran American official as "the finest athletic performance by a woman skater that I have ever seen." And in the free skate, she landed the first triple Axel by a woman at a world championship to move from third to first.

The following year, Ito finished 10th in the compulsories at the 1990 World Championships, the final year of figures, and although she won both the short program and the free skate, she had to settle for the silver medal behind American Jill Trenary.

It was testament to Ito's impact on skating's movement away from figures that her struggle with them was viewed not as an indictment of her, but of the outdated tracings. Although she holds the record for most perfect 6.0 scores in technical merit at the Worlds (five each in 1989 and 1990), arguably, her imperfections endeared Ito to the skating public nearly as often as her jumping superiority did.

For example, Ito had long been cautioned, prophetically, that she attempted most of her jumps too close to the arena boards. Just after landing her triple Lutz-double toe combination in the short program of the 1991 Worlds, she plunged right through a gap in the boards carved out for a TV camera. She scrambled back onto the ice to thunderous approval, only a few beats behind the music, and eventually finished fourth overall.

In the short program of the 1992 Albertville Olympics, Ito suffered a rare fall on her triple Lutz to put her in fourth, virtually out of reach for the gold. She also fell on her triple Axel in the free skate but incredibly, just a few seconds from the end of her program, she landed an unscheduled triple Axel, the first-ever by a woman in the Olympics. She won the silver medal behind Kristi Yamaguchi, but in a touching TV interview apologized to all of Japan for not taking gold.

Ito had nothing to apologize for. With her barrier-smashing amateur career, successful domestic professional tours, and her inspirational lighting of the Olympic Torch to open the 1998 Winter Olympics in Nagano, she inspired thousands of young Japanese to take up a sport that they would soon come to dominate.

Michelle Kwan

Aside from the glittering accomplishments that easily place her among the best half-dozen women ever to lace up skates, Michelle Kwan has served figure skating in an even more symbolic way.

As the lightning rod of skating's most popular era, Kwan unwittingly helped create the template by which all skaters are now judged. The blend of artistry and athleticism she possessed is what skating officials are *now* seeking when judging skaters on the new points-based marking system.

The daughter of immigrants from Hong Kong, Kwan was the first megastar of skating's TV generation. She came of age on the world stage and matured into the consummate performer in an era when more people watched figure skating, and got

their skating news, from television than ever before. Or since.

She was *the* celebrity during skating's celebrity-mad era — when television, surging from multiple Olympics and the Harding-Kerrigan affair — transformed the sport in people's eyes from interest to obsession.

And while she didn't seek the mass attention, she accepted it as part of becoming the most decorated U.S. skater in history. She treated her many highs and her few, but heartbreaking, lows with equanimity and was loved for that trait as much as for her skating.

Kwan was at the focal point of four Olympic Games: two in which she didn't compete (one at the beginning of her career and one at the end); and two in which she took a medal, but not the one she wanted or was favored to win.

The world first took serious note of her as the 13-year-old who was to replace Tonya Harding at the 1994 Olympics, until the disgraced Harding cut a late deal to skate at Lillehammer. Kwan was probably the most interviewed Olympic alternate of all time.

By then she was already accustomed to being watched closely. The year before, she had made her U.S. senior debut at the age of 12 (she waited until disapproving coach Frank Carroll was away before doing the qualifying tests), and finished sixth in the toughest women's Nationals in the world. A few months later, she became the youngest winner of the U.S. Olympic Festival, in front of more than 25,000 people in San Antonio, the largest audience ever to witness a competitive skating event.

Before age requirements were raised for the 1998–99 season it was not uncommon to see girls in their very early teens competing at the World Championships, but most were hot-house flowers: they bloomed quickly, competed for a short time in senior-level amateur competition, and left for the pros, or oblivion, just as quickly.

But Kwan had more staying power than anybody of her time, or of any time. Consider, among other evidence, that she is both the 4th-youngest and 10th-oldest women's champion in U.S. skating history. The cornerstones of her longevity among the world's elite were consistency of performance, a deep well of physical and artistic talent, a strong work ethic and an

unparalleled resiliency.

Kwan, who successfully defended only one of her five World Championships, is the only skater to reclaim the world title three times, and twice she did so after heartbreaking Olympic losses. In 1998, Kwan put on a dominating display in Minneapolis to win her second World Championship only a month after losing a 6–3 judging split at the Nagano Olympics to 15-year-old teammate, Tara Lipinski. In 2003, a year after leading the Olympic short program at Salt Lake but dropping to third in the final, she won her fifth world title in Washington, D.C.

Both times, the American audience accorded Kwan a standing ovation *before* she skated, in response to the gracious manner with which she handled her profound Olympic disappointments. Outside the Games, though, she had few setbacks and the extent of her success is staggering.

Her nine world championship medals (five gold, three silvers and one bronze) are the most by a U.S. skater, three beyond Dick Button's six. Sonja Henie, with 10, is the only woman to win more world titles, while fellow American Carol Heiss and Austrian star Herma Szabo are the only other women to win five championships. Kwan appeared at 12 straight World Championships and, for eight consecutive years, she won either the gold or silver medal.

She won nine American titles, tying Maribel Vinson, and eight in a row, a U.S. record, often beating a bevy of young, jumping talent.

Kwan earned 12 perfect 6.0 marks at the World Championships, more than any other singles skater, taking six of those in 2004, the last year of the old scoring system. Her 42 perfect 6.0s at the U.S. Nationals are three times what anyone else has ever managed, and in 1998, she earned a total of 15 sixes over the short and free skate programs.

"There has never been anyone like her," marveled Frank Carroll.

Carroll became Kwan's, and her older sister Karen's, coach when Michelle was 10 years old. He remained her mentor until four months before the 2002 Olympics, when she decided she wanted to take more control of all parts of her life. Without a formal coach, she finished third behind long-time rival Irina Slutskaya and surprise winner Sarah Hughes, whose

Michelle Kwan victorious in front of her home country at the 1998 World Championships in Minneapolis, Minnesota, her second world title.

OPPOSITE: Kwan performing her famous spiral during her gala performance at the 2005 U.S. Figure Skating Championships. It was her last appearance at the competition and her ninth domestic title.

younger sister Emily was the replacement for Kwan when injuries forced her to surrender her berth in the 2006 Olympics.

Ironically, one of Kwan's early role models was Harding because Kwan, too, was working on a triple Axel at that point in her career. In time, and with a maturing body, she became known much more for her artistry, and her signature spiral, although she retained speed and a precise jumping technique.

Carroll initially had trouble convincing Kwan's parents to allow her to wear the kind of makeup and skate the more worldly routines necessary to win a

Kwan's near-perfect scores at the 2004 U.S. Championships, a competition she has won a record eight consecutive times.

world championship. But after she was eighth and fourth respectively at the 1994 and 1995 Worlds, riding unsophisticated programs, Carroll upped the ante with the pivotal, and decidedly risqué, Salome program in 1996 — which won Kwan her first world championship in a brilliant battle of artistry over Lu Chen. It was the only time two women ever won 6.0s for artistry in the same world championship free skate competition.

While she competed, Kwan attended UCLA and, later, the University of Denver. And through competition, touring, seasonal TV specials, and a raft of endorsements, she became one of the most familiar sports faces in America.

In recognition of her larger-than-sport status, in 2006 she was named as the U.S.A.'s first public diplomacy envoy — she was later joined by baseball star Cal Ripken Jr. and actress Fran Drescher — making public appearances around the world to help promote a better international image of America.

Irina Slutskaya

Irina Slutskaya is, without question, the best and most accomplished female singles skater Russia has ever produced.

Slutskaya was the first Russian or Soviet woman to win a European championship (1996); the first to win an Olympic silver medal (2002); and the first to win a

second Olympic medal (2006, bronze). She is one of just two Russian women to win a world championship, and the only one to win a second. And in 2006, a full decade after her first continental triumph, she captured her seventh European title to break the record she shared with Sonja Henie and Katarina Witt, arguably the two greatest female skaters in history.

At the 2000 Grand Prix Final, Slutskaya landed the world's first triple Lutz-triple loop combination by a woman, and the following year she became the first woman to land a triple Lutz-triple loop-double toe loop combination. Along the way, she also pioneered the spine-torquing double-Biellmann spin with a foot change.

But even more impressive than her thick catalogue of record-setting championships and technical innovations was her ability to prevail over serious personal setbacks. She was the arch-enemy of adversity.

Stoked by kinetic energy and a palpable zeal for skating, Slutskaya has rebounded multiple times: from her ligament-damaging accident at the 1997 Worlds; from her shocking omission from the 1999 Russian world team; from choosing to miss the 2003 Worlds in order to tend to her ailing mother; as well as missing the better part of the 2003–04 season with a severe vasculitis that nearly cost her her career.

"After I was second in the Olympics and won the 2002 Worlds, I used to think, 'Do I need to skate more? Do I need to work hard?'" Slutskaya said after her sensational comeback from her mother's and her own illnesses to win the 2005 World Championship. "When I got sick, oh my God I wanted to skate. It was a life lesson for me. And this story can serve as an example for those who doubt that they are able to overcome their illness and return to a normal life."

Slutskaya's skill, tenacity and accessibility inspired thousands of young Russian girls to take up skating, and her loyalty to her native land won her widespread national support. When most of the top Russian skaters and coaches left for western Europe or North America in the wake of economic woes in the early 1990s, Slutskaya and Zhanna Gromova, the only

Irina Slutskaya poses with her Olympic bronze medal from Turin in 2006, her second Olympic medal.

Slutskaya performing her back-breaking Biellmann spin during her free skate at the Turin Games.

coach she ever trained for, stayed in Moscow, other than a summer in Connecticut in 1997 when her home rink was under repair.

"Irina is not a diva or star who became a champion, then became distant from the public," Gromova said in 2001. "She is very open and the public loves her. She is a leader."

Slutskaya's mother, Natalia, first put her four-year-old daughter on skates in the hopes that the cold air would improve her ailing health. At age 6, Slutskaya joined one of Gromova's mass classes, and year after year her speed, flexibility and work ethic separated her from the others. By 1994, at the age of 15, she won her first big international medal, a bronze at the Junior Worlds.

The winner that year was Michelle Kwan, foreshadowing a rivalry that defined women's skating for nearly a decade, although both women insisted there was no competition off the ice. Each won Olympic silver and bronze medals, but neither won the Big Prize. Kwan took five world championships to Slutskaya's two. But it was Slutskaya who initiated, and continued to master, the big, new elements that set the standard for the next generation.

Like most skaters who make their initial mark with advanced athleticism, Slutskaya had to work on her presentation continuously. And, also like the most athletic skaters, she suffered from inconsistent results in her early career.

After winning the 1995 Junior Worlds, Slutskaya made a thunderous debut in senior skating. In 1996 she became Russia's first European women's singles champion, won three Grand Prix events and finished third in the World Championships behind Kwan and Lu Chen. In 1997, she won the Europeans again but at the Worlds crashed hard into the boards the morning of the free skate, and was carried off the ice with a back injury. Barely able to walk, she should have withdrawn, but elected to skate and finished fourth overall. The following year she was fifth at the Olympics, second at the Europeans and second at the Worlds.

But in the 1998–99 season, undertrained and overweight, she could finish no higher than fourth at the Russian Nationals, and was left off the world team. In her absence, Maria Butyrskaya became the first Russian woman to win the Worlds, a milestone most of the skating world had assumed would be Slutskaya's.

With the help of her husband, fitness instructor Sergei Mikheyev, Slutskaya made an astounding comeback in 1999–00, landing her record-setting triple Lutz-triple loop combination at the Grand Prix final and winning a silver medal at the Worlds, a result she repeated the next year.

A month after finishing second at the 2002 Olympics — a result the Russian federation protested, arguing Slutskaya should have been placed higher in the short program, which would have won her the gold — Slutskaya won her first world championship. She was unable to defend her title in 2003 because her mother was suffering from kidney failure and Slutskaya was needed at home.

"Everyone in the world is just trying to stay alive; it is the way things are," she said stoically.

The next year, Slutskaya experienced devastating bouts of fatigue, coughing and fever. She was hospitalized, eventually diagnosed with vasculitis and prescribed strong medicine that made her legs swollen and painful. She missed all but the final event of the competitive season. Slutskaya said she returned for the 2004 Worlds because she couldn't stand being away from the ice, but many felt she was under pressure from the Russian federation. Slutskaya, exhausted, and more than a year out of competition, finished ninth.

But, true to form, she rebounded again to win the Europeans, the Grand Prix Final and Worlds in 2005, at the age of 26, a decade older than many of her ascending rivals. She went into the 2006 Olympics as a favorite but, in position to win gold, she skated tentatively in the free skate, fell halfway through, and dropped to third overall, holding onto the bronze.

"I am a professional person," she was fond of saying during her career. "I can win and I can lose."

And after any kind loss, she almost always fought back to win. Others might have won Olympic golds, or been blessed with more natural gracefulness, but no skater of her time could match Slutskaya's resilience and irrepressible, scrappy athleticism. By repeated example, she defined for an entire generation of female skaters exactly what it means to "compete."

Katarina Witt

With all of the controversies surrounding her costumes, her sensuality, her financial instincts, her constant support of a repressive regime, there is one undeniable truth about East Germany's Katarina Witt: She was the greatest competitor of her era. And, likely of all time.

Witt had many natural gifts — strength, athleticism, a strong sense of rhythm and a favorable body type for the lines and grace of figure skating — but it was her hunger for victory that set her so far apart from her contemporaries.

While most skaters don't like the idea of being

Katarina Witt performing a spiral during her "Robin Hood" short program at the Lillehammer Olympics where she competed as a reinstated athlete.

Witt as Carmen in the Emmy winning production *Carmen on Ice*, which also earned her and her co-stars Brain Boitano and Brain Orser, Emmys.

world title in 13 years. With gold medals at Sarajevo in 1984 and Calgary in 1988, she joined Sonja Henie as the only women figure skaters to capture successive Olympic championships. And she won six consecutive European championships from 1983 to 1988, at which time she graduated to the professional ranks.

With her competitive success and natural beauty, Witt became one of the few female European skaters in history to penetrate and influence the North American market. *TIME* magazine once called the East German "the most beautiful face of socialism."

Witt rarely criticized the government or the policies of the totalitarian German Democratic Republic she represented. In fact, when her files from Stasi (the East German secret police) were opened, among the 1,354 pages was evidence that she considered the dreaded secret police her partners and that she was to be allowed to tour professionally in the United States if she won a second Olympic gold. Accordingly, she faced negative audiences in the reunified Germany of the early 1990s, but that friction soon dissipated.

And, in fairness to Witt, it's relevant that the Stasi had begun trailing her when she was just nine years old. They spied on her throughout her career, recording intimate details *and* although it was later revealed that one of those providing information was eventual world pairs champion Ingo Steuer, Witt readily forgave him.

In the second half of her amateur career, Witt's sometimes insensitive competitiveness came under fire. She would stare down potential rivals during warm-up, she would stretch near easily rattled competitors and confidently hoist her heavily muscled leg to the boards, and as Caryn Kadavy practiced her free skate at the 1987 Worlds, Witt improvised moves to it — inadvertently, she said, because she was just reacting to the music. Witt also faced grievances about her revealing costuming, with opposing coaches accusing her of selling sexuality. After she wore a legless costume — to which she added feathers to quell complaints — to accompany her 1988 short program about a show girl, the ISU tightened costuming rules, requiring women to wear skirts.

After Witt had skated what was the best performance of her amateur career, to beat reigning

the last performer of the evening, Witt craved that pressure of "feeling the fists in your neck."

Once she had stopped competing, Witt was almost apologetic about her single-minded competitiveness. "I kept my head down, seeing no obstacles, like someone who could walk right through a wall," she said with some regret.

But it helped her win with stunning regularity.

After skating timidly as a 16-year-old to finish second at the 1982 World Championships behind Elaine Zayak, then dropping to fourth behind Rosalynn Sumners in 1983 because of poor compulsory figures, Witt bore down with fierce intensity.

She won four of the next five world championships, becoming the first female to successfully defend her champion Debi Thomas for the 1987 world title in Cincinnati, the American said she admired Witt's toughness. And when Thomas wouldn't shake her hand on the podium of the 1988 Olympics, Witt forgave her, understanding the bitter disappointment of her rival.

Witt was born near Berlin, but raised in Chemnitz, known as Karl-Marx-Stadt during the communist regime. Her father sold farm seeds and her mother was a physical therapist. Witt started skating as a five-year-old kindergarten student, at age six, she took part in a mass skating tryout, and at seven she won her first competition. At nine, she was skating at the famed Hohenschoenhausen rink for legendary coach Frau Jutta Müller, who also handled world champions Jan Hoffmann and Anett Pötzsch (who eventually married Witt's brother).

Witt attended a state-of-the-art sports school for prospective Olympians, where sport ranked ahead of classes. The training regimen included hours of ballet, soccer and off-ice training, which was more demanding than skaters elsewhere faced. And the harsh, stone-faced Müller always had Witt training with older skaters, a practice which, combined with her innate competitiveness, made her reach higher. Eventually, she became the first woman to land a triple flip, at the 1981 World Championships in Connecticut.

After finishing fourth at the 1983 Worlds, she gained competitive confidence by beating Sumners for the 1984 Olympic title. The margin of victory was one-tenth of a point on one judge's card.

As she started to win international events, Witt had a "handler" from the government, who controlled her bank account. She didn't have to wait 10 years to buy a new car, as so many people in East Germany did, but she was also under extreme pressure to keep winning.

After she fell in the short program and lost the 1986 world title to Thomas, Witt was made to feel personal failure and Müller pounded on her psyche for the entire next year.

She won in 1987, and also took the famed Battle of the Carmens — when both she and Thomas skated to music from the famed Bizet opera — at the '88 Olympics, cementing her reputation in North America, although it was actually Elizabeth Manley who was the best free skater that week.

Witt toured professionally in a mega-show with fellow gold medalist Brian Boitano for a number of years, and was also a headliner with Stars on Ice and Holiday on Ice. She won an Emmy for a *Carmen on Ice* telecast, has done countless TV specials, has written books, has her own jewelry line and posed naked in what was then the hottest-selling issue of *Playboy* since Marilyn Monroe's appearance in 1954.

But in 1994, in spite of knowing her four triples could not cut it against a new generation of young jumpers, she still put her professional career on hold for nearly a year, and self-financed her return to the Olympic Games because she had a message to deliver. Dressed all in red, she skated to a haunting rendition of the protest song "Where Have All the Flowers Gone" as a tribute to war-torn Sarajevo, site of her first Olympic victory.

Skating last, she missed two jumps and mouthed "I'm sorry" into the TV cameras, but the program's elegant simplicity and soulful message yanked the mesmerized audience to its feet.

Ironically, in the final amateur appearance by Witt, the ultimate competitor, the competition itself really didn't matter.

Kristi Yamaguchi

If it's a question of balance, then the answer is Kristi Yamaguchi.

No female skater of the modern era has been as versatile, or as busy, as the 1992 Olympic champion, while still managing to maintain a calm, but fiercely determined, equilibrium.

Yamaguchi was the only elite skater of the post-war generation to win both the U.S. women's championship and the national pairs title. She was the first woman to take home two gold medals from the same World Junior Championships: she and Rudy Galindo won the 1988 pairs title, while Yamaguchi also won the women's singles — the second of three consecutive American world junior champions.

For seven years, she juggled the extraordinary physical requirements and time demands of the promising pairs partnership with Galindo and her own ascending career in singles (which then included the extra time-consuming element of compulsory figures).

Kristi Yamaguchi skating to gold at the 1992 Olympics. Her gold medal was the first Olympic gold for American women since Dorothy Hamill's 1976 win.

In a skating world that has become ultra-specialized, Yamaguchi doesn't receive nearly enough acclaim for the determination, sheer stamina and precise organizational skills that it took to rise to the occasion five times — short program and free skate in both disciplines, plus compulsory figures — during each competition. Once she decided, after the 1990 season, to concentrate on singles, Yamaguchi quickly rose to the top of the women's division, which was in a state of flux. She found the perfect balance between what had become warring philosophies of ballistics and showmanship.

"All the articles in the newspapers before the 1992 Olympics were about the battle between artistry and athleticism," she said. "I hope in some way I did show that artistry and athletics can be combined."

She not only combined them, the stitch she sewed

between kinetics and presentation formed the pattern for an ensuing wave of all-round skaters such as Oksana Baiul, Michelle Kwan, Shizuka Arakawa and Sasha Cohen.

She was deservedly described as the "complete skater," a compliment not only to her physical prowess and interpretative skills, but also to her prodigious work ethic and sense of purpose.

Yamaguchi, whose mother was born in a Japanese-American internment camp during World War II, is the middle child in a California family of achievers. Her brother was a basketball star, her sister a champion baton twirler.

She was born with clubfeet and her parents enrolled her in skating as a form of physical therapy. Inspired by Dorothy Hamill's fame and success, Yamaguchi turned that therapy into an exemplary career that rivaled that of her childhood idol. She set lofty goals, and drove herself to achieve them.

"Kristi has the ideal temperament for a championship skater," veteran coach Don Laws said.

When she was 15, Yamaguchi and Galindo won the American Junior Pairs Championships and were fifth at the Junior Worlds. They moved up to senior domestically but stayed junior on the world stage, winning the bronze medal in 1987. The skill level of their pairs partnership was underscored when Galindo won the 1987 world junior single men's title, and Yamaguchi won the women's event the following year as part of her unprecedented and unmatched golden double.

Their advanced individual skating gave Yamaguchi and Galindo the potential to become the first American world pairs champions since 1979. They were doing side-by-side triple flips, still considered a difficult pairs element, and spun in opposite directions — she counter-clockwise, he the less common clockwise — giving them a unique on-ice look that could be exploited choreographically.

In 1989 and 1990, Yamaguchi and Galindo were national champions and ranked fifth in the world, but while his singles career appeared to have stalled (he did rebound to win the 1996 U.S. men's title in a massive upset), hers was on a meteoric rise. She had dreamed of an Olympic championship since she began skating, and won silver medals in her first three

U.S. Senior Nationals, beginning in 1988.

But Yamaguchi's singles coach Christy Ness had moved to Edmonton's Royal Glenora Club, and Yamaguchi followed her. The 1,000-mile trip back to Galindo and their coach Jim Hulick was too taxing and after the pair finished fifth at 1990 Worlds, while Yamaguchi was fourth in the women's division, she told the disappointed Galindo that she would concentrate on singles.

In the late 1980s and early 1990s, no competition in the world was as difficult to survive as the U.S. Women's Nationals.

In Yamaguchi's four years as a senior skater, five different American women won medals at the Worlds. Yamaguchi herself was already a world champion before she won her only U.S. title in 1992. In 1991, Yamaguchi, Nancy Kerrigan and Tonya Harding finished 1–2–3 at the Worlds, the only time in world championship history one country had swept the women's podium.

Once she dropped pairs, there was more artistic flow and maturity in Yamaguchi's singles skating, which also had a high degree of technical difficulty. She mastered the high-end triple Lutz-triple toe loop combination and it's usually forgotten that she was successfully landing triple Axels in practice, although not consistently enough for the perfectionist in her to allow them into competition.

She didn't need the Axel anyway. Her high level of artistry and technical skill won her the 1992 Olympic gold, the first for an American woman since her idol Dorothy Hamill, 16 years earlier. She made a couple of major mistakes, but the ice and atmosphere in Albertville were not conducive to best performances and no competitor skated cleanly.

Yamaguchi went on to become one of the most successful professional skaters of all time, headlining Stars on Ice, the genre-altering skating revue, for 10 years with Scott Hamilton and her old Royal Glenora teammate Kurt Browning.

While there were initial concerns that her Asian heritage did not appeal to major American advertisers, Yamaguchi eventually built a portfolio of endorsements, wrote two books, started her own foundation, was featured in videos and electronic games, skated in numerous television and live specials and still found time to raise two children with her husband, NHL defenceman and Stanley Cup winner Bret Hedican.

And in 2008, she burst back into international prominence by taking off her skates and winning the sixth season of *Dancing with the Stars* with professional dancer Mark Ballas. She had the highest celebrity marks in the history of the ultra-popular TV show, and judges said she was the most consistent performer — as she had been in her skating career.

"If I have my mind set on something, I work toward it and try not to get distracted," Yamaguchi once said.

That proved to be an understatement.

Yamaguchi waves to the crowd as the 1992 U.S. Figure Skating champion; her first domestic title after three years of finishing runner-up.

NATIONALISM AND THE BUILDING OF CHAMPIONS

On carved animal bones over frozen rivers, or on steel blades in the private clubs of better society, skating's earliest attraction was as a winter pastime.

So it was natural that figure skating took root and generally still thrives in areas where winter can be most formidable: Russia, northern Europe, Canada and colder parts of the U.S.A., plus, in latter years, China and Japan.

Indoor artificial ice and ice-resurfacing improvements have extended the reach of figure skating into less reliably frigid regions of Japan, Europe and the United States.

Television has spread the message even further and deeper, while videos, CDs, e-mail and other forms of mass communication have disseminated technical knowledge. Skating has become so widespread that there are now more than 60 full member countries that belong to the International Skating Union.

However, the impact of figure skating and the fashion in which it is embraced vary wildly from country to country. Even among the sport's great powers. There are many factors creating that diversity, including economics, sociological ideals, seminal stars, national organizational strength, access to ice time, sustained success in the sport, and the manner by which the sport first took hold in a country.

For example, demonstrative American Jackson Haines was not welcomed with open arms in Britain, where he made his first stop after leaving the U.S. in the middle of the 19th century. England is acknowledged as the birthplace of modern figure skating, enjoyed in elite society, and Haines' exuberant stylings clashed with the precise, rather snobbish, English style.

But Haines' live orchestras and theatrical approach entranced music-crazy Vienna

---

Sasha Cohen, proudly draped in her nation's flag, shows off her silver medal at the 2006 Winter Games in Turin, Italy.

113

A young Karl Schäfer in Vienna in 1930, the year that marked his arrival as the world's premiere men's skater.

and spawned a whole school of "international" skating. "To the Viennese, skating meant something to see, to the British it meant something to do," was Nigel Brown's concise description in his 1959 book *Ice Skating: A History.*

The variations in the way skating nations view the sport didn't end with Haines' contrasting visits to two European centers of culture. These differences continued and expanded through the century and a half that followed.

In general, when a nation does well in figure skating, it tends to continue to do well, unless interrupted by a catastrophic event, such as war or economic depression. Success breeds success, especially after an Olympic year, when a medal-winning performance can inspire the children of that skater's country to take up the sport in increasing numbers. Spikes in American skating registration have almost always followed an Olympic gold or a period of international domination by a U.S. skater, particularly by a woman.

In more recent years, international success has usually translated into higher income from domestic TV rights, which the national association of the country can sink back into identifying and nurturing talent, and publicizing the sport.

Further, when the Iron Curtain split Europe from the end of World War II until 1989, skating became a political instrument for the Soviet-dominated countries. Success was used to shore up national morale, the pitch being that victories came because the system was working. And the Eastern Bloc mounted many victories. But stretches of dominance do not necessarily make a country a perennial power.

WESTERN EUROPE

Consider Norway, which, through 1936, had won six Olympic medals (three gold, two silver and one bronze) and 17 world championship medals (10–2–5),

but hasn't made a single trip to the podium at the Worlds or Olympics since then. All of the gold, plus one World silver, were won by the irreplaceable Sonja Henie. She arrived on the heels of a couple of strong men and pairs teams in an era when skating was a favorite of the Norwegian royal family, and a lot of money was invested in developing Henie (particularly by her father) and other skaters. Henie in turn inspired the likes of 1927 bronze medalist Karen Simensen and 1933 pairs medalists Randi Bakke and Christen Christensen.

But continuity halted when Henie left permanently for America, and this adieu was soon followed by World War II ravaging northern Europe and Scandinavia. Cross-country skiing and ski jumping have become the winter sports that now frame Norway's current athletic identity.

The nations that founded or dominated figure skating competition through the early 20th century were Austria, Sweden, Great Britain, Hungary,

2002 Olympic dance champions Marina Anissina and Gwendal Peizerat competing in Salt Lake in 2002.

Germany, Russia, Holland and sometimes Switzerland. Of those, only Russia, and periodically Switzerland or Germany, were still significant forces by the end of the century, although all were still playing host to major competitions and most could exercise a degree of influence within the International Skating Union.

There has been a gradual decline in the strength of skating in continental Europe since the late 1970s, and nowhere was this more pronounced than in Austria, the country that had welcomed Jackson Haines with open arms and staged the first national skating competitions.

Austria has won 117 medals at the World Championships but none since Claudia Kristofics-Bender's second straight bronze in 1982. The country had been a major power broker in the sport from the beginning of the International Skating Union in 1892, often determining the path that world skating competitions would take. It was Austria that helped form the rule of no more than one judge per country after three Norwegian judges outweighed the German and Austrian judges (who often worked as a unit) to give Sonja Henie her first title. It was alleged to be Austrian backroom influence that cost Canadian pair Frances Bowden and Norris Dafoe the 1956 Olympic and world titles.

Austria managed to produce medalists after World War II despite, like many European countries, losing most of its arenas in the war, but once compulsory figures began their rapid decline, it never produced another champion. Beatrix Schuba, perhaps the best ever at the compulsories, was Austria's last Olympic and world champion in 1972. The country that gave skating multiple world champions like Willy Böckl, Gustav Hügel and Karl Schäfer had exactly one male entrant in its 2006 Nationals at Innsbruck, only one

ice dance entry and not one pairs team.

In Austria and most other European countries, interest in figure skating waned in the latter part of the 20th century as their international results diminished. TV ratings also sagged, even in once skating-mad Germany. During isolated periods, when a sudden skating star appeared, there were surges of national interest: in Italy and Bulgaria, respectively for world champion dancers Barbara Fusar-Poli and Maurizio Margaglio and Albena Denkova and Maxim Staviski; in Switzerland for repeat men's winner Stephane Lambiel. But the attraction fades once the skaters move out of the competitive limelight. The number of children attracted to skating may have increased during those skaters' peak years, but often the infrastructure wasn't there to sustain the impulse.

European skating also lagged behind popular culture, which exploded, particularly musically, in the 1960s. Skating taste worldwide is still influenced by what social historian Ellyn Kestnbaum deftly called a "Euro-American repertoire of movement," which was associated with the higher art of classical music and body carriage, but it was most deeply rooted in Europe, and therefore harder to shake.

Only France bucked the general trend, through a concerted effort by its national federation. Skaters became national icons, acting almost like rock stars, and pushed their sport to upper-tier status, beginning with Canadian-raised-and-trained ice dancers Isabelle and Paul Duchesnay and continuing through Surya Bonaly, Philippe Candeloro, 2002 Olympic dance champions Marina Anissina and Gwendal Peizerat and 2007 men's world champion Brian Joubert.

French skating, which had strings of international successes just before and after World War II and again in the early 1960s, fell on hard times for a quarter of a century. But in the late 1980s, the country returned to world prominence, competitively and politically, and stayed there, led by a federation that was hyperaggressive, gusting up to scandalous.

Among the factors in the decline of European skating was the rise of other skating nations. There was a shift in financial and podium power to North America, particularly the U.S., after World War II; the Eastern Bloc countries, mostly the USSR, began devoting resources to sports and created, in essence, professional athletes in an era of amateur ones; and Japan and China began investing in the sport, the former through mostly private enterprise, the latter through government funding.

Because European skating had sprung out of aristocratic society, there was a hesitancy to make it more democratic. The sport gathered interest and new athletes as a natural fallout of world success. Few countries had widespread public programs designed to increase skating participation. Few funded networks of accessible rinks as the Canadians did or formed structured identification and recruitment strategies as the communist nations did. Most European nations had fallen behind long before the results began to show.

Figure skating was clearly codified, if not founded, in Great Britain. It was in England that indoor rinks first made a significant impact. Depending upon your historian, skating clubs were formed there in either the mid-17th or mid-18th century. Membership included nobles, clergy and professional people, usually men. At the Scotland Skating Club in the mid-19th century, the criticism that skating was effeminate was countered by the claim that it was a sport of sophistication, for gentlemen.

Proper skating style was tightly defined in Britain even before the Victorians took over general society. The body carriage, formal and erect, combined with the popularity of ballroom dancing, made England a natural leader when ice dancing finally worked its way onto the competition scene.

Britons dominated dance in the 1950s, its inaugural decade, and again with the incomparable Torvill and Dean in the early 1980s, but haven't seriously challenged in any discipline since then.

Paradoxically, considering its roots as an elite male-dominated club sport, with a rather rigid form, British skating has produced its major share of innovators. Madge Syers was the first woman to enter an international competition against men; Cecilia Colledge and Megan Taylor, two jump-oriented youngsters who arrived near the end of Sonja Henie's reign, won back-to-back world championships; Renaissance men John Curry and Robin Cousins helped redefine artistry; Torvill and Dean altered ice dancing forever. Additionally, the first female international judge was British, and the national federation was among the pioneers with input from strong female members and leaders.

In the 18th and 19th centuries, figure skating was for the British club set, while "fen skating" (or speed skating) on the frozen marshes of the agricultural counties was for the working class and was often surrounded by gambling. So, within figure skating circles, professionalism came to be associated with crassness. It is interesting to note that it was the city council of Nottingham, not a national skating association, that gave Torvill and Dean the training money they needed to become world champions, and that even into the 1980s, the national association didn't pay for coaches to travel to international championships.

Britain had been among the early leaders in building indoor arenas, but many of these facilities had become too old and too small for proper training. Several new ones were built approaching the turn of the 21st century, which may eventually increase the depth of British skating.

NORTH AMERICA

Arena availability was a major factor in the first golden age of North American skating. In contrast to war-torn Europe, rinks in Canada and the U.S. not only survived World War II, but most of them remained open during the conflict. Only one complete Canadian Championships was cancelled (1943), while only women competed in 1944; the United States cancelled only the 1944 and 1945 men's championships.

The post-war era opened with two charismatic teenage stars from North America dominating international competition. Graceful Barbara Ann Scott of Canada won at the 1947 World Championships in Stockholm (the first held since 1939), and the 1948 Worlds and Olympics. Athletic American Dick Button was second in 1947 (and perhaps should have been first), and then won five straight world titles and two Olympic gold medals.

These youngsters kicked off the Golden Age of North American skating. American men won 12 straight world championships and four consecutive Olympic gold medals. Beginning in 1953, Americans Tenley Albright and Carol Heiss combined for seven gold medals and three silvers at the Worlds, plus three Olympic golds and one silver. Karol and Peter Kennedy won a world pairs championship and four silver medals. And within eight years, three different Canadian teams won 10 world pairs medals, seven of them gold.

Ironically, although Scott was Canada's first world champion, and Button the first American world champion, men's skating eventually became the most popular event in Canada, while in the U.S., the women's champion is almost always the face of the sport.

And in Canada the tandem events are popular and respected, especially pairs, while, outside of a couple of pairs champions and a recent growth in ice dancing, the U.S. has always been about singles.

Brother and sister Peter and Karol Kennedy, known as "The Kennedy Kids," took home numerous medals during North America's golden age of figure skating.

American coaches have often theorized that U.S. culture is obsessed with the ideal of individualism. So it's singles or nothing.

With the largest number of registered skaters in the world, Canada has always had enough partners for pairs and dance, while early success in pairs established the discipline as one worthy of attention.

Figure skating has always been Canada's winter alter ego to hockey and was regarded as mostly a women's sport until Canadian men started winning. And it wasn't just the victories themselves. The almost reckless abandon by which those victories were achieved had an echo of hockey's free-form aggressiveness. Canadian men were usually so far

Debi Thomas in 1986 as the world ladies' champion; the banner year for Thomas included life as a fulltime college student and the U.S. National title.

to 1997. Over their careers, the trio won four Olympic silver medals, eight world golds, seven silver and two bronze, and each of them became, and remained, a national idol. In 2008, well-polished, all-round skater Jeffrey Buttle became Canada's sixth men's world champion.

By contrast, since Barbara Ann Scott's Olympic win and second world title (both in 1948), Canadian women have won just two world championships (Petra Burka, 1965; Karen Magnussen, 1973). The 1988 Olympic and world silver medals by Elizabeth Manley were the only podium positions since 1973 for Canadian women until Joannie Rochette's silver at the Worlds in 2009.

American women have won 25 world championships in the post-war era, just two more than the men, but the place of honor always goes to the female champion.

That derives from the first two skaters to have a widespread impact on American society. Both were queenly performers whose essential athleticism was packaged in heavy glamor. Charlotte Oelschlagel (who was generally known as just "Charlotte") began performing at the New York Hippodrome in 1915, and her brand of demure, stunning skating, emphasizing the pliability of the female form, became a general template for women skaters. The arrival of Sonja Henie in the U.S., first for the 1930 World Championships in New York, and then for the 1932 Lake Placid Olympics, increased the leading lady image in figure skating.

Both "Charlotte" and Henie made Hollywood movies which projected that image — a princess, prom queen, gracefully gymnastic athlete with a wholesome personality and an understanding of the power of her sexuality — far past the boundaries of

behind after figures — in itself a nod to Canadian sporting culture's disdain for restraint — that they had to be dynamic free skaters. Other than Toller Cranston's revolutionary style, those free skates usually depended upon daring technical work.

For more than a quarter-century, every one of the world's major jumping advances for men came from Canadians. Don Jackson needed the world's first triple Lutz to win his only world title. Vern Taylor landed the first triple Axel, while Brian Orser successfully executed the next three and most of the next dozen. Kurt Browning landed the first quadruple jump in competition, and Elvis Stojko landed the first quad-double and quad-triple combinations.

Following a Canadian men's drought which lasted 25 years, Orser, Browning and Stojko combined for eight world titles in a stunning 11-year run from 1987

skating. Some U.S. champions, such as Debi Thomas, Nancy Kerrigan and, most notoriously, Tonya Harding, justifiably struggled against that typecasting. But no matter what the reality, for the most part the stereotype remains and has proven successful as a marketing vehicle for an array of product advertising aimed at the mostly female audience.

In Canada, interest in skating is more stable than anywhere else in the world. Registrations tend to rise steadily, and TV and live audiences don't fluctuate as wildly as they do in other countries.

In the United States, when an American woman wins the Olympics, there is a huge spike in young athletes entering the sport for the first time. For example, after three Olympics in six years and the Harding-Kerrigan affair in 1994, figure skating became the second-most popular televised sport in the U.S., following only football.

Interest faded and leveled off with excessive and repeated TV exposure, and with teenage champions Tara Lipinski and Sarah Hughes peaking and departing before they became well-known. And as the 21st century began to produce more singles champions from Asia (women) and Europe (men), skating lost some resonance in the U.S., where the wider public cares mostly about American athletes.

Things really plummeted with the judging scandal at the 2002 Olympics in Salt Lake, which became a media feeding frenzy. Shortly thereafter, the value of U.S. broadcast rights for skating events fell to a minor fraction of its former level.

ASIA

For the ISU, much of the financial slack due to U.S. lack of interest was taken up by a phenomenal surge of skating interest in Japan. When Japanese skaters made their international debuts — Kazukichi Oimatsu was 9th and Ryoichi Obitani 12th at the 1932 Olympics — there was only one rink in Japan, and it was only 20 percent the size of an international rink. The skaters had never seen world-class competitors and learned their skills from books, practicing on frozen mountain lakes.

Even when Midori Ito won Japan's first world championship in 1989, she said that although she was known at home, and people watched the Olympics and World Championships, skating was "only so-so in popularity and baseball players are the real heroes."

But then Japan held the 1998 Winter Olympics; Shizuka Arakawa won a world title and the 2006 Olympics; Miki Ando and Mao Asada won back-to-back world championships; and Takeshi Honda and Daisuke Takahashi won three men's world medals within six years. Additionally, young Japanese women were setting new athletic benchmarks in triple Axel and quadruple jumps and won three straight world junior titles. Suddenly, skating had become huge in Japan and the ISU could not provide Japanese TV with enough events to feed the growing national appetite.

One of the issues facing Japanese skaters, according to renowned Canadian coach Doug Leigh (who has coached several of these skaters), has been their cultural reluctance to express themselves openly on the ice. Coaches such as Leigh, Tatiana Tarasova and Nikolai Morozov have worked on improving the confidence and presentation of their Japanese pupils. With this teaching and the drive of the famed Japanese work ethic, the once shy, inward-looking Japanese skaters are more willing to accept the marquee treatment they garner, as they are treated like rock stars, trailed all around the world by a thick throng of media.

Korea began showing similar stirrings early in the 21st century, and China, which had once labeled skating as too bourgeois (which it often is), began committing resources to it in the early 1980s, with technical help from the Canadian Figure Skating Association which provided some coaching seminars to the country. The graceful Lu Chen won a world title and two Olympic bronze medals, and Chinese pairs, led by the masterful pair of Xue Shen and Hongbo Zhao, became dominant. But a promising crop of athletic men, riding quad after quad, failed to forge the expected breakthrough.

The spiritual grandfather of Chinese skating was Li Yoaming, known only as Leader Li. He taught Bin Yao who made his debut as a pairs skater at the 1980 Worlds and endured countless humiliations. He finished last most years, and sometimes received scores under 2.0, especially in the short program, with its mandatory deductions. But Yao developed into a master coach, and the frigid northern city of Harbin became the home of skating's revival.

Lu Chen, two-time Olympic bronze medalist, performs in the gala at the 1996 Worlds where she placed second to Michelle Kwan.

China was beginning to venture out into the world community, and sport was a favored vehicle. It was understood that funding directed toward sports came with the expectation of good results, which, in turn, would reflect favorably upon the government and foster national morale. Skating delivered the promise, and Shen and Zhao became celebrated national icons, permitted, like Chen, to seek training and choreographic help outside the country.

But there are huge expectations placed on the skaters and the government maintains control. In the mid-1990s, Chen was suddenly pulled back from tours and training in North America, her results suffered and she intimated that she wasn't receiving

proper treatment for a minor foot injury. Shen and Zhao, clearly in love and later betrothed, were forced to live in separate dorms and were discouraged from public displays of affection. And the 2006 Olympic prospects were housed at a state training center in Beijing for 11 months before the Winter Games and lived a spartan existence.

While skating is a favored sport in China, and it is one of only six nations that can support a yearly Grand Prix event, there are always concerns that if results diminish, so will the funding, especially because of the heavy government expenditures on the 2008 Summer Olympics.

EUROPE'S EASTERN BLOC

The nation that perfected the use of skating as a political and social policy tool was the Soviet Union, comprising Russia and several smaller nations it had annexed during and after World War II.

Long before then, Russia, with its long and brutal winters, was a natural for figure skating and as far back as 1697, Peter the Great had a pair of skates made that could be permanently fastened to his boots. St. Petersburg played host to some early major competitions, including what is now regarded as the first world championship in 1896. But figure skating was an aristocratic pursuit, and by the time the world championships resumed after World War I, the Russians had undergone the Bolshevik Revolution and disappeared from the international skating scene.

They did not return until 1958, and only then because the Soviets believed some of their athletes were ready to succeed. Nina and Stanislav Zhuk seemingly came out of nowhere to win three consecutive silver pairs medals and the European Championships, but in fact, Soviet officials had been at international championships for three or four years with cameras and video equipment, returning home with ideas and tips on how to prepare their skaters.

The Soviet Union had a vast talent pool, an aggressive — and not entirely voluntary — selection system to steer potential stars into advanced programs, new indoor arenas and immense outdoor rinks, and government funding for coaching, research and off-ice training. Usually attached to the military (without actually having to serve), their skaters were essentially pro athletes, raising concern and protest in the West, which was jealousy guarding antiquated notions of "amateurism."

Succeeding internationally gave Soviet competitors special privileges and put them near the head of the line for apartments, cars and freedom to travel. That stimulated dedicated, obedient training and intense internal competition. And bushels of medals that government could trumpet as validation for the Soviet way of life.

With a cultural depth in ballet, music and theatre, Soviet skating concentrated on pairs and ice dance in the early years. Their most talented women were shunted into pairs, rather than singles, so the athletic component of Soviet pairs skating was light years ahead of other nations. In the 38 world championships after the Protopopovs' first title in 1965, until Canada's Isabelle Brasseur and Lloyd Eisler won in 1993, all but three world pairs championships were won by Soviets/Russians. And the country has won every Olympic pairs gold medal since 1964, except for the second gold medal awarded to Canada's Jamie Sale and David Pelletier after the 2002 judging scandal.

It became a similar domination in dance once Liudmila Pakhomova and Alexandr Gorshkov won the Worlds in 1970. Since ice dancing became an Olympic event in 1976, the only non-Russian winners have been Torvill and Dean and the French team of Gwendal Peizerat and Russian-born-and-developed Marina Anissina.

While pairs and dance were highly regarded because of cultural history and, partly, due to the emphasis on teamwork in communist countries, the Soviets were slower to develop singles stars. Sergei Chetverukhin started winning medals in 1971, although there were suspicions he often had extra judging help, and Sergey Volkov and Vladimir Kovalev won world titles in the late 1970s. No Soviet/Russian woman (outside of Oksana Baiul, then skating for Ukraine) won a world title until Maria Butyrskaya in 1999.

Tellingly, it wasn't until communism collapsed, beginning in 1989, that Russia began to be a dominant power in singles skating. Butryskaya and Irina Slutskaya combined for three world titles in seven years, Russian or Soviet-developed men won

five straight Olympic golds beginning in 1992 and seven straight world titles beginning in 1998. Many of those athletes began skating under the Soviet system, but triumphed in the free market system when skating success could lead to financial freedom.

Through the 40-plus years that the Soviets ran its international program, Russian skating was used as a political and propaganda weapon. Skaters were monitored by secret police while outside the country, and after the involuntarily "retired" Protopopovs defected in 1979, they were never officially mentioned except in reproachful terms. They were not even

Maria Butyrskaya, the first Russian woman to win the World Championships, performs at the 2002 Olympics, where she placed sixth.

included in a 1985 book that documented the Soviet's great Olympians.

This almost obsessive need to have system-validating champions produced judging alliances split along Cold War lines. Controlling many satellite nations politically and economically, the Soviet Union could also influence their skating judges. The '70s and '80s in particular were fraught with national and bloc alliances from all nations, but none so overtly as the Soviet Union, which in 1978 was prohibited from having any international judges for a whole season.

Skating was also a government instrument elsewhere in the Eastern Bloc, particularly in the sport's historical hotbeds of Hungary and the now-defunct countries of East Germany and Czechoslovakia. The East Germans, with state-backed technical and biomechanical advances (some later proven illegal and immoral), concentrated on power sports. In skating, that meant singles and pairs. They developed champions in each discipline who became national icons, and in the case of Katarina Witt, an international one.

But, Witt says in her book *Only With Passion*, her country used her "as a political tool, in a way. It's not just you who lost, it's your country. It's your political system. You've let down everyone. That's how they make you feel. You come home and you feel like a complete loser, even though you'd won a silver medal."

When the Russian economy collapsed along with the communist era, skaters and coaches left for North America and western Europe. But eastern Europe had even more political power in skating because nine new skating federations were created out of former Soviet Union republics.

There was such a deep-rooted history of skating in Russia that when the economy revived, many skaters and coaches returned, and successful touring shows sprung up, playing, like U.S. tours, on star power. The Protopopovs were officially asked back in 2004 and have been restored as national idols.

Leader Vladimir Putin, himself a sportsman, appointed hockey idol Vyacheslav Fetisov as sports minister, and sport has again become a political lever. The new Russian billionaires are strongly urged to invest in many different sports, including skating. The Russian government is still using sport as a way to build national pride and a sense of well-being.

"INTERNATIONALIZED" SKATING

The International Judging System, in use in ISU championship events since 2005, was, in part, a reaction to judging improprieties — the darker side of skating nationalism. Two of the key components of the IJS are anonymity (the marks are no longer attached to the specific judges that allotted them) and the random selection of whose marks will actually count in the final score (all judges score, but their scores may or may not be included in the final score). Both components are an acknowledgement that national skating federations have put so much pressure, intentionally or otherwise, on the judges assigned to major events that it sometimes affected their objectivity. That pressure was exerted because to the domestic market, medals and championships are the indicators of a healthy skating nation.

The IJS has also internationalized the aesthetics and hierarchy of the sport. Demanding and assessing proficiency in all aspects of performance, the new system does not allow for a dominating asset or two to over-compensate for shortcomings elsewhere in a skater's repertoire.

The byproduct of that has been that countries which have traditionally been known for certain elements or themes have seen their historical strengths spread to skaters in every nation. Conversely, nations that have historically been weak in some skills have had to emphasize the development of those areas.

For instance, the long history of brilliant spinning by Swiss skaters — none of them can explain why, other than tradition, the blurring, creative rotations are a Swiss specialty — is no longer theirs alone. Skaters from every country, in every discipline, must now excel at spins or forego any chance at a medal. The increase in spinning proficiency is one of the most noticeable positive effects of the IJS. Similarly the spiral, a beautiful gliding maneuver in which the hand holds the back of one leg high over the head, has often been a calling card of top American female skaters, including Michelle Kwan and Nancy Kerrigan. But now every female single skater must demonstrate proficiency in the spiral; and the ones with the best spirals now have trouble finding time in their jam-packed programs to highlight the move a little longer than their competitors do.

On the other side of the coin, despite their prowess in other technical areas the leading Chinese pairs of the 21st century were not naturally good spinners. Chinese coaches used to say they didn't train long enough on spins. Those spins weren't as crucial in the old 6.0 scoring system as they are in the IJS, so now the Chinese pairs find themselves devoting more training time to improving the element.

The IJS has also had an interesting impact on the two traditionally strong North American nations.

The U.S. women's field has always run deep but the podium finishers had usually emerged from a small predictable group of contenders, rarely numbering more than four. But in the first four years after the U.S. Figure Skating Association adopted the IJS for Nationals in 2006, there were four different national women's champions — it was just the second time this happened since the 1961 Sabena Flight 548 crash had wiped out the entire American team. And, from 2007–09 the nine possible woman's medals available at U.S. Nationals were won by eight different women. While that partly reflected the absence of a lead female skater, it also verified that past champions and medalists could not count on a little judging help based on their reputations, as they might have before the institution of the IJS.

The U.S. men, not known over the past three decades for producing technical pioneers (other than Brian Boitano), started to again make waves internationally under the IJS. In 2009 Evan Lysacek won the first men's world championship by an American man in 13 years and just the second in 21 years. Johnny Weir, who had never reached the world podium, won the bronze medal in 2008. Neither American used a quadruple jump in those medal wins.

Canada continued its impressive post-1980 harvest of men's world medals with Jeff Buttle's compelling championship in 2008 and Patrick Chan's solid silver in 2009. But neither of those two men — representing the country responsible for a half-dozen major men's technical breakthroughs — even considered attempting a quad at Worlds. Canada is not only re-inventing the tone of its men's skating, but its strength in women's skating has also been revived with the IJS's emphasis on all-round skills and presentation. In 2009, Joannie Rochette's world silver ended a 21-year Canadian medal drought in the women's division.

In many ways, the IJS has "internationalized" skating away from some unique national traits, which may, in turn, alter the kind of impact skating makes in certain nations. But rest assured, there will always remain a wide range of reasons as to why, how much, and for what reasons, skating matters to individual countries.

Alissa Czisny performs at the 2009 U.S. Figure Skating Championships where she became the fourth consecutive first-time champion.

THE PAIRS

Pairs skating is arguably the most difficult of the four figure skating disciplines because it requires that "two people skate as one."

This unison has to occur while the man and woman — who most often differ significantly in height and physique — are performing taxing athletic maneuvers at high speed. And the partners are often separated by noticeable space: by the length of the man's arm in a perilous lift; by the distance the female travels in a throw jump.

And pairs skating is by far the most dangerous genre in figure skating. The windows for disaster are numerous: the woman is flung several dangerous, torque-building feet during complex throw jumps; she is left vulnerable to the slightest stumble by the male during an overhead lift which can send her crashing to the ice; and errant elbows, knees and skate blades can become near-lethal weapons during lifts, throws and side-by-side spins.

Pairs skating combines its own unique maneuvers with almost all of the basic requirements of singles skating, and, at its best is a perfect blend of the exciting and the lyrical. The magical partnership of Ekaterina Gordeeva and Sergei Grinkov raised the performance bar in the 1980s and 1990s, as the pair crossbred the highly artistic style of the Protopopovs and the gymnastic power of the pioneering Irina Rodnina and her partners, Alexsei Ulanaov and Alexandr Zaitsev. Since Gordeeva and Grinkov, a pairs team cannot ascend to superstar status without a seamless combination of high risk maneuvers and harmonious artistry.

Despite pairs skating having been a world championship discipline since 1908, many countries cannot find enough capable skaters to create top teams, as the genre requires so much skill and fearlessness. But for those nations that do succeed in generating elite partnerships, pairs skating is a highly-respected event — and for all, it is the discipline in which the total of the two skaters far exceeds the sum of their individual parts.

Ekaterina Gordeeva and Sergei Grinkov pose in a lovers' embrace. The young couple, whose time was cut short by Grinkov's sudden death, is best remembered for their chemistry, on and off the ice.

PIONEERS AND TRENDSETTERS — *Pairs through to the 1950s*

Andrée Brunet and *Pierre Brunet*

When the lure of the ice proved too strong for Pierre Brunet, engineering lost a skater, but skating gained an engineer, and he gained a partner and wife. Pierre and Andrée dominated pairs skating from 1926 through 1932, and elevated the event from an echo of ice dancing to a well-respected discipline that demanded precision, athleticism and creativity.

Although they spent more than half their lives in the United States, the Brunets are still revered in France for winning the nation's first medal at a world championship (silver in 1925), its first world championship (1926, and three times thereafter), and first Olympic skating golds (1928 and 1932).

In 1920, Brunet was a 19-year-old mechanical engineering student at Paris Technical Institute when he met Andrée Joly on Paris' only indoor rink,

located on the Champs Élysées. She was about to win the first of her 10 consecutive national singles championships, and he had already decided that his future was going to involve blades, not slide rules.

"When I saw a couple engaged in skating pairs for the first time, I gave up the idea of a career in engineering," Brunet recalled to *New Yorker* magazine in 1954. "I could see that there was so much to be done . . . from an engineer's point of view."

Brunet and Joly formed a friendship, a skating partnership and, in 1929, a marriage union. And together they modernized pairs skating.

She was the daughter of a well-known French equestrian who introduced her to skating while the family was spending World War I in the winter sports hub of St. Moritz. As well as her 10 national singles

---

Andrée and Pierre Brunet at the 1924 Chamonix Olympics, where the pair captured bronze in the first true Winter Olympics.

titles, Joly finished fifth in the first true Winter Olympics, which were held at Chamonix, France, in 1924. Tellingly, though, she finished second in free skating, which highlighted her strong stroke and interpretative strengths.

He was the son of a French industrialist and naturally gifted in mechanics. He skated incessantly on ponds around Paris and on the canals near the Palace of Versailles. Brunet won seven national singles titles and he applied the principles of mechanics to skating training, much the same as Willy Böckl, an engineer and the men's world champion of that era.

The Brunets skated with a youthfulness and vigor that won them numerous admirers. Pierre devised precise and daring routines for their pairs skating that contained many elements — at the Chamonix Olympics so many elements were packed into their routine that some judges punished them for it, and they finished third.

"Their obviously more difficult programs seemed to be skated practically as well as the winners'," American competitor Nathaniel Niles wrote.

The Brunets finished second at the 1925 Worlds, won again in 1926, and then began an unusual habit of winning only every second year They won the 1928, 1930 and 1932 World Championships and also the 1928 and 1932 Olympic titles.

All the while, they were re-sculpting pairs skating, making it more athletic and precise. Using thrilling lifts with fluid entries and uncorking spectacular side-by-side jumps, they exuded excitement and a sense of continuous motion.

They introduced mirror skating, in which the partners perform the same moves but in opposite directions, and at the 1932 Games, unveiled a revolutionary one-hand lift. And Andrée broke the tradition of women wearing white, by matching her outfit to Pierre's dark suit.

"They have everything: program, rhythm, speed, style and personality," marveled American judge Joel B. Liberman. "One cannot think of them apart. Even their separating moves are part of a pairs picture."

The Brunets were originally prepared to defend their Olympic title at the 1936 Winter Games in Garmisch-Partenkirchen, Germany, but balked after the rise of Nazism, and instead, they turned professional.

They performed in England before touring North America in 1938, and eventually settled in the U.S. two years later. The Brunets became world-renowned coaches, although Andrée had to retire after a car accident re-injured her back, which she had first hurt skiing in 1933. Pierre led Carol Heiss and many others to a slew of world championships.

The couple's son, Jean-Pierre Brunet, won the U.S. junior and two senior pairs championships with Donna Pospisil, and there were hopes that the Brunet world championship legacy would extend to a second generation. But, tragically, at the age of 19, Jean-Pierre was killed in a car accident in the summer of 1946.

The Brunets, justifiably known as the world's first great pairs team, spanned 70 years of figure skating; Pierre died 1991 in Boyne City, Michigan, where his lifelong partner, Andrée, died in 1993.

Frances Dafoe and Norris Bowden

Frances Dafoe and Norris Bowden invented several elements that are still important parts of today's programs, and they pushed Canadian pairs skating down a road of success that has become almost a national birthright.

It was in the 1950s that Dafoe and Bowden introduced early versions of the lasso lift, the twistlift and throw jumps, which have been refined and amplified, but are still pairs staples. The frightening "Leap of Faith" made famous by Underhill and Martini 30 years later was also a Dafoe-Bowden invention. In the gasp-inducing move, both partners are skating backward and the woman picks and jumps, blind to her partner, who catches her just as she turns forward.

During their competitive prime, Canadian skating officials rarely gave Dafoe and Bowden the respect they deserved as pioneering national heroes. Often, they were more celebrated in Europe than in their home country, where they faced numerous impediments.

For instance, the Canadian Figure Skating Association originally denied them permission to enter the 1952 Olympics and World Championships

Frances Dafoe and Norris Bowden at the 1953 World Championships in Davos, Switzerland. The pair took silver, scoring the gold the next two years.

because it was felt they weren't good enough.

But, after they won their first of four consecutive national pairs championships and, for good measure, all three gold medals in the dance divisions, "we were put on the Olympic team that very night," Dafoe recalls. The Games, though, were only 10 days away, and had Dafoe and Bowden not been coached by the innovative Sheldon Galbraith — who'd already had them practicing outdoors in all conditions, just in

case — they would not have been ready. They finished fifth at the Oslo Olympics, matching the second best Canadian pairs result ever, and were fourth at their first Worlds soon after.

Dafoe and Bowden were engaged (although they eventually did not marry each other), and thought skating as a team would be fun and give them more time together. The couple's first foray as partners was in ice dance, which was then separated into several divisions, by type of dance. They won the 1950 and 1951 national waltz titles before sweeping all three titles in 1952 (waltz, tenstep, ice dancing), when they had also taken on pairs skating as a discipline.

"Being dancers made us more aware of the many nuances of musical arrangements," Dafoe said.

They were the first pairs team to "cut" pieces of music together, which allowed them to properly demonstrate the new skills that had evolved in North America while Europe was engulfed in war.

Bowden's uncle, who was director of the Toronto Skating Cub, saw him roller-skating when he was nine and urged his parents to register him at the club. Dafoe came from a well-known Toronto medical family. Her father, a doctor, was also hockey coach at University of Toronto and her uncle was the doctor of the famous Dionne quintuplets. Her parents started her in skating to strengthen her muscles because she had been ill.

By the time of the pair's 1952 Olympic and World debut, Bowden had already won the 1945 Canadian junior pairs title with Suzanne Morrow and the 1947 Canadian senior men's title, but turned down his berth in the 1948 Olympics because of his engineering studies at the University of Toronto. After earning his engineering degree he added a business degree to his portfolio and entered the insurance business, which gave him the time to continue training.

Bowden, who died in 1991, was a serious thinker and very methodical because of his experience with singles compulsory figures. A writer of the era described him as blond, with penetrating eyes, "set deep in a sensitive face."

Dafoe was much more animated and creative with a love of line, color and design. She created their costumes, and eventually had a 35-year career designing costumes at CBC-TV.

Their contrasting personalities complemented their shared creativity, musicality and superior athleticism. But when they first hit the international scene they were criticized for being too athletic.

"I often thought that was used an excuse for the Europeans not understanding pairs skating and how to evaluate the new trends," Dafoe says today. "For them, it was mostly two singles skaters skating in unison, performing the same elements, with low lifts barely off the ground."

Thanks to Galbraith's training, not only did the Canadians take the lifts into the air, but they were original, inspired thinkers who possessed great velocity and edgework.

Dafoe and Bowden soon became crowd favorites and in 1954, a year after losing the 1953 Worlds to Jennifer and John Nicks in the then-closest pairs finish (one-tenth of a point) in world championship history, they won Canada's second world championship and first in the pairs discipline. They repeated in 1955, beating Austrians Elisabeth Schwartz and Kurt Oppelt right in Vienna by a mere .06 of a point.

But the Austrians rebounded to win the 1956 Olympic gold at Cortina, Italy. Although the audience and journalists thought Dafoe and Bowden were better, a falter on a late lift gave the judges the window they needed, and Schwartz and Oppelt won on a majority of second-place votes. It was Canada's first Olympics pairs silver medal. Shortly after, the Canadians went to the Worlds in Garmisch-Partenkirchen, West Germany, where they found their room reservations botched and their music repeatedly interrupted. Sabotage by other skaters, or their supporters, was suspected as the Canadians had neither their coach, nor a team leader, with them to look after their interests. They clearly gave the best performance, and the German crowd cheered them off the ice and right into their dressing room. But the judges again opted for Schwartz and Oppelt and the spectators pelted the judges with oranges and other flying objects. Austrian coach Arnold Gerschwiler shook the skaters hands and called them the "true champions."

"The results at Garmisch proved to me that even with a perfect performance at the Olympics, the results would not have changed," Dafoe says.

To make matters worse, Dafoe and Bowden came home to find Canadian officials had suspended the two for five years because of a confidential report Bowden wrote to the CFSA, in his name only, suggesting ways to prevent some of the organizational problems that had plagued him and his partner in Europe.

Dafoe and Bowden had decided much earlier that they would not turn professional, because they each had fulfilling outside careers, and had planned to give back to their sport by judging.

"We had five years of international competition, more than any other skaters or officials in our association," Dafoe recalls. "Unfortunately, I think this experience was a threat to others."

But Dafoe and Bowden took the high road and remained invaluable contributors to Canadian skating. They both eventually became respected international judges, but much later than they should have, because of the undeserved suspensions.

The legacy left by Dafoe and Bowden was carried on by two astounding Canadian pairs — Barb Wagner and Bob Paul and Maria and Otto Jelinek — who between them won an Olympic gold and five straight world titles, to further entrench pairs skating as a Canadian institution.

Frick and Frack

Just like Ping-Pong or Band-Aid, their brand name has become part of everyday vocabulary.

Their passports may have said "Werner Groebli" and "Hansruedi Mauch," but the marquees screamed Frick and Frack.

The Swiss-born show skaters became American legends — to the point that people assumed they had borrowed Frick and Frack from the popular catchphrase, meaning two close friends who are also a little zany.

But it was the other way around. Their Ice Follies comedy act was so popular that, in fact, it was Frick and Frack who lent their names to the catchphrase.

Frick (Groebli) estimated that he had performed more than 12,000 times before he retired at the age of 65 (after badly injuring his knee hitting the rink boards on New Year's Day, 1980). Frack (Mauch) had died a few months earlier.

Mauch hadn't skated since 1953 when a bone disease forced him to the sidelines, but Groebli continued to perform, sometimes with another partner but often solo as Mr. Frick. However, it was his 15-year, North American barnstorming career with Mauch that clearly had established his popularity.

While current skaters were inspired to take up the sport largely by televised competitions or Christmas specials, previous generations were most often influenced by the touring professional companies.

Debi Thomas, the 1986 world champion, said she asked her parents for skates after seeing Frick perform when she was only three years old.

Groebli and Mauch were childhood neighbors in the northwestern Swiss canton of Basel. Groebli built a rink in his own backyard, and eventually became national junior champion, but he preferred the creatively unfettered routines he would work out with his close friend Mauch, who was four years younger. They gathered a local following by performing goofy routines on nearby ponds.

Their parents wanted them to pursue serious careers — Mauch in banking, Groebli as an architect — so they camouflaged their skating activities with fictitious names. First they went by the evocative moniker Zig and Zag. But eventually, and with no specific rationale, they adopted the names Frick (a small town in the area) and Frack (local dialect for "frock coat").

Growing in fame, Frick and Frack were invited to perform in a show at St. Moritz, with Egypt's King Farouk in attendance. Their routine included a hilarious send-up of Ethiopian emperor Haile Selassie. From there, they were signed to London's Covent Garden, forging a reputation that led to a slot in the new American revue, St. Moritz Express, in late 1938.

Frick and Frack joined Shipstad and Johnson's Ice Follies in May 1939, just as show skating was entering its golden era. With their sense of timing, their precise near-collisions, their hilarious contortions and their innate feel for the audience, they were usually the most popular act of the night.

Frick's signature move was his "backbend cantilever." He'd nonchalantly splay his feet straight out to each side, bend his knees and lean back so that his torso, thighs and head were almost parallel to the ground. Meanwhile, Frack would skate in the other direction, not cantilevered, but approximating what is known today as hydroblading.

During the 1940s and 1950s, Sonja Henie was the only figure skating name which was recognized more widely in North America than Frick and Frack.

No skaters of the 1930s, '40s and '50s, aside from Sonja Henie, exemplified the great show tour era better than Frick (right) and Frack (left).

Frick (Werner Groebli) demonstrates his "backbend cantilever" as Frack (Hansruedi Mauch) narrowly avoids a collision.

They performed as often as three times a day with Ice Follies and also appeared in two flimsy but widely-viewed movies (*Silver Skates*, 1942; *Lady, Let's Dance*, 1943), which helped immortalize their nicknames. Comic artist Charles Schultz was a huge fan and Frick appeared in Peanuts TV specials and Snoopy often referred to him in the legendary comic strip.

"You know you are a living legend when you have to keep reminding people you are still alive," Groebli said famously, while on tour in 1976.

Groebli, who died in April 2008, preferred that he and Mauch be remembered as athletes. And there is no doubt that Frick and Frack were among the physical elite. But their impact extends far beyond the limits of athleticism. They introduced massive audiences and future skaters to their sport; the thread of their humor still runs through the best comedic routines of skating's modern era; and they contributed a new phrase, Frick and Frack, to North American colloquial language.

"The nicest thing is," Groebli told a newspaper in 1997, "that it stands for friendship, for being together."

Maxi Herber and Ernst Baier

Until the 2002 Games, which promised distinction but delivered disgrace, there had never been a more intriguing Olympic pairs field than the 1936 event in Garmisch-Partenkirken, Germany.

Immortal French pair Andrée and Pierre Brunet had decided a few years earlier that they would not remain amateurs for an Olympics that might glorify the Nazis, and had retired after the 1931–32 season. Hungarians Emilia Rotter and László Szollás succeeded the Brunets and came into the 1936 Games as reigning three-time world champions. Rotter and Szollás were Jewish and hoped to crown their careers — which already included a bronze medal from the 1932 Olympics — with a symbolic victory in Germany, which, by then, was being run by Adolf Hitler.

The other two contending teams for pairs medals at Garmisch-Partenkirken Games were comprised of three wide-eyed teenagers and one well-seasoned veteran.

Austria's Ilse Pausin was only 16 and her brother Erich two years younger, when they won the silver medal behind the Hungarians at the 1935 Worlds, their first international event. Less than a year later the teenage duo were making their Olympic debut. The home-crowd favorite was the improbable May–December partnership of Maxi Herber, a fleet-footed 15-year-old with classic movie-star looks, and the polished 30-year-old Ernst Baier, who already had won four world championship medals in singles and was also challenging for the 1936 men's Olympic gold medal.

In a very well-skated Olympic pairs competition, it became obvious that no one was going to beat the innovative Herber and Baier, who won the gold with a visually stunning performance on their way to a sweep of the 1936 Olympic, World and European titles. Rotter and Szollás finished third, repeating their bronze medal of the 1932 Games, while the Pausin siblings delivered an admirable, crowd-pleasing performance claiming another debut silver medal. The Austrians would continue to be runners-up to Herber and Baier in most major events until World War II curtailed all of their competitive careers.

"Rarely touching, the dark male hovered over the speeding Maxi like the adoring shadow of a gorgeous weightless gem," one Olympic journalist wrote of their Olympic victory.

Herber and Baier excelled at "shadow skating," in which pairs would synchronize the same movements in close proximity to each other.

But their lasting contribution was to extend what the Brunets had started in urging pairs away from that very shadow skating, the dominant style of the 1920s, and toward the more robust motif which North Americans would make popular just after World War II.

Herber and Baier were the first to perform side-by-side jumps in their programs, a revolutionary development but one that also seemed perfectly natural because of their individual skills.

Baier was a five-time German champion and four-time world medalist in singles skating and was the crowd favorite in the 1936 Olympic men's event, but finished second to Karl Schäfer. Baier's gold in pairs and silver in singles made him the only man ever to win two figure skating medals at the same Olympics, a distinction he still holds.

Herber, driven to succeed by her strict father, won her first of three consecutive national singles titles in 1933, when she was only 12 years old. She was also in the early stages of her partnership with Baier, and the following year they each won their national singles title, and combined to start their string of five German pairs championships. At the 1934 Worlds, the only time they both entered into singles and pairs competition, Herber was seventh in singles, Baier was the men's silver medalist and, in their major international debut as a pairs team, they won the bronze medal. As a pair they never finished anywhere but first again.

Baier, an architect by profession, was the pilot of the partnership, pushing his younger partner toward

Maxi Herber and Ernst Baier practicing at the 1936 Winter Olympics; between 1935 and 1939 the pair placed first in every competition they entered.

excellence. With their timing, new technical moves and a sense of presentation nurtured by singles competition, their skating was celebrated as a unique combination of art and science. A few months before the 1936 Olympics, the German government made a decision that was years before its time, as they filmed the couple's free skate and paid a composer to write music to match their routine. The process, much more painstaking than it is today, led to a finely finished look and helped them win seven of nine Olympic judges (the other two voting on nationalist lines).

Herber and Baier were married in 1940 — and headed for skating practice right after the wedding reception. They had three children, skated professionally in ice shows and founded the successful Berlin Ice Revue. Herber, a talented artist, illustrated their book *Maxi and Ernst Baier Tell*. Divorced in 1964, the pair briefly remarried, but were divorced again. Baier died in 2001, and until her death in 2006, Herber was Germany's oldest surviving female Olympic champion.

Barbara Wagner and Bob Paul

What began as a remedial project for two singles skaters turned into the most decorated partnership in Canadian skating history.

Barbara Wagner and Bob Paul won five national pairs titles, four world championships and the 1960 Winter Games for a skating-mad country: a country that would then go 42 years before capturing another Olympic skating gold medal. It's a record no other Canadian skaters — singles, pairs or dance — can match.

Near the end of their amateur careers, they did hear the charging, athletic footsteps of fellow Canucks Maria and Otto Jelinek, but from late 1956 through 1960, Wagner and Paul were essentially without equal.

"I think what really amazed me looking back is that in four world championships, we had a second place from only one judge and the rest were firsts," Paul says. "I look back at what [Frances] Dafoe and [Norris] Bowden went through, and all the pairs after us right up to Irina Rodnina, and they all just squeaked out wins."

Nothing squeaky about Wagner and Paul: this was a well-oiled unit, with a synchronization vastly superior to the norm of their day. Their fluid unity was all the more surprising given their difference in size, with Paul at 6 feet tall and Wagner only 5-foot-1, the pair were built more like a modern pair than what was considered standard for a 1950s team.

They were equal in height when brilliant coach Sheldon Galbraith brought them together in 1950. Wagner was 13 and Paul 14, and Galbraith teamed them up not to build a pairs team, but to work on their weaknesses as singles competitors.

"Bob was a strong skater, but because he was a pretty shy kid, his free skating was too inhibited," Galbraith explained to *Sports Illustrated* in late 1958. "Barbara, on the other hand, was vivacious, showed a wonderful abandonment in her free skating, but wasn't taking a long enough stride."

But they were good enough to be runners-up at the 1953 Canadian Junior Championships, and be winners of the junior title the next year — so the newly developed, less-inhibited style and lengthened strides never made it back to singles skating.

After finishing second in the Senior Nationals to two-time world champions Frances Dafoe and Norris Bowden, Wagner and Paul were fifth in the 1955 and 1956 World Championships and sixth in the '56 Olympic Games. Because the Canadian championships were held after the Worlds and Olympics, and Dafoe and Bowden had retired, Wagner and Paul won their first Senior Nationals in 1956, and were never threatened again.

Within three weeks in February 1957, they won the Canadian, North American and World Championships.

Their differences complemented each other perfectly and, under Galbraith's expert state-of-the-art-coaching (he was filming skaters for instructional purposes long before any other coach was), they learned to minimize the effects of height difference. "Bob had to start the lifts unusually low," Galbraith

Four-time world champs Barbara Wagner and Bob Paul at the 1958 World Championships in Paris. The competition would be the second of four straight World wins.

providing their accompaniment skidded across the record and the music came to a stop. They began again and were absolutely perfect, the nerves of trying to live up to their own reputations becalmed by the extra warm-up. Months later, it was revealed that Galbraith had inadvertently banged into the table while positioning his camera.

The pair went directly from Squaw Valley to Vancouver for the 1960 World Championships, the first Worlds held in Canada in 28 years. Before a wildly enthusiastic crowd, Wagner and Paul were Canada's only gold medalists, but silvers in men's (Donald Jackson) and dance (Virginia Thompson/ Bill McLachlan) made it Canada's best world championships to that point.

It was only later, when they got to a public reception on the city hall steps in Toronto, where a young Paul had watched Barbara Ann Scott honored a dozen years earlier, that their phenomenal success really sunk in.

They turned professional after the 1960 World Championships and toured for four years with Ice Capades.

Wagner married a Capades skater, Jimmy Grogan, and left the show for a life of coaching in California and Atlanta.

Paul coached Peggy Fleming to a World bronze medal in 1965 and choreographed Fleming for most of her amateur and professional career. He was also Disney on Ice choreographer for 15 years, an echo of the 1960 Games when Walt Disney himself directed the Olympic pageantry.

And, Paul did indeed get into show business, choreographing the Osmonds in their *Donnie & Marie* TV series.

explained. "And if Barb didn't give him enough spring at just the right time, he had trouble getting her up there."

That rarely happened.

Wagner also designed the couple's skating costumes to draw attention away from their size difference, but what really served that purpose best was their incredible timing and harmony, on the ice and above it. Audiences — and judges — couldn't keep their eyes from the perfect illusion of two skaters performing as one.

"I have seen photos of our jumps together," Paul says, "and even though there's a foot difference in our height, there is an absolute unison in mid-jump, the amount of rotation, where our feet and hands are." Paul says they owe that to "hard work and Sheldon."

They'd train five hours a day during the season and a full eight hours per day at summer school in the small northern town of Schumacher, Ontario.

In 1960 at Squaw Valley, California, Wagner and Paul won Canada's second Olympic gold skating medal, and first in pairs, with a polished performance that was aided by a re-start. They had made a couple of passes around the rink, done a lift and their single Axels, when the needle on the record player that was

AGENTS OF CHANGE — *Pairs from the 1960s through the 1970s*

Irina Rodnina

with Alexsei Ulanov
and Alexandr Zaitsev

Irina Rodnina was often described as a little dynamo, but there was nothing small about the way she conducted herself. On the ice, or off. In fact, Rodnina was among the frankest and most fascinating international sports personalities of the 1970s.

She is the most successful pairs skater in history, combining with two partners to equal Sonja Henie's record of 10 World and three Olympic titles.

Like Henie, she redefined her event. Since Rodnina exploded onto the international scene in 1969 with Alexsei Ulanov, pairs skating has belonged almost exclusively to athletic partnerships of larger, strong men with smaller, powerful and bravely determined women.

Although two of the most stirring public memories of Rodnina's extraordinary career involved her tears (on the podium of the 1972 World Championships, and after her final amateur performance at the 1980 Olympics), she was a fierce competitor, ice-cold in her resolve. Most tellingly, in an era of complete control by the USSR skating federation, Rodnina was able to convince officials to let her and second partner

---

Irina Rodnina and Alexsei Ulanov at the top of the podium at the 1971 World Championships in Lyon, France. Notice the difference in height between partners in the gold-medal pair.

Rodnina and her second partner, Alexandr Zaitsev, proved to be a flawless team—in their eight-year career the pair never lost a competition.

Alexandr Zaitsev escape the chilly autocratic coaching of Stanislav Zhuk.

Rodnina recalls in her autobiography *Uneven Ice* that she was so scared of Zhuk that if he warned her to be at their Moscow training rink 40 minutes before practice, she'd leave home a full two hours in advance to arrive even earlier.

"Zhuk didn't have enough with three hours of training," Rodnina explained, "but then eight hours weren't enough for him either."

But Zhuk was the most knowledgeable coach in the Soviet Union, and his gruelling approach provided Ulanov and Rodnina with excellent technical skills, precision and harmony.

Zhuk and wife Nina had been the first Soviet skaters to medal at the Europeans, winning three straight silvers between 1958 and 1960, but were supplanted by the sublime Protopopovs. Turning to

coaching after his retirement from competition, Zhuk realized it was impossible for his students to match the elegance and cohesion of the popular Protopopovs, so he established the basic principles of the Moscow school of pairs: power, jumps, excitement and speed.

Rodnina and Ulanov made their international debut at the 1969 European Championships in Garmisch-Partenkirken "on a bolt of lightning" according to one writer, defeating the Protopopovs. A month later, they won their first of four consecutive world titles.

They blended together new combinations of jumps, speed, athleticism, muscular lifts, intricate footwork and dynamic music to become the world's dominant pair. Their throw Axel became a trademark and, respectfully, they credited Americans Cynthia and Ron Kauffman for sharing it with them.

The pair skated with precise harmony but, as in ice dancing, when Rodnina and Ulanov skated, the audience and judges couldn't take their eyes off the woman — Rodnina's vibrant energy was the center of attention. That may have helped in the 1972 Olympics, when Ulanov did a single Salchow instead of a double and many judges missed the error.

Off ice, there was no unison. Rodnina was known to be in love with her partner, but he was in love with Ludmila Smirnova who teamed with Andrei Suraikin as the silver medalists behind Rodnina and Ulanov in three world championships and the 1972 Olympics.

After the 1972 Games, Ulanov flew to Moscow to marry Smirnova, and then traveled on to Calgary for the World Championships, his final event with the heartbroken Rodnina. During practice at the Worlds, with Smirnova and Suraikin in the same session, Rodnina fell from a lift, suffered a concussion and spent the night in hospital. She recalls skating the next day in a trance and accepting the gold medal with tears streaming down her cheeks.

Dispirited and facing an uncertain future, Rodnina became apathetic about skating, but Zhuk strongly lectured her against what he called accepting the failure wished upon her by others. He organized a massive search for a new partner, and out of a field of 100 candidates the two chose Alexandr Zaitsev from Leningrad.

Quiet, and somewhat in awe of Rodnina, Zaitsev was fast, strong and nearly a foot taller than his famous partner. They worked so hard on difficult elements that other skaters recall seeing slashes across Zaitsev's chest, reportedly inflicted by Rodnina's skates during the triple twist.

With their blazing lifts and strong side-by-side jumps, Rodnina and Zaitsev were an immediate success. Nine months into their partnership, they announced their impending domination with perfect 6.0s from eight of the nine judges in the short program, on the way to winning the 1973 European title.

At the 1973 Worlds, their music stopped because of a technical glitch during their free skate, but Zhuk motioned for the pair to continue skating anyway. They finished the program exactly when their music would have, and won their first of a record six titles. Satisfyingly for Rodnina, the runners-up were Ulanov and his new wife.

Rodnina was the buffer between Zaitsev and the dictatorial Zhuk, but it soon became obvious the trio couldn't work together. Increasingly independent and outspoken, Rodnina brokered a deal with her Central Red Army Club to have little-known Tatiana Tarasova take over as coach in 1974.

Only two years older than Rodnina, Tarasova came from a musical and ballet background, and began shifting the champions' style away from the athletic run-and-jump toward a smoother, more artistic style.

The couple married in 1975, and in 1979, Rodnina took a year off to give birth to her son, Alexandr. Americans Tai Babilonia and Randy Gardner won the 1979 Worlds in their absence. Inspired by the Lake Placid Games, Rodnina returned quickly and in remarkable shape and she and Zaitsev won their second Olympic gold, her third.

They retired without ever losing a competition, returned to Moscow and later divorced. As the Soviet Union began to crumble, Rodnina moved to California to coach, and in 1995 mentored Radka Kovarikova and Rene Novotny to the first world pairs title ever won by Czechs. Zaitsev also spent time in California and for five years the pair collaborated on coaching projects in Lake Arrowhead, California.

They both returned to Russia where they remain national icons. Zaitsev now coaches at the Russian Army Sports Club and travels the world giving

coaching seminars. In 2005 Rodnina was made part of President Vladimir Putin's first Public Chamber, a group of 42 prominent Russians which monitors the country's political, legal and cultural institutions.

Ludmila Belousova and Oleg Protopopov

When Ludmila Belousova and Oleg Protopopov joined forces in 1954, their skating federation thought they were already too old. But more than 50 years later, they were still drawing crowds and training 15 hours per week.

Somehow, skating officials in the Soviet Union always managed to misunderstand — and underestimate — the vigor and appeal of the world's most durable and poetic pairs team.

From the beginning, the Protopopovs have dedicated themselves to each other (they married in 1957), and to their art.

"That is our life," she once said. "It keeps us healthy, mentally and physically. We move our wings."

And what wings! Skating has never seen a pairs team as understatedly elegant as the Protopopovs. They brought a lyrical, musical sense of movement and grace to pairs skating that was eventually trampled underfoot by the stampede toward power and ballistics in the early 1970s.

By then, the Protopopovs had already given the USSR its first four world championships and first two Olympic gold medals, in any skating discipline.

But, rather than feeling indebted, Soviet officials decided that the Protopopovs had outlived their usefulness on the world scene. They wanted to herald the dynamic Irina Rodnina (who, paired with both Alexsei Ulanov and Alexandr Zaitsev) and similar pairs types and felt that the Protopopovs' unassailable refinement was in the way.

"They said, 'You're too theater-like, and we're into athletic direction now,'" Oleg recalled during a Russian radio interview some 30 years later. "We were taken out of competitions."

The Protopopovs wouldn't retire after their second Olympic gold in 1968, as their federation wanted them to, and without the important political support

The husband and wife team of Oleg Protopopov and Ludmila Belousova at the 1968 Olympics in Grenoble, France, where they took the gold.

of their home country, they were ultimately relegated to third at the 1969 Worlds, behind Rodnina and Alexsei Ulanov. The federation didn't name them to the 1972 Olympic team, so they reluctantly retired. They were allowed sporadic outside tours, and won the first World Professional Championship in 1973. But when it took them more than a year to land positions with the Leningrad Ballet on Ice, they realized they weren't going to be allowed to perform very often.

So, during an exhibition tour in Zug, Switzerland, in September 1979, they defected on the very day they were to return to the Soviet Union. They sought asylum in Switzerland, moved to the small mountain resort town of Grindelwald (where they still train), and accepted a contract with Ice Capades.

Their defection was huge news in the West, but in the Soviet Union, their names were never mentioned except in a derogatory sense. They were called traitors,

but the Protopopovs have said many times since that the real treason would have been had they remained in the USSR — they felt they were destined to skate, and to be seen skating.

"They are true artists in technique and style," Olympic champion John Curry told *The New York Times* after their defection. "So intensely lyrical and musical. I was awe-struck."

The Protopopovs were a rarity in Cold War skating: Russians who succeeded despite, rather than because of, the communist system. Neither of them skated until they were 15 years old. Ludmila Belousova was studying to be a locomotive engineer in 1950 when she moved from Ulyanovsk 400 miles west to Moscow. At 5-foot-4, thin and light, she had a perfect physique for ballet but took up skating instead. She formed a pair with Yuri Nevsky, but in 1954 met Protopopov, a tall, blond student from Leningrad, three years her senior, who had finished third in the Soviet Nationals with his former partner.

Initially, no Soviet coach would handle Ludmila and Oleg because, at 19 and 22, they were deemed too old. Eventually Igor Moskvin — the first Soviet to compete at the Europeans, with his partner Maia Belenkaia in 1954 — took the reins.

In 1958 the Protopopovs and national champions Nina and Stanislav Zhuk became the first Russians to appear at the Worlds since Ivan Malinin and Sergei Vandervliet in 1914. They finished 13th, moving up to eighth at the 1960 Worlds.

With their balletic style and psychic awareness of each other, they finished second at the 1962 and 1963 Worlds before winning the 1964 Olympics on a 5–4 split of judges (with the U.S. the swing vote) over Germans Marika Kilius and Hans Baumier, to whom they'd lost 13 straight competitions.

The judging split was reversed at the 1964 World Championships — in Germany, perhaps a hometown vote — but the Protopopovs won four straight Worlds after that, before losing a gallant battle to Rodnina–Ulanov in 1969. When the Protopopovs won the 1968 Olympics at 36 and 33 years of age, they became the oldest pairs winners since Finland's Ludowika and Walter Jakobsson, 48 years earlier.

"They are truly masters in the art of beautiful skating," American impresario and skating icon Dick

The pair deemed "too old" by their federation when they were in their 20s have continued to skate; here the Protopopovs perform in Moscow at the 2007 Ice Symphony.

Button wrote after the 1965 Worlds. "Their program never gives way to cheap sensationalism and no individual move is performed for its own sake."

Their major legacy was the impossible beauty of their skating, and its mesmerizing effect on the audience, which inspired a generation of pairs skaters. But the Protopopovs were also responsible for several technical advances. They developed new twists and spins and introduced three new death spirals: forward-inside, forward-outside and backward-inside.

The death spirals became such Protopopov trademarks that they'd perform them as encores. They showed the same control and nuance in their forward spirals, which British journalist Dennis L. Bird described as "Ludmila gliding away from her partner, then returning to him as though drawn by a magnet, with the hint of a kiss."

They were drawn home, finally, in 2003 to be introduced and honored at the Grand Prix Final in St. Petersburg, in the very arena where they had trained for so many long, hard hours. For the first time in 24 years, they were celebrated and worshipped by Russians, in Russia.

BREAKING THE LIMITS — *Pairs from the 1980s through the 2000s*

Elena Berezhnaya and *Anton Sikharulidze*

When the partnership of Elena Berezhnaya and Anton Sikharulidze sprung out of near-tragedy in 1996, many respected skating insiders compared them to the great Gordeeva and Grinkov.

The new Russian pair was fast, creative, extraordinarily light on their feet, had an exemplary triple twist and excelled at side-by-side jumps.

Although Berezhnaya and Sikharulidze never approached G&G's status, self-confidence or competitive achievement, they enjoyed excellent careers in one of the most tumultuous and talented eras in the history of amateur pairs skating.

They won two European titles, two world championships and managed to run the Russian/Soviet Union string of Olympic pairs' gold medals to 11 in a row, when they eventually (and retroactively) shared the top of the podium with Canadians Jamie Sale and David Pelletier at the scandal-drenched 2002 Games at Salt Lake.

Berezhnaya-Sikharulidze, Sale-Pelletier and Chinese legends Xue Shen and Hongbo Zhao pushed each other to new heights and created an

OPPOSITE: Anton Sikharulidze gracefully throws his partner Elena Berezhnaya during the short program at the 2002 Olympics in Salt Lake City.

Berezhnaya and Sikharulidze performing in the free skate at the 2002 Olympics. The duo shared the gold with Jamie Sale and David Pelletier after a French judge admitted to corrupt voting.

unprecedented interest in pairs skating, even in the U.S., never a fertile ground for pairs' support.

But there was always the sense that the world never saw the very best of Berezhnaya and Sikharulidze, at least not on the grandest stages. Early in their time together, competitive nerves, and sometimes spats, interfered with their potential for perfect performances. Their Olympic program at Salt Lake was very good, but not great, and not up to the emotional level of the Canadian pair. And many critics felt it was the Chinese, not the Russians, who should have won the 1999 World Championships at Helsinki. There was also the shadow of a positive drug test at the 2000 European Championships (attributed to a cough syrup containing ephedrine, which Berezhnaya had naively taken, under doctors orders, for a cold). They were forced to forfeit that European title, and withdraw on the eve of the World Championships.

Yet there are few pairs teams who have ever faced the massive financial, emotional and physical hurdles overcome by Berezhnaya and Sikharulidze.

As they were beginning their individual careers, the Soviet economy collapsed and the two skaters, not yet partners, suffered severe deprivation, along with most other athletes in the crumbling states of the former Soviet Union.

Berezhnaya skated for Latvia in a friction-filled partnership with Oleg Shliakov, finishing seventh at the 1995 World Championships and eighth at the 1994 Winter Olympics. The two were training at a deserted rink in Riga in January 1996, when the toe pick of Shliakov's skate became embedded in his partner's head during side-by-side camel spins. Berezhnaya underwent emergency brain surgery and there was legitimate concern that she might not survive. She spent a month in hospital and experienced severe difficulties with her speech, and there was a strong possibility that she would never skate again.

Sikharulidze, already a star who had finished sixth at the 1995 Worlds with Maria Petrova, had shared ice time with Berezhnaya and Shliakov in St. Petersburg and came to Latvia determined to take her back to Russia. He had long been concerned about Berezhnaya feeling intimidated during her sometimes-abusive partnership with Shliakov and, ever protective, he was determined to become her new partner. When she was well enough to travel he and coach Tamara Moskvina took Berezhnaya out of Latvia by train at night, almost cloak-and-dagger style.

Berezhnaya said that she had always trusted Sikharulidze and "knew I could come back and skate with him so I didn't listen to people who said, 'No, no don't go back to the ice.'"

Moskvina forced the couple to take small steps in their training, emphasizing that health was more important than sport, and constantly reminding Sikharulidze that his partner was a "crystal vase that has already been broken once."

The two were briefly romantically involved, but it was their professional relationship which really flourished. She calmed his well-known temper; he made her feel safe as she fully recovered. They had natural on-ice affinity and skating styles which blended together seamlessly.

Exceeding everyone's expectations, Berezhnaya and Sikhuralidze finished third in the 1997 Europeans, just their fourth competition together. And although they suffered severe nervousness at the 1997 Worlds, resulting in a disappointing ninth-place finish, they were brilliant the next season, winning a silver medal at the Nagano Olympics and taking their first world championship a month later at Minneapolis. They won the Worlds again in 1999, although many observers felt Shen and Zhao deserved the gold.

After the 1999 season, Moskvina moved to the U.S., and the pair was forced to follow her to an unfamiliar country with unfamiliar customs and language. Berezhnaya was homesick, and the stress took a toll on the pair's relationship and performance level.

Then came the unwanted hurricane of the 2002 judging scandal. Nobody ever accused Berezhnaya and Sikharulidze of being complicit in the judges' vote-swapping and they were praised for their stoicism during the media storm. The upbeat Sikharulidze would later admit that all the media focus got them more attention — and professional touring dates — than if they'd won outright.

The pair became popular touring performers in North America, and later Europe, and in 2007 Sikharulidze, who as David Pelletier has stated, has "always been a person with really interesting ideas," was elected as a St. Petersburg representative to the Duma (Russian parliament). The following year he was made chairman of the Duma committee responsible for Russian physical culture and sport, so, in effect, Russian figure skating now reports to him. Berezhnaya took time away from skating for

the birth of her son Trysten, which she and her partner (fellow professional skater Steven Cousins) celebrated in late 2007.

Artur Dmitriev
with Natalia Mishkutionok and Oksana Kazakova

There were stretches during his amateur career when easygoing Artur Dmitriev would get a little soft around the edges, smoke cigarettes and look anything like a world-class athlete. But, when it really mattered, the superlative Russian pairs skater was right in the moment physically, emotionally and mentally, with the focus of a hawk and the instincts of a champion.

No other man has done what Dmitriev accomplished: partner two different women to Olympic pairs skating championships. He realized the feat by winning with Natalia Mishkutionok in Albertville in 1992 and Oksana Kazakova in Nagano in 1998.

And had it not been for a silver medal at the 1994 Games in Lillehammer, Dmitriev's career mark would be equal to Irina Rodnina's record of three Olympic pairs gold medals.

Without the ISU's one-time decision to allow former amateurs turned professionals to become eligible participants, Dmitriev would have never even gotten a chance at the milestone. That silver medal performance in Lillehammer, which many veteran witnesses have said was worthy of the gold, was the final event of the Mishkutionok-Dmitriev partnership, and they split amicably. She wanted to return to professional touring, where she and Dmitriev had made a solid debut after winning the 1992 Olympics, but Dmitriev's competitive appetite had been whetted, and he wanted to maintain his eligible status.

Mishkutionok eventually met (then married, and divorced) American hockey player Craig Shepherd, with whom she formed an unlikely professional pairs partnership, in a storyline that mimicked the skating movie *The Cutting Edge*.

Dmitriev, meanwhile, searched for another partner and in February 1995, at the famed Yubileyny Sports Palace in St. Petersburg, he officially teamed with

Kazakova, a native of St. Petersburg, who had finished 15th at the 1993 World Championships with former world junior champion Dmitri Sukhonov.

Many observers felt that the new combination wouldn't click because he was 27 and she just 19, and Kazakova's skills were well below the level of her partner's. But insightful coach Tamara Moskvina felt Dmitriev could quickly bring her up to speed and as usual, the dynamic coach had it right. Her pair won the 1996 European Championships. They finished only fourth at the Russian Nationals the next year and didn't qualify for the Europeans, but a second-place finish at the Grand Prix Final earned them a berth at the 1997 Worlds. They won the bronze medal, but that hardly made them favorites for the 1998 Olympic title.

Then, at the Nagano Games, despite a weak death spiral in the short program, Kazakova and Dmitriev rode a passionate and energetic free skate past reigning world champions Mandy Woetzel and Ingo Steuer, 1997 World silver medalists, Marina Eltsova and Andrei Bushkov, and European champions Elena

Natalia Mishkutionok and Artur Dmitriev skate to a silver medal at the 1994 Games in Lillehammer.

Berezhnaya and Anton Sikharulidze.

Dmitriev and Kazakova went on to tour professionally and Dmitriev eventually became a coach and choreographer in the U.S for a time, before moving back to Russia in 2007.

It was a different Russia than it had been 20 years earlier when he teamed up with Mishkutionok in the then-Soviet city of Leningrad. Both were outsiders — he from the far north, she from Minsk.

Dmitriev was a singles skater, but at 16 he was rapidly approaching his eventual height of six feet, a height that generally makes it difficult for singles skaters to launch and maintain the lift necessary to execute the powerful jumps needed in the singles discipline. He came south to Leningrad and to pairs training with the renowned Moskvina. Meanwhile, in 1987 Mishkutionok's ailing mother brought Natalia to Moskvina, hoping she could learn to coach, so she

Dmitriev and Oksana Kazakova, with their coach Tamara Moskvina, receive their gold-medal winning marks with excitement at the Nagano Olympics.

would have a profession if her mother died (happily, she did survive). Moskvina teamed the delicate and cool, almost aloof, Mishkutionok with Dmitriev who was a full ten inches taller.

With his thick curly hair, slightly brooding on-ice demeanor and strong skating skills and her refined suppleness, they were a striking pair, blessed with innate musical and dramatic sense. They moved together as if their bodies were magnetized.

In their signature element, usually appearing at the end of the program, Mishkutionok would have her face down at her partner's boot, one leg pointing straight up, and would grab hold of Dmitriev's calf as they both spun. Moskvina called it Natalia's Spin, but freely acknowledged that she'd copied the move from Canadian skater Lyndon Johnston.

After finishing third at two Europeans and one Worlds, they took over from Gordeeva and Grinkov

as world champions in 1991 and 1992. Liszt's Dream of Love, which they used both years, is considered one of the classic pairs programs although, trained to strive for perfection, Mishkutionok was dissatisfied with their 1992 Olympic gold medal performance because she had made two mistakes.

Mishkutionok and Dmitriev represented three different "nations" in that confusing period of the 1990s: the Soviet Union, the Unified Team (a loosely-defined, anthem-less collection of former Soviet States at the 1992 Games) and Russia.

Through it all, they worried about food, power and ice-time shortages due to the decline and fall of the Soviet system. Mishkutionok's mother stood in food lines, and made costumes, to save them money and time, and Moskvina found them money-earning exhbitions when food prices shot up a hundredfold in the early 1990s.

Few of their peers outside Russia faced anything like that harsh reality, but it was just another opponent eventually beaten by Dmitriev and his partners.

Ekaterina Gordeeva and Sergei Grinkov

At about 11 o'clock on the morning of Monday, November 20, 1995, 28-year-old Sergei Grinkov launched his wife into a throw double Axel during a practice at Lake Placid, New York. Accelerating as usual toward her landing, he inexplicably stopped, skated a few rudderless strides to his right, and then gently lay down on the ice.

And Ekaterina Gordeeva, a world champion at the age of 14, became a widow at the age of 24.

Only death could have separated this pairs team, which most of their contemporaries considered the greatest ever. It was an ideal, and yet firmly grounded partnership, on and off the ice, a love story that the entire skating world basically watched unfold before them.

The soft-spoken, strong, reliable Grinkov and wispy, but steel-tough Gordeeva were the perfect blend of the contrasting styles that had divided pairs skating since the late 1960s. They combined the elegance, softness and emotional connection of the Protopopovs with the raw speed, athleticism and mammoth tricks of the Rodnina era.

The couple who became known simply as G&G, were raised and trained under the old Soviet Russian skating regime. Gordeeva's father was a dancer in the Red Army dance company in Moscow, but she preferred the rink to the dance floor. She began skating at the Central Red Army school when she was just four, and at 10 was paired with 14-year-old Grinkov, a tall, promising singles skater.

Neither was sure the partnership would work, because he was so tall and she so small and frail-looking, and at first they skated as if they were younger sister and protective big brother. But they had extraordinary cohesion, excellent skating skills and their size difference enabled them to perform the highest level of elements, such as the quadruple twist.

In 1985, Gordeeva and Grinkov won the World Junior Championships. They finished second to world

The epitome of elegance and grace, Gordeeva and Grinkov perform the routine that earned them the gold at the 1988 Calgary Olympics.

champions Elena Valova and Oleg Vasiliev at the 1986 Europeans, but eight weeks later, two months before her 15th birthday, Gordeeva and Grinkov won their first of four world championships. They became the first pair to jump directly from junior world champions to senior world champions.

They quickly evolved from a tricks-team into a superlative, all-round pair, with great sensitivity to music and an unearthly seamlessness to their programs. But despite more obvious assets, their greatest strength was their blade work. It was often said of G&G that their touch was so soft you could not hear their skates carve the ice, even when the music was off. That same softness extended to their on-ice demeanor, as it seemed the pair never removed their adoring eyes from each other during a performance.

G&G won the 1987 World Championships, and at the 1988 Olympics in Calgary, the pair captivated judges, the live audience and millions of TV viewers to win gold. In the post-Olympic emotional letdown, they lost the 1988 world title to Valova and Vasiliev, but came back to win the Worlds again in 1989 and 1990 with sophisticated ease, before turning professional with Stars on Ice. Like so many Russian skaters after the fall of communism, they moved to the U.S. east coast.

Meanwhile, it was clear to skating observers, perhaps before it was clear to the skaters themselves, that Gordeeva and Grinkov had fallen in love. They married in 1991 and their daughter Daria was born a year-and-a-half later.

When a brief window was opened for pros to return to eligible skating in 1994, G&G took advantage, winning the Europeans and their second Olympics, the only Games gold won by returning pros. They suffered two uncharacteristic major mistakes, but carried the night with exquisite skating melting right into the music.

Eighteen months later, with his tiny grieving widow standing alone and vulnerable, Grinkov's funeral was held in the very Moscow rink where the two had trained for so many years.

Heartbreakingly, Gordeeva performed alone at a tribute to Grinkov soon after his death, and continued a solo career, mostly with her close friends in Stars on Ice. Later she married 1998 Olympic champion Ilia Kulik and their daughter Elizaveta was born in 2001.

Gordeeva and Grinkov's beautiful, and ultimately sad story transcended skating and caught the imagination of North Americans. She wondered aloud whether their life was too perfect to last and her book, *My Sergei*, was a runaway bestseller.

Choreographer Marina Zueva understands why. She was on the ice the day Gordeeva and Grinkov teamed up in Russia and was the only other person on the ice with them the day Grinkov died in America.

"People lose their dreams in life, and it was like they were the dream for everyone."

Jamie Sale and David Pelletier

It is unfortunate that the worst judging scandal in history chased Jamie Sale and David Pelletier from the eligible ranks before they could elevate the art of the competitive pairs program even further.

Sale and Pelletier spent only four seasons together in "amateur" competition and in that time left indelible impressions with iconic free skates Tristan and Isolde, Orchid and, of course, Love Story.

In an era that featured three other legitimate, and lasting, world champion pairs — Maria Petrova and Alexei Tikhonov; Xue Shen and Hongbo Zhao; and their chief rivals, Elena Berezhnaya and Anton Sikharulidze — Sale and Pelletier dominated their final two years, winning 12 of the 13 competitions they entered, finishing second to Russians Berezhnaya and Sikhuralidze in only the 2000 Lalique Trophy.

But one of those gold medals left such a bad taste in their mouths, that they immediately turned professional.

On a night when their revived Love Story had clearly beaten Berezhnaya and Sikhuralidze's solid, but uninspired skate, the Russians were awarded the 2002 Olympic gold medal on a 5–4 split. There was an immediate media uproar which reached an unprecedented intensity with the ensuing revelation by the French judge that she'd been pressured to vote for the Russians. Every major news outlet in North America immediately dispatched extra reporters and crews to Salt Lake and, for four days, the rest of the Olympic Games was completely overshadowed by the scandal. Hardened journalists, not usually assigned to sports stories, pressed the slow-reacting International Skating Union with demands for resolution and explanation. Sale and Pelletier appeared on major late-night talk shows and on the covers of the U.S.A.'s most influential weekly magazines. Four days after the original competition, and after an angry intervention by the International Olympic Committee, the Canadians were awarded a second gold medal, sharing the top spot with Berezhnaya and Sikhuralidze in a repeat podium ceremony.

The scandal created massive credibility issues for

figure skating and also fast-tracked the radical International Judging System that replaced the 6.0 Judging System for all ISU championship events starting the 2004-05 season.

"What we've created out of what we've been given, lifestyle, recognition, is great," Sale says. "But we got robbed of that 'moment.' And there was that national pride thing, everyone in Canada wanted to hear their national anthem on that night."

Adds Pelletier: "A lot of people tell us it's our fault that the marking system changed," Pelletier says. "But it really had nothing to do with us, they did it to themselves."

Sale and Pelletier became instant legends as the massive U.S. media mill relentlessly took up their cause. The self-effacing, often humorous, way they conducted themselves on national TV endeared them to people even more.

By then, in just four years together, Sale and Pelletier had become the masters of the seamless, evocative pairs program.

It helped that that they were beautiful, athletic and in love (they eventually married and started a family), and that their personal electricity was obvious on the ice.

It also helped that each had a deep and successful skating background. Pelletier, born in a small village in eastern Quebec, figure skated and played hockey until he was 15. He was second in the national junior singles championship, the same season he and partner Julie Laporte were national junior champions and finished seventh at the Junior Worlds. He then partnered Allison Gaylor to a national silver medal and 15th-place World finish in 1995, while also finishing fourth in the Canadian men's championship.

Sale, raised in Red Deer, Alberta, took

Gold medalists Jamie Sale and David Pelletier dazzle the crowd during their gala performance at the 2002 Salt Lake Olympics.

gymnastics before concentrating on skating, and in 1994, she finished third in the Junior Nationals as a singles skater and was fifth in Seniors the next year. Skating pairs with Jason Turner, Sale won a bronze medal at the 1994 Nationals and finished 12th at the Lillehammer Olympics.

Sale and Pelletier originally auditioned together in 1996 but at the time it didn't quite take and they decided not to pursue a partnership. Then two years later, when Sale, back in singles, suggested to the partnerless Pelletier that they try it again, things were entirely different and they began training together in Montreal.

"The first time out there, I felt 'it' and skating became easy again," Pelletier says. "Jamie and I both thought skating was telling a story beyond the elements, and when you have the 'it' factor, it's easier to tell the story."

Choreographer Lori Nichol provided those stories, as the new team finished second at their Canadian Nationals debut in 1999, but were forced to miss the rest of the season due to Pelletier's back injury. The next season they won their first of three straight national titles, but were fourth at the Worlds when Sale made some technical mistakes.

During the short program at the Vancouver Worlds in 2001, Sale stepped out of a triple toe loop, the element that was bedeviling her at the time, and they stood third heading into the free skate. In the free skate, they landed the triples with perfect timing "and the crowd was so loud I had to tell Jamie to settle down, but we just rode the wave all the way home."

Their gold was just the fourth (Wagner-Paul, Underhill-Martini and Kurt Browning) ever won by Canadians on home ice, and it gave them momentum for the notorious 2002 Olympics, where they would be at the center of a storm that changed skating forever.

Xue Shen and Hongbo Zhao

The colossal significance of Xue Shen and Hongbo Zhao was reflected in Bin Yao's wet eyes. The normally impassive Chinese master coach could not hide the emotional and historic gratification after his star pupils won both their second and third world championships, more than any of their pairs skating contemporaries and more than any other Asian skaters in history.

In 2003, Shen ignored the searing pain of a bad ankle injury to deliver the performance of her life, as she and her appreciative partner doggedly repeated as world champions. Four years later, Shen and Zhao concluded a crammed, undefeated 2007 season with an untouchable performance at the Worlds in Tokyo and skated off into semi-retirement,

Sale and Pelletier on *The Tonight Show With Jay Leno* days after the IOC issued the pair gold medals in retribution for judging improprieties carried out during the pairs competition.

OPPOSITE: Hometown favorites Xue Shen and Hongbo Zhao skate at the 2006 Cup of China. The duo won by 21 points over fellow Chinese pair Qing Pang and Jian Tong.

which, given their dominance, still left skating fans wondering about a return for the 2010 Olympics. At the end of their 2007 Worlds free skate, Zhao knelt to the ice in part to thank Japan for being a good host, but mostly to ask Shen to marry him. Later, they formally announced their engagement celebrating the love they'd been forced to hide, but which most skating fans had seen for a long time.

The final half-minute of their 2007 free skate was accompanied by a heartfelt standing ovation, acknowledging how far the once shy and awkward pair had come.

For their coach Yao, the wheel had completely turned. He and partner Luan Bo were the first pairs team to represent China internationally, and audiences actually laughed at them when they finished last at the 1980 Worlds.

When he retired in 1984, Yao succeeded Li Yaoming, the legendary Leader Li, as national coach and began the long, meticulous process of developing champions. For the next seven years, no pairs left China for competition, while Yao built the program.

Yao is the fulcrum of Chinese skating history. He had been a seven-year-old skater when the Cultural Revolution of the 1960s banned the sport as too bourgeois. And when it suddenly regained status, he was part of a spartan training regime that relied upon detailed study of still pictures (and some tapes) of western pairs, because no one in China knew anything about the discipline.

Shen and Zhao perform in the gala at the 2007 Four Continents Championships, part of an undefeated season that included the 2007 Worlds.

Yao was based in frigid, northern Harbin, known in China as Ice City. In 1992, against the instincts of other skating officials, Yao teamed the unknown, far less talented Shen with Zhao to replace Maomao Xie, with whom Zhao had finished 11th of 16 teams at the 1991 Junior Worlds. That was the first time a Chinese pair had not finished last at an ISU event.

Zhao had made the Chinese national team without ever skating. Leader Li saw him playing kindergarten basketball, liked his strength, power, foot movement and coordination and said he should be a skater. At the age of seven, he moved into a team dormitory a few miles away, and never lived at home again.

Where Zhao is outgoing and blessed with innate skill, Shen overcame a lack of native talent with a rigorous work regimen that is almost impossible to fathom. Shy, undersized, and sickly, she trained outside in the bitter cold for as many as eight hours a day, starting when she was just five. Wretchedly poor, she, her father and mother would sneak through an open window of an arena under construction at 4 a.m. to scrape up some extra ice time.

She pressed on despite feet that were often frostbitten or bleeding from wearing skates that were deliberately purchased too big. She could, as Joy Goodwin described in her excellent study, *The Second Mark*, "eat more bitterness" than other skaters, and it was that quality, and her unworldly determination that eventually prompted Yao to team Shen with Zhao when she was just 13.

Impossibly, she trained even harder to catch up to the skills of the 18-year-old Zhao, who could already do five triple jumps. They moved to Beijing with Yao to live in state dormitories and soon developed huge throws and lifts and elite jumps. But without access to a culture of pairs skating, they had no unison or finesse and struggled mightily with spins and smooth jump entries, as well as with western artistic standards.

They debuted internationally in 1994, finishing an unimpressive 21st at the World Championships and, after skipping the next Worlds, inched up to 15th in 1996. With his photographic memory, Yao was studying the world's top pairs and adding incrementally to his students' still-thin arsenal of tricks and artistry.

Shen and Zhao smashed through a huge barrier

in 1997 at the NHK Trophy, where their victory was the first international win by a Chinese pair. Two years later, they were the inaugural Four Continents winners, the first ISU championship for any Asian pairs team. And in 1999, they won China's first world pairs medal, finishing a controversial second to Elena Berezhnaya and Anton Sikharulidze. "They should have won," said Canadian pairs coach Paul Wirtz. "You could have driven a tractor-trailer under those throws."

They were second and third in the next two years, and won the bronze medal at the 2002 Olympics, the fearless Shen just missing her attempt at history's first throw quadruple Salchow. Patience, which Shen possesses in greater quantity than any other athlete, finally paid off a month later in Japan. Ten years after being forced together, they won China's first world pairs championship and became the planet's dominant team.

Zhao's tendinitis kept them out of the 2005 Worlds, and when he snapped the Achilles tendon completely the next summer — while practicing a triple-triple combination — their chances at competing for the 2006 Olympic gold seemed gone. But right after surgery he said he was inspired by Shen's courage at the 2003 Worlds and would be ready for the Turin Games. Two weeks before the Games, he landed his first triple loop and, despite clearly being subpar, he and Shen skated to their second Olympic bronze medal.

By the time they won their third World title in 2007, they had risen from unthinkable deprivation to become one of the most memorable and respected pairs teams ever.

Shen and Zhao had stimulated a tidal wave of popularity for pairs skating in China and even Japan; inspired young imitators in their home country; and, perhaps most surprisingly, had moved their stoic coach to tears.

Barbara Underhill and Paul Martini

Rarely do reverence, nervous anticipation, patriotism, vindication and acute awareness of significance collide as spectacularly as they did in one moment at the

Ottawa Civic Centre in March 1984.

Forty seconds from the end of the final free skate of their amateur careers, Paul Martini launched his partner Barbara Underhill into a soaring throw double Axel, as the crowd of 10,000 held its collective breath.

The throw Axel was considered an extremely difficult element at the time, and only a month earlier, the Canadians had botched it at the Sarajevo Olympics, hastening their descent to seventh place and nearly causing them to retire before the World Championships in their home country.

Because of natural interest and repeated exposure, Ottawa is among the most educated skating cities in the world, and the audience knew what was at stake. They knew that Olympic champions Elena Valova and Oleg Vasiliev of the Soviet Union had skated competently but not superbly, and had left enough room for the wildly popular Canadians. They knew that the crisply synchronized Underhill and Martini had yet to fulfill their vast potential, that the couple had felt humiliated and frustrated about their Olympic results, and that they had wanted to skip the Worlds. They also knew that the throw double Axel was the key to everything.

So the spectators knew that when Underhill triumphantly touched down on one foot, Canada had won its first figure skating world championship in 11 years, its first pairs gold in 22 years and that the second golden era of Canadian skating was indeed upon them.

The reaction was immediate and explosive. Sound becomes trapped and amplified under the low slanted roof of the Civic Centre, and the cheering nearly drowned out the final half minute of Underhill and Martini's music.

"I can't tell you the number of people who, to this day, have come up to me and said, 'I was in the building that night,'" Martini says.

"It was one of those experiences that if you get more than one in a lifetime, man you're living right. The disappointment of the Olympics, then in front of the whole country, basically pulling together what you were capable of doing but for whatever reason had never been able to quite get done.

"Had we been anywhere else, I know it wouldn't have been nearly as effective or had as much impact."

Barbara Underhill and Paul Martini a few years before their 1984 World title.

That victory, and the 14 years that still remained in their careers, had a wide-reaching effect on Canadian skating.

In the moment, it was a verification that the country was coming in from the wilderness after nearly two decades of sporadic results, and that the recently formulated "team concept" of the national association, which provided resources, experience and emotional support for Canada's top skaters, was working. Martini was Canada's first team captain.

The victory provided Underhill and Martini with the confidence and cachet they needed to embark on a long, post-amateur career.

They first toured with Ice Capades and assumed they might spend four years in the professional ranks. Instead, they became the greatest professional pairs team of all time, adapting to each era and maintaining their upper-tier marquee status despite a steady graduation of amateur champions to the pros. They toured with performance-based Stars on Ice, won seven world professional titles, and when professional competitions sprouted up everywhere in the mid-1990s, they won nine championships and 15 medals.

And because of TV, as performers, competitors and analysts (they were longtime broadcast commentators at the Worlds and Nationals) Martini and Underhill influenced Canadian skating more profoundly as pros than they did as amateurs.

They made the dramatic "Leap of Faith" their signature move, and although never romantically involved, they could sell an emotionally rich program such as Unchained Melody, as if they were lifelong lovers.

"Some of us in the pros realized that you could take it to another level, and that skating could be a far more emotional and theatrical experience as opposed to just an athletic endeavor," Martini says. "The environment allowed you the time and space to let that happen.

"There was a group of us who came out of the early '80s era and sprang into the pro world when there were probably more avenues than there had ever been and it continued to grow. And most of those avenues provided you with network television. So the ability to influence the sport, and attract viewership to the sport, was at your disposal."

Although they were mismatched in size, the difference was only noticeable on their biggest tricks. Otherwise, Underhill and Martini evolved into a fluid unit, and they could attract an audience just to watch the perfection and power of their basic stroking technique.

After spending three years competing against each other with different partners, Martini and Underhill were paired by legendary coach Louis Stong at a Toronto summer skating school in 1977. Within nine months, they won both the Canadian and World Junior Championships.

Graduating to seniors, they won their first of a record-tying five national titles, but stalled at the world level, finishing 11th in both 1979 and 1980, and seventh in 1981, before vaulting to fourth in 1982. In 1983, skating last, it appeared that they had beaten champions Elena Valova and Oleg Vasiliev but seven of the nine judges saw it differently, and they finished third.

That put them among the favorites for the 1984 Olympic gold. In Sarajevo, Underhill caught an edge and was propelled into Martini, ruining the short program, and the throw double Axel helped destroy the free skate and they finished seventh.

Shattered and dejected, they had decided to retire two weeks before the Worlds, but Brian Orser, Underhill's best friend, convinced her to try an old pair of skates during their goodbye practice. The comfort and familiarity of those old boots contributed to a good run-through, they decided to stick it out until Ottawa, and their lives changed because of it.

"Without Brian's advice our careers would have been completely different," Underhill said gratefully in early 2009 when she and Martini were inducted into the World Figure Skating Hall of Fame. Only the mystical Protopopovs had a longer run than Underhill and Martini's 21-year partnership.

And the floodgates opened for Canadian skating. In the 10 world championships prior to that unforgettable night in Ottawa, Canadians had won just four medals, all bronze. In the next 10 years the haul was 24 world medals, including seven gold and 10 silver.

It had become possible, often probable, that Canadians could win again.

Pivotal Moments

Every field has critical eras and entities that alter or accelerate its history. And, not surprisingly, timing is usually everything. When the milieu wasn't right, or the right person wasn't the one commanding the spotlight, figure skating only inched ahead. Those individuals and events with the most profound impact on figure skating's narrative usually arrived in, or arose from, an environment that was ready for them. Revolution meeting evolution.

For example, at the 1956 Winter Olympics, confident coach Gus Lussi told the press that his student, the dynamic American Ronnie Robertson, had been landing triple Axels with ease in practice and would do one in that evening's free skate. But, as Lussi later explained, they eventually decided Robertson didn't need the Big Daddy of all triples to win the free skate. Robertson did win that portion of the competition, but not by enough to dislodge countryman Hayes Alan Jenkins from the top of the podium. Had Robertson gone after the new jump, as he had in landing the world's first triple Salchow the year before, he quite possibly could have won the title and pushed men's skating's clock ahead 22 years. One of the most dynamic skaters ever, Robertson never won a world or Olympic title. And it would not be until 1978 that Canada's Vern Taylor landed the first triple Axel in competition and Brian Orser, another Canadian, made it de rigueur, igniting a sensationally athletic era.

Similarly, in 1969 Britain's Diane Towler and Bernard Ford won their fourth straight world ice dance championship, and had accomplished all they could as amateurs. American Mark McCormack, the pioneer of the burgeoning field of athletes' representation, flew to London to discuss with Ford the possibility of representing the pair professionally and creating a major tour around their stylish routines. But Towler didn't want to leave Britain, and the idea withered on the vine. It was not until two decades later that McCormack's company, International Management Group, used the very same concept to create Stars on Ice around their client Scott Hamilton, dramatically changing the way touring shows were presented.

Sonja Henie's celebrity status as both an athlete and an actress greatly increased
North America's interest in competitive figure skating.

This Currier and Ives print titled "Central-Park, Winter; The Skating Pond" illustrates the growing popularity of ice skating in 1860s America.

SHAPING SKATING'S PATH

Despite a number of those squandered moments, figure skating is still crammed with collisions of individuals, technology and sociology that have shaped its path.

Among the earliest important developments was the appropriation of skating by Europe's elite class, once the Dutch had invented "schaats" during the 16th century and taken them onto their frozen canals for business and pleasure.

In 1648, during the English Civil War, some members of the English Royal Family escaped into exile in continental Europe. James, the Duke of York, spent the early part of his exile in Holland and learned to skate on the country's frozen canals. When his older brother regained the throne in 1661 for the family as King Charles II, James returned to England and took his love of carving figures on ice with him. The "hard frost" of 1662 froze the Thames River and the new royal sport could be practiced immediately.

Meanwhile, in 1660 Dutch engineers had drained the fens at Cambridge and had skated on the frozen remains, intriguing the local populace and marking the arrival of speed skating in England. With speed skating thus introduced to the commoners and the elite society of London adopting the Duke of York's interest in figure skating, that two-year period started the general division of skating in England into figure skating for the upper classes and speed skating for the masses. That polarity was further entrenched when the Duke of York became King James II in 1685.

In North America, skating had reached a modest level of popularity just before the U.S. Civil War, partly because of the steel-bladed skate, which Edward Bushnell of Philadelphia began mass marketing in 1850. The steel allowed for deeper edges and faster movement, which coincided nicely with the popular rise of Jackson Haines in the 1860s.

Haines won several important championships in the U.S., but as he began to apply more balletic principles and movements to the inflexible, uninspired "British" style of skating in vogue at the time, he lost favor in the New World. Convinced he was on the right track, Haines emigrated to Europe in 1865 and got the same chilly reception in England before enjoying wild success in arts-astute Vienna. He was expressive from head to toe, performed to music, and invented a process to screw his skates directly into his boots, which created more stability and freedom to perform jumps. All those radical concepts set the standard for a new version of skating called the International Style, which quickly obliterated the stiff British fashion and formed the foundation of today's sport.

When Haines last performed in North America, in Montreal in 1864, he was reportedly watched by three-year-old Louis Rubenstein, who grew up to become a seminal figure in North American skating history. A renowned skater himself, Rubenstein spearheaded the formation of the Amateur Skating Association of Canada, now called Skate Canada, plus the National Amateur Skating Association of the United States and the International Skating Union of America, predecessors of what is now United States Figure Skating.

The national associations united the various clubs that had sprung up across the continent and provided a "grapevine" for information and technical advances — they also set performance standards, and, eventually, organized competitions. The first formal club in North America was the oddly named Philadelphia Skating Club and Humane Society.

The Europeans were well ahead in organizational evolution, with Scots in Edinburgh forming the world's first skating club in 1742. Prospective members had to show they could complete a circle on each foot, and be able to jump over three hats piled on top of each other. It wasn't until a century later, in 1830, that England got its first club, The Skating Club, which became the Royal Skating Club in 1932.

The National Ice Skating Association of Great Britain, combining clubs in the two countries, was formed in 1879, some 14 years before the *Internationale Eislauf Vereinigung* (IEV) brought together existing national unions for speed skating (and eventually included figure skating). The IEV evolved into the International Skating Union, which still runs the sport.

With its structural roots in private clubs, rather than more accessible forums, the die had been cast for the perception that figure skating was an elitist, expensive sport, an image it has never been able to completely shake.

As the sport became more popular and better organized, major competitions began springing up, beginning with the first recorded international event in Austria in 1882. By 1891 there was a European championship, with Austria and Germany as co-hosts. In 1896 the IEV staged its first major annual competition in St. Petersburg, Russia. In 1924 those events were formally, and retroactively, recognized as world championships.

THE "LADIES" ENTER THE SPORT

Until the beginning of the 20th century, the only competitors were men. This situation changed with the 1902 world championships in London, when Britain's Madge Syers, wife of 1899 World silver medalist Edgar Syers, entered and won the silver medal behind the legendary Ulrich Salchow. The IEV wasn't impressed and kept women out for the next three years. Eventually, under great pressure from English interests, in 1906 it established the first women's championship, which Syers won.

It is ironic that there should have been such fierce resistance to women competing in the sport that has the longest history of female stars and was the earliest to sanction women as athletes, officials and judges.

In fact, societal mores and, frankly, elitist attitudes have often stunted skating's development. For instance, figure skating didn't get its first female international judge until Mollie Phillips was appointed in 1947. It was felt the "frailer sex" couldn't handle the rigors of standing outside all day to judge figures. But, over the course of World War II, the years of men and women working side by side in war factories had reduced that argument to ashes. Fifteen years earlier, Britain, through Philips, achieved another first for women, as the figure skater became the first woman to carry the British flag at an Olympic Opening Ceremony when she held the honor at the 1932 Lake Placid Games. And today, when most other sports don't dare mention the archaic word, female skaters are still referred to as "ladies."

TECHNOLOGICAL DEVELOPMENTS

The Olympics would not have a separate "winter division" until 1924, but the British were keen to show the country's superiority in large-scale refrigeration and included skating in the 1908 Summer Games. London was a last-minute substitution for Rome, which had to bow out as host because of the huge costs of recovering from the devastating Mount Vesuvius eruption.

England had had artificial ice rinks since 1876 when the first one in the world opened in Chelsea, with short-lived success because of the expense and misty atmosphere. John Gamgee, the same man who invented the slot machine, developed the process and several other such venues sprung up across England and in North America (where New York's Madison Square Garden, six times the size of the Chelsea rink, opened in 1879). That established skating in the heart of the continent's emerging megacity, preparing the entertainment capital for the later arrival of Charlotte Oelschlagel, Sonja Henie and the ice shows.

Eventually, artificial ice made figure skating a year-round sport, allowing its athletes to hone their skills and routines during the off-season, thus elevating the performance and competition level.

There was no artificial ice available for the 1912 Games in Stockholm, but in 1920 figure skating was back at the Antwerp Olympics, before the first Winter Games were established at Chamonix, France, in 1924.

Sixteen years after the first Winter Olympics, Californian Frank J. Zamboni was worried that it was still taking too long to resurface the ice at a rink he had opened in 1940. By 1942 he was tinkering with an ice-resurfacing machine that would replace the shovels, tractor-towed watering barrels, and labour-intensive squeegeeing needed to resurface arena ice.

In 1949 Zamboni had the machine, which eventually bore his name, in full use. Sonja Henie bought two for her show, and Ice Capades also invested in one. With an hour-long process reduced to 15 minutes, revenues increased and arenas became more financially viable. It also meant that rinks could be built in any region, and resurfacing would not be a time issue.

THE STARS and THE SHOWS

With formal competition figure skating began to develop stars, many of whom became legends, in spite of the strict amateur rules, which didn't permit skaters to trade on their titles. The first icon was, of course, Haines, whose spirit hovered over the early competitions. He was followed by Axel Paulsen, who invented the sport's toughest jump (the Axel), and Ulrich Salchow, the first major player of the competition era, who won 10 world championships, the most by any man. Salchow also won the first men's Olympic championship in 1908.

Among the competitors at the 1908 Games was Irving Brokaw, 1906 American champion, who finished sixth at the Games in the first appearance by an American at an international skating competition. He returned to provide the U.S. its first important demonstration of the International Style, which it had not seen since Haines left the country. Combined with the earlier efforts of George H. Browne, who had studied the sport in Switzerland, Brokaw's zeal for skating established the International Style in North America. Browne organized the first U.S. Championships using the International Style at New Haven, Connecticut, in 1914.

The World Championships were suspended later that year because of World War I, and when they resumed, the same countries that had dominated the medals before hostilities — Sweden, Austria and Germany — took up where they had left off, a sharp contrast to the dramatic power shift that would happen after World War II.

The U.S. Championships, meanwhile, continued through the global conflict and were in their infancy when Charlotte Oelschlagel arrived in the U.S. from Germany. Going only by her first name, Charlotte starred in *Flirting in St. Moritz* a skating extravaganza

Sonja Henie drew attention to figure skating both at the rink and on the silver screen. Henie poses with a trophy in the 1939 movie *Everything Happens at Night*.

which, in 1915, played Broadway's Hippodrome for 300 consecutive days. Within the next year, some 400,000 pairs of skates were reportedly sold in the U.S., and many major U.S. hotels installed small indoor rinks of tank ice for entertainment acts.

Charlotte was also the headliner of *The Frozen Warning* (1917), skating's first movie. She, far more than the new national championships, helped popularize the sport across the nation, not just as an activity, but as a spectacle.

While Charlotte got Americans interested in skating as both an athletic endeavor and as entertainment, the legendary Sonja Henie accelerated the process years later. She arrived in New York, a city now ready for her showmanship, for the World

Championships in 1930, and she returned for the 1932 Olympics at Lake Placid, taking the country by storm both times. She generated an enormous interest in the sport at a time when American entertainment and sport were in their first great period of star culture, which turned silent movie stars Mary Pickford and Douglas Fairbanks and athletes such as Babe Ruth and Jack Dempsey into icons.

Henie was among many Europeans, including the Brunets and Frick and Frack, who sensed the

1947 World champion Hans Gerschwiler at the 1948 Olympics, Gerschwiler finished second behind Dick Button, who lost to Gerschwiler at the 1947 Worlds.

The Henie-triggered rise in skating popularity in the United States was aided by the founding of Ice Follies in 1937 by Oscar Johnson and Eddie and Roy Shipstad. Ice Follies, which became the first large-scale, all-pro touring show, kicked off a frenzy of new skating shows. Ice Capades was founded shortly after in California by John Harris in 1940, and applied the concepts of operettas and musicals to an ice-show format. Capades headliners Robert Dench, Rosemarie Stewart and Rona and Cliff Thaell became national stars and helped popularize ice dancing which, in turn, helped soften the attitudes of skating federations for dancing as a competitive division.

Holiday on Ice, the other long-term survivor of the ice-show boom, was born in 1944, and was the first company to own portable ice-rink equipment, which allowed it to spread the skating gospel to smaller towns that had never seen such a show.

But while these shows, and local, large-scale club carnivals were enormously popular, there were usually only a couple of headliners who performed pure skating numbers. Figure skating still wasn't big enough that pure skating could carry the show. It had to be cross-pollinated with the theatrically-costumed chorus routines of other mass entertainment genres.

THE WAR and ITS AFTERMATH

While North America was building stars, the world was at war. The World Championships were cancelled from 1940 to 1946, the 1940 and 1944 Olympics were scrubbed, and the infrastructure of European skating was nearly destroyed. Many arenas in Europe did not survive bombing attacks — popular skating centers in Bristol and Southampton, England, were wiped out by the earliest raids — and in Great Britain and some places on the continent, rinks were decommissioned for the duration and retrofitted into factories or armories.

By the time World War II ended, European skating had been devastated. Ravaged economies could not afford to rebuild arenas or operate those that had somehow survived. Some prewar stars, such as 1939 world silver medalist Freddie Tomlins of Great Britain, had been killed in action. Others, such as 1939 champion Graham Sharp of England, an army captain, had fought with distinction but had lost six or seven of their best skating years. Some coaches

winds of war and emigrated to the U.S. in the late 1930s. Henie retired after her third Olympic title in 1936, but continued to stimulate a North American interest in skating that remained unparalleled on the continent until the spectacular spike of the mid-1990s. Henie appeared in several movies, had her own touring show and, amplifying Charlotte's image, established the American stereotype of the athletic, attractive, flirty, but ultimately moral female skating champion, which exists to this day. Her most influential effort was the Hollywood Ice Revue, which played cities across North America from 1938 to 1950 and was promoted by Chicago Blackhawks hockey team owner Arthur Wirtz.

were killed, others had fled to North America. And a younger European generation hadn't been able to take up the sport.

The North Americans, while facing some deprivations during the war, had continued to skate and compete. The U.S. Championships, aside from the 1944 and 1945 men's competitions, were held every year during the war, while Canada cancelled the 1943 national tournament and only held a women's championship for 1944. All the while, the ice shows were creating new fans and attracting potential athletes.

So it is no surprise that, with the resumption of the World Championships in 1947, power had shifted dramatically westward. Hans Gerschwiler of neutral Switzerland won the first men's post-war world title, then the U.S. won an unprecedented, and unmatched 12 straight men's championships. Also, the first Golden Age of Canadian skating began immediately, when Barbara Ann Scott won the 1947 Worlds, the first time a non-European had won a global championship. And North American women won a dozen world titles in the next 20 years.

There were shortages everywhere in Europe, leaving no room for frills such as skating lessons and attire. For example, while finishing second to Scott in 1948, Austrian Eva Pawlik skated with gaping holes in her tights and wore boots that had become too abused to clean.

THE CHANGING FACE of FIGURE SKATING

In the 1950s, two major forces arrived which would re-sculpt the face of skating.

In 1952, ice dancing officially became part of the World Championships (but would wait until 1976 to gain Olympic status). This new discipline carved out a new fan base which liked what seemed to be common dance-floor moves on ice, and didn't so much care for the technical aspects and falls of the other three more athletic disciplines. But precisely because there were no falls, dancing quickly became the discipline where judging was most subjective, predictable and often dishonest.

Then in 1956 the Winter Olympics were televised for the first time. TV would eventually make the sport more popular than anyone had dreamed, but would also become its controlling force, both financially and artistically.

Coinciding with these two developments was the rise of Russia as a figure skating power. In 1956, three men and two pairs teams from the Soviet Union had entered the European Championships, without a placing higher than eighth. By 1958, the Russians had won a medal at the Europeans, and later that year entered the World Championships. Soon, Russia was producing prodigious pairs and dance teams that had seemingly acquired squatters' rights on the pairs and ice dancing podiums.

Russia had been absent from international skating since before World War I, as the communist government considered the sport too bourgeois. But after World War II, the Soviets saw skating as an arena for potential Cold War advantage and began marshalling its forces. When they arrived, they were ready.

"They had been at the Worlds and went to the practice sessions to tape everything we did," recalls four-time world ice dance champion Courtney Jones. "All of Russian ice dancing is based on what we did."

The Soviet Union quickly dominated the mixed events so well that soon the Russian National Championships became the measuring stick for all pairs and dance teams — the Russian Nationals became more important and influential than the World Championships.

"It was a war, there was huge secrecy, and people would prepare 'secret weapons,'" says two-time Olympic champion Evgeny Platov, of the USSR. "It was worse than the World Championships. It was amazing...and I loved it."

But because Russian skaters were completely state supported, it raised the issue of professionalism. Skating, with its leisure-class origins, had prided itself on rigid amateurism and forbade even a whiff of money, placing a limit of $25 on the value of gifts or prizes a skater could earn. And national federations counted upon skaters and their families to bear the expense, limiting both the prospective talent pool and the stars' ability to remain in the game for long.

"My parents beggared themselves so I could skate," Courtney Jones said, and his partner Doreen Denny

U.S. Champion Maribel Vinson in 1935. Vinson, along with her daughters Maribel and Laurence (whom she coached), were members of the U.S. team lost on Sabena Flight 548.

concurred. "We were given one-third of the land fare to the World Championship by our federation," she recalls. "That would get you the taxi to the airport."

It took nearly 30 years until "amateur" skaters were allowed trust funds in the 1980s. By the mid-1990s, amateurs were making as much as, or more than, they could as professionals. But it was the arrival of the Soviets that initiated the debate, which led to Olympic-eligible skating becoming a full-time profession rather than a full-time athletic hobby.

THE TELEVISION ERA and the DEATH of COMPULSORY FIGURES

The Americans, meanwhile, were faring so well internationally through the 1950s that it seemed

only natural for U.S. TV to discover figure skating. In 1960, Canadian Johnny Esaw, sports director for CTV, a new private network that hadn't yet aired, negotiated for the World Championship rights on behalf of ABC. The American network thought it would be forced to pay too much to the ISU, and that a Canadian-brokered deal would be cheaper.

Concurrently, CTV became the Canadian broadcast voice of international and national skating, a distinction it held with only a few interruptions before opting out of the sport in 2007. From 1981 on, the private network was a virtual partner with the Canadian Figure Skating Association and its successor Skate Canada, investing money and air time to improve Canadian skating under a deal brokered by Esaw and CFSA head David Dore. That was one of a number of steps that returned Canada to the forefront of international competition in the early 1980s.

The early years of Canadian and American TV rights heavily influenced the way the sport was broadcast, right into the new century — with more emphasis on personal interest and artistry than on the purely athletic. Part of that was because figures, a discipline TV shunned, often determined champions before the free skating reached the airwaves.

ABC was scheduled to televise the 1961 World Championships from Prague, but the event was cancelled after the crash near Brussels of Sabena Airlines Flight 548 from New York on February 15, 1961. It was the first major crash of a Boeing 707, and killed 72 crew and passengers, including the entire U.S. figure skating team bound for Prague. Coaches, judges, team officials and skaters' families were also lost.

The American skating program was shredded by the loss of skaters who were to form the building blocks of the next Olympiad. A development fund for American skaters was set up after the accident and has been a factor in dozens of gold medals since. European coaches, most notably Carlo Fassi and John Nicks, were quickly recruited to help rebuild shattered programs. And within a couple of years, the results began to show.

Unknown Peggy Fleming finished sixth in the 1964 Olympics, and then began winning world championships. As the lightning rod for a sport suffering so much obvious heartache, Fleming was

Peggy Fleming in 1967 after her second world title; one year prior to her unprecedented rise to stardom.

promoted heavily by ABC. She was a perfect spokesperson for skating, and her startling rise to the top accelerated the American recovery from the 1961 tragedy. Fleming's victory at the 1968 Olympics in Grenoble grabbed an entire nation's attention and heartstrings, and made skating the comeback sport of the era.

An enterprising rock and roll promoter named Tom Collins saw a North American marketing opportunity created by Fleming fever, and in 1969 started an annual post-Worlds tour featuring medalists and rising stars to capitalize on the increased television coverage of the global championships. The tour, which went by various titles over the years — including Champions on Ice, its final name before it went out of business in 2007 — was the first extended tour to be completely star-based, rather than production-based, and it formed a template for IMG's wildly successful Stars on Ice 20 years later.

In 1964, the ISU introduced the short program (initially called the "connected" program) to give an extra dimension to pairs skating, which had never included compulsory figures as singles and dance had.

So, a supplementary free skating event was already established when concern about figures' inordinate influence on singles' results reached a crescendo in the early 1970s. TV executives didn't like showing a battle for second and, along with other forward thinkers in the sport, lobbied heavily for changes after marketable free skaters like American Janet Lynn and Canada's Karen Magnussen repeatedly fell victim to figures' specialists like Austria's Beatrix Schuba. Schuba, a capable but uninspiring free skater, won two world championships and the 1972 Olympics because she was so adept at compulsory figures. In 1973, the short program was introduced, and the long death spiral of compulsory figures began.

As expected, there was a surge in free skating achievement, and in 1978 Canada's Vern Taylor landed a triple Axel, the first major jumping milestone for men in 15 years. Brian Orser

quickly followed, making it a necessary part of a championship repertoire. As figures declined in importance, other free skating breakthroughs followed. And once the compulsories were finally eliminated after the 1990 World Championships, skaters were freed from those mundane practice hours to work more on technique and showmanship. Simply put, the overall product became better, more competitive and artistically packed.

Internationally, the performance level absolutely soared from the 1990s onward. Much of that had to do with the shedding of compulsory figures, but there were other important factors: the rise of Asian skating increased the number of bona fide championship contenders; the fall of the Iron Curtain and subsequent economic chaos in the former Soviet republics sent top Russian coaches and skaters around the world; skaters were competing more often in major ISU events that offered prize money; and in making a significant income, top eligible skaters could afford more and better technical support, costuming and musical accompaniment.

No skating era ever approached the popularity the sport achieved in North America in the mid-1990s. Not the Sonja Henie years. Not the Button-Jenkins

THE NIGHT TO REMEMBER

IT'S A cowboy town, so there were thousands of white Stetsons in Calgary that week. But everybody remembers just one.

In the flood of joy and madness that immediately followed Elizabeth Manley's spectacular free skate at the 1988 Olympics, a delirious fan tossed the oversized hat onto the littered ice. The image of Manley wearing that Stetson and hurling herself at the Saddledome audience which — in decidedly unCanadian fashion — had gone crazy, is an enduring piece of Canadiana.

But Manley's unanticipated surge to a silver medal in Calgary, and her sweeping free skate victory over two media megastars, did not belong to only one country. It was pure Olympics. An extraordinary, four-minute response to the quadrennial demand to stand and deliver.

By marshalling all the flashes of brilliance she'd shown but could not sustain in her eight-year senior career, Manley completely overshadowed the Battle of the Carmens, which was supposed to rival the Battle of the Brians as the marquee event of the Games.

American Debi Thomas, who had won the 1986 world title, and East German Katarina Witt, the reigning world and Olympic champion, had both chosen to skate to music from Carmen in their long program. Coming into the Games, no one seemed to care what Manley was skating to. Witt's press conference drew close to 1,000 media attendees while Manley's, later that day, attracted nine reporters, all Canadian.

It was not that Manley didn't have talent. Nine years earlier, while still a junior, she had become the first Canadian woman to land a triple jump in combination. She had blazing speed, a bubbling on-ice personality when she was in sync, and she could launch big jumps quickly — with tight rotation. She had been third in the Junior Worlds, won three national titles and just a year before Calgary was poised to reach the world podium for the first time when a disastrous free skate relegated her to fourth.

But, by her own public admission, Manley struggled with pressure, often falling prey to attacks of nerves, which robbed her of the consistency required to run off two strong programs in a row. She even left the sport briefly in 1983, deflated by a fourth-place finish at the Canadians, as well as an earlier loss of hair from a nervous condition and the constant financial strain on her single-parent family.

Manley said she "was just trying to get through the Olympics" because only 10 days earlier she'd been bedridden with a pneumonia, which was still weakening her as she headed into the Games.

But in Calgary she finished a career-high sixth in figures and stood third after the short program, which buoyed her confidence, even though Witt had only to beat Thomas in the free skate to win her second Olympic gold.

In the free skate, Witt was conservative, Thomas was a disaster and Manley was on another planet. From the moment Manley landed a huge early triple Lutz, the skating-savvy crowd knew they were witness to something special.

"The thing that sticks out about that night — still — was the energy she created in the building," recalls Brian Orser (who also won a silver medal that week). "It just kept getting better and better as she went long."

Long before she finished with a flourish, the audience was on its feet screaming. Manley, hands pressed to her face in shock, took a moment to recover then exploded in unrestrained celebration. And found the Stetson.

"I didn't know how to handle skating that well," she recalls. "I just remember shaking and being in disbelief that after the hell we went through for three weeks I could have done the best I ever did."

She had annihilated the world's best female free skaters and claimed a silver medal that seemed like gold. It was Canada's first Olympic medal in women's singles since 1972, and a month later she proved it wasn't an isolated incident, winning silver at Budapest, the only women's world medal Canada had won since 1973. Her performances along with Orser's Olympic and World silver, as well as Tracy Wilson and Robert McCall's Olympic dance bronze and World bronze, reignited skating participation in the Canadian populace.

Manley signed with Ice Capades and went on to a successful professional career. And the night of her life still resonates loudly with skating fans and with the skater.

"Even on the days when I'm complaining," she says, "I thank my lucky stars."

string. Not even the reigns of Peggy Fleming and Dorothy Hamill.

It began with Scott Hamilton's popular tenure as world and Olympic champion in the early 1980s, and built up a head of steam with the 1988 Calgary Olympics' Battle of the Brians (Boitano and Orser) and Battle of the Carmens (Katarina Witt and Debi Thomas). The creation of Stars on Ice around Hamilton in 1989 maintained the momentum. It was then spiked by the International Olympic Committee decision to separate the Summer and Winter Games (moving the Games to a two year cycle with four years between each seasonal Olympic event), which resulted in the need for an extra Winter Games in order to make the Olympic Games rotation work. Those games, the 1994 Lillihammer Olympics, gave winter athletes two extravaganzas within three years.

And when associates of Tonya Harding clubbed rival Nancy Kerrigan on the knee during a practice session for the 1994 U.S. Nationals at Detroit's Cobo Hall, an entire continent became fixated on the sport. CBS coverage of the ladies technical (short) program at the 1994 Olympics was the sixth-most-watched program in U.S. TV history.

The extra hordes of viewers tuned in out of morbid curiosity, but many became intrigued by skating's more traditional beauties and developed into fans. At one point, skating was ranked the No. 2 favorite sport in the U.S. behind only NFL football. In another poll which further subdivided sporting taste, skating's four disciplines finished 2nd, 3rd, 4th and 5th behind only NFL football. It was, and still is, the favorite sport of women in the prime demographic of 18 to 40, creating enormous marketing and sponsorship opportunities.

When CBS lost its NFL broadcast rights in 1994, it went to alternative programming and started airing professional skating competitions on Sundays. That stimulated a stunning surge in the number of pro events, which reached a peak at mid-decade with 17 such competitions. The International Skating Union, a rather antiquated body, wasn't quite ready for the runaway success of the TV coverage and began losing its young stars — like 16-year-old 1994 Olympic champion Oksana Baiul — to the pros before they had accomplished all they could as "amateurs."

But Ottavio Cinquanta, an aggressive Italian former speed skater, ascended to the presidency of the ISU in 1994, and in a series of bold strokes wrested power back from the professional world. Amateur skaters were renamed (Olympic) "eligible" skaters and most restrictions against skating for money were removed. In 1995, the ISU began paying prize money at its major events and elevated its top six once-independent fall internationals into a high-profile Grand Prix series with a prestigious final.

The revamping of amateur skating went so well it kept many of its athletes in the game *too* long and created a bottleneck. They liked the career exposure, rock star treatment and many made more money from the ISU than they could have as pros.

As a bubble, the popularity of skating couldn't possibly have lasted. Athletes, professional and eligible, were overexposed and there weren't enough new dynamic stars. By the turn of the century it had found its level of acceptance — still far higher than a decade earlier — but the 2002 Olympic judging scandal at Salt Lake weakened skating's underpinning. The casual fans, and many lifelong devotees, turned away in droves while ratings and rights fees plummeted, particularly in the rich U.S.A.

Cinquanta, raised on the timing and finish-line mentality of speed skating, had already been talking about a change in the scoring system. The humiliation of Salt Lake accelerated the process and the radical new International Judging System, based on keeping judges' marks secret from their deal-making federations, item-by-item marking and reduction of subjectivity, was in full use by the 2005–06 season.

The new system has created a statistical base which skating had sorely lacked in comparison to other sports. There are now world records, segment records and all kinds of other data that fans and media can use for comparisons. The sport will never be totally quantifiable, and will never be totally acceptable to some, but it's become far less subjective and corruptible. The new system will eventually breed a new generation of fans with a deeper understanding of what goes into a program.

And the judges, once the focus of attention as soon as the music ended, have become anonymous — the attention is now cast back upon the athletes, and that's a good thing. After all, they are the real stars.

THE DANCERS

Ice dancing did not gain world championship status until 1952 or a berth on the Olympic roster until 1976, but it is always one of the first events sold out at the Worlds and Olympics. Many casual fans relate to ice dancing more readily than they do to pairs and singles skating because dancing is similar, by intent and by practice, to dancing in a ballroom or nightclub.

Ice dancers often start out as singles or pairs skaters but switch disciplines because they reach a competitive plateau, or because their body structure is not conducive to the powerful spins and jumps required in other disciplines.

But ice dancing has its own exacting demands. There is a heavy emphasis on the proper use and rapid change of blade edge. Skating in unison, and a strong sense of musicality are also heavily weighted. And because there are far fewer falls in ice dancing, the discipline has historically relied upon more subjective judging, which demands that dance couples find a way to stand out from the crowd artistically and choreographically while meeting the exacting technical demands.

Until the 21st century, ice dancing was dynastic, with champions tending to hang onto their positions throughout a four-year Olympic cycle. The inclination might be to reduce ice dancing dynasties to no more than judges playing favorites, but, in reality, this era produced some of the most influential performers in skating history. Without these dynasties skating might not have witnessed Diane Towler and Bernard Ford, Liudmila Pakhomova and Alexandr Gorshkov, or Jean Westwood and Lawrence Demmy. Furthermore, the run of four world titles, an Olympic gold medal and a record number of perfect scores by Jayne Torvill and Christopher Dean comprised the most dominant four-year period by any figure skaters, in any era.

Although there are still suspicions of subjectivity, the International Judging System has made ice dance judging far more objective. World and Olympic medals are now being won by an ever increasing number of nations — but the legendary performers of ice dancing's past are all due the accolades of the stars of any other discipline.

Two-time Olympic ice dancing champions Oksana Grishuk and Evgeny Platov pose
in an embrace symbolic of the passion and theatrics of ice dancing.

PIONEERS AND TRENDSETTERS — *Dance Pairs through to the 1970s*

Courtney Jones

with June Markham
and Doreen Denny

If some are born great, some achieve greatness and some have greatness thrust upon them, then Courtney Jones is among the latter group.

"I was never planning to be a champion," Jones likes to explain. "I sort of became one by mistake."

And he made the mistake with two different partners.

Jones, who skated as a hobby in Bournemouth on England's south coast, had come to London in 1956 to try his gold dances, the top rung on the skating discipline's national skills-testing ladder. But his coach, the legendary Gladys Hogg, was ill and unable to partner him through his tests and suggested that he team with June Markham, another skater trying for her golds. Further, Hogg recommended that Markham and Jones get familiar with each other's

style by entering a dance competition in Richmond.

"And to our amazement, we won," Jones says.

So they tried the British Championships soon afterwards, and finished second there, the placement landing them on the national team. That sent them on to the 1956 European Championships, where they finished second to their compatriots Pamela Weight and Paul Thomas.

"I was in the air force and had to get special dispensation to attend," Jones says. "I left camp just in time for the first practice and couldn't even stay afterward for the banquet and prize-giving. On the way home, my mother met me at the airport and gave me my air force uniform to wear back to camp. It was very difficult, and I did that twice."

A few weeks later, Jones and Markham finished second at the Worlds, and in 1957 and 1958, they swept the British, European and World Championships.

But after the 1958 Worlds, Markham decided to emigrate to Canada to teach skating.

"I was very disheartened because it was a very sudden stop," recalls the tall and regal-looking Jones. "I was working in a factory. I had three jobs actually. And I gave up."

But Hogg didn't, and soon spotted another partner for him.

Doreen Denny was a tall, beautiful singles skater with an enormous personality, who had been sixth in the national championships and second in the Commonwealth Games. But she had no desire to be an ice dancer and didn't even have her gold dance tests.

"I said, 'Courtney Jones? He's the world champion, I can't skate with him,'" Denny laughs. "I was scared. I had never had a dance partner in my life. I didn't know what he was going to do. But he was wonderful. After we skated together for the first time, he stood there with Gladys Hogg and then he put his arm around me while Gladys made the decision."

Courtney Jones with second partner Doreen Denny, with whom Jones continued his streak of World Championship gold medals, numbering four.

Squaw Valley Olympics, but dancing was 16 years away from being admitted to the Games.

"Watching all the Olympic athletes go off in their uniforms, it was very disappointing to have to sit at home," Denny says.

Ironically Jones, a four-time world champion who didn't have an opportunity to participate in any Games, designed the Olympic team uniforms for Great Britain in 1976 — the first year ice dancing was an official medal sport. And the bronze medalists that inaugural year were Americans Colleen O'Connor and Jim Millns, coached by Denny.

All through his skating partnerships, Jones worked at his designing career and usually made his partners' costumes.

When he was teamed with Markham, he worked in a lining factory from 6 a.m. to 6 p.m., while Markham worked in a dress shop all day. They never began training until 10 p.m.

When Denny became his partner, she worked 9-to-5 in Richmond, walked almost a mile to the train station for the hour ride to London, where she and Jones would practice at night, usually amid two or three hundred other skaters in a public session. They'd remain on the ice, alone, until it was time for Denny to take the last train back to Richmond. Jones would then shovel the ice clean in payment for the free practice time.

"We had no money so we had to do that, and to hold jobs," he said.

With no Olympic prospects and four world titles under his belt, Jones felt he'd done all he could in skating, and retired to pursue his burgeoning designing career. It wasn't until 40 years later that he told Denny they'd had an offer from Ice Follies, but he had turned it down.

Denny married Italian dance champion Gianfranco Canepa and eventually moved to Colorado Springs, where she was still coaching 40 years later. American dance pioneers Judy Blumberg and Michael Seibert were among her students.

It's a monumental testament to Jones' ability as a partner, and Hogg's as a coach, that in the five months before the British Championships, without ever having ice danced in competition, Denny was somehow able to learn 16 compulsory dances and a free dance.

At the British Nationals, she and Jones won, and then won again "by a hair's breadth" over fellow British couple Catherine Morris and Michael Robinson at the Europeans. Then, in what was just Denny's third dance competition, the couple captured the 1959 World Championships in Colorado Springs.

In 1960 at Vancouver they were world champions again, beating Canadian champions Virginia Thompson and Bill McLachlan. A month earlier skaters from all other disciplines had been in the

After a 10-year absence from the sport, Jones returned to the administrative chain, and eventually became a member of the ISU dance technical committee. He and Peri Horne are credited with creating the Starlight Waltz and Silver Samba dances.

Jones and Denny have kept in close touch "and are still the best of friends."

Irina Moiseeva and Andrei Minenkov

Even if they hadn't won two European titles, two world championships and two Olympic medals, Russians Irina Moiseeva and Andrei Minenkov would still be legends.

They popularized the single-theme programs which soon became ice dancing's calling card. They jump-started the coaching career of the dynastic Tatiana Tarasova, who was an unheralded 22-year-old coach in 1969 when she began working with 13-year-old Moiseeva and 14-year-old Minenkov.

But, more pointedly, they influenced two of the most influential dance couples of the last 30 years: the incomparable Jayne Torvill and Christopher Dean from Britain and the athletic duo of Tracy Wilson and Rob McCall from Canada.

"I was a singles skater and didn't want to be an ice dancer until I saw them skate," said Wilson who, with partner McCall, won an Olympic bronze medal and pioneered an athletic North American ice dancing revival, which began to bear full fruit in the early 2000s.

"They [Moiseeva and Minenkov] had grace, elegance and a sense of theater," Wilson continued. "Dramatic, strong, balletic."

Skaters and skating fans were more consistent in their love for the Russian husband and wife team, known familiarly as "Min and Mo," than their own federation was. After winning their second world championship in 1977, Moiseeva and Minenkov remained on the Worlds podium for five more years, but never stood at the top of it. In the rigid, politically dictated ice dancing hierarchy of the 1970s and 1980s, that was a stern message that they were out of favor, no matter what the rest of the world thought, and that they had overstayed their welcome. So, after finishing third at 1982 Worlds, Moiseeva and Minenkov left the amateur ranks, just as the British couple they had inspired was climbing to record-setting heights.

The Russian pair had had a stunningly influential international career, which debuted with seventh-place finishes at the 1973 European and World Championships and eventually harvested 18 medals, six of them gold, from the Europeans, Worlds and Olympics.

They had excellent technique and an obvious chemical connection (they eventually married), but their lasting impact was their refusal to remain within traditional ice dancing forms,

"Min and Mo" revolutionized ice dancing with the help of young coach Tatiana Tarasova. The two-time world champions display their trademark artistry in 1982.

or to accept the dictates of national and international judges. They became the torchbearers for avant-garde ice dancing, and planted the seeds of possibility in the minds of rising young dance teams.

"We don't regret anything," Minenkov said in a 2007 Russian TV special. "We always agreed with Tatiana's main concept of the newer, the more interesting. We always had to have something new, we should never repeat ourselves, not in our movements, not in our thoughts, not in our music."

As inexperienced as she was, Tarasova recognized that the way to reveal the romantic young couple's strongest assets was through their music. But, she recalled years later, she felt restrained by dancing's accepted program structure, which relied upon four distinct segments, two to a slow beat and two to a fast one, performed mainly to traditional European operas or operettas.

Tarasova began selecting single-concept pieces to emphasize her students' sense of theater and ability to interpret the dramatic theme of the music, rather than just its mood and tempo. That resulted in several memorable, seamless programs including Carmen, Romeo and Juliet, and their signature program, the trend-setting West Side Story. Choreographer Irina Klenskaya, who worked with Moiseeva and Minenkov, said that Carmen brought Minenkov into his own and he became more than just a supportive appendage to his proud, energetic partner.

In the absence of Liudmila Pakhomova and Alexandr Gorshkov, they leapt from fourth at the 1974 Worlds to the gold medal in 1975. They were second behind Pakhomova and Gorshkov at the 1976 Olympics and Worlds, and then won the 1977 Worlds after their revered compatriots retired.

The dancers themselves first suggested West Side Story, a modern, western Romeo and Juliet, perhaps because it reminded them of their own situation. Tarasova created an advanced, daring program that drove appreciative audiences wild, but which left judges less enthused, and they finished second at the 1978 Worlds.

After 10 years with Tarasova, Moiseeva and Minenkov switched to Pakhomova, who was just beginning her coaching career. Part of the decision was political, based on the lukewarm reaction of the judges to West Side Story. Later, they were trained by Natalia Dubova, another coaching superstar, but despite lessening their fierce intensity and amending their style, their world status never improved from third place.

Eventually, Min and Mo took up coaching and at a training camp in 1990 they suggested that Isabelle Delobel and Olivier Schoenfelder join forces. It took 18 years, but the French couple went on to win the 2008 world title — coached by Tarasova who by then was a superstar.

While the general public may have lost touch with Moiseeva and Minenkov, their ground-breaking work still resonates with athletes. Skaters they inspired have inspired another generation.

"At our first Worlds [1982] we were in a practice group with them," says Tracy Wilson, now a coach and a respected TV analyst. "And I was in awe. I felt like the Ugly Duckling because here was The Goddess. I wanted to skate just like them."

Liudmila Pakhomova and Alexandr Gorshkov

As a skater, Alexandr Gorshkov ruled the world of ice dancing. As an official, he does the same thing. Now the chairman of the ISU's extremely powerful ice dance technical committee, Gorshkov was one half of the memorable team that started the Soviet Union and Russia down the path of ice dancing domination.

"My experience as an ice dancer helps me now as we try to make ice dancing better and a more popular sport around the world," Gorshkov says.

Gorshkov and his late wife Liudmila Pakhomova, were the first ice dancing world champions (1970) from the former Soviet Union, the first Olympic ice dance champions (1976) from any country and they still hold the record of six world titles in the discipline.

"And thanks to them, dancing came into the Olympics," says Tamara Moskvina, the master pairs coach who was a national teammate of Pakhomova and Gorshkov.

When the ISU finally accorded ice dancing full championship status in 1952, the first dynasties

Liudmila Pakhomova and Alexandr Gorshkov at the 1971 World Championships; their second of what would be a string of five straight world titles, a record six in total.

were primarily British, reflecting the country's tradition of ballroom dancing.

Russia, then the dominant republic of the massive Soviet Union, didn't enter a dance team at the Worlds until 1966 when Pakhomova, teamed up with her former coach Victor Ryzhkin, finished 10th out of 13 entries. Their free dance was creative, but their compulsory dances were hopelessly ragged, because they had had little exposure to them. The year before, Britain's Bernard Ford and Diane Towler, about to become world champions, had met Pakhomova and Ryzhkin at the Europeans in Moscow and had taught them a couple of the compulsory dances.

Pakhomova soon decided to find a new partner and the Soviet skating world was shocked when Gorshkov was chosen, as his ability and experience were clearly beneath her level.

But both skaters were driven to succeed, and when they began working with coach Elena Tchaikovskaia, the total became far greater than the sum of the individual parts.

"I still remember the time when we knew nothing," says Tchaikovskaia, who still coaches elite skaters. "I used every opportunity to learn, and I watched."

What emerged was a new style of ice dancing, combining classical ice dance with Russian folk music and dancing and the principle elements of the Russian ballet school. (Pakhomova herself was accredited to teach ballet.)

"We were trying to change the face of the sport." Gorshkov recalls. "So we used the type of folk music which hadn't been used before."

What was then new has become standard ice dancing fashion.

"We skated in the old style of erect upper body," Ford recalls. "But she was the first to add choreographic details. She'd emphasize an ankle, a flick of the wrist, a lift of the finger. I'm sure it all came out of ballet.

"When they skated, she was everything. He was in the shadows."

Which may be why the partnership worked. The charismatic Pakhomova brimmed with energy and emotion and the sophisticated, but reserved, Gorshkov would virtually present her to the audience, a role ice dancing insiders cynically refer to as "The Waiter." But without that kind of partner, Pakhomova would say later in her career, she would not have been able to project her unique skills and personality.

In 1969, the emerging couple won the Soviet Union's first international dance medals, with a bronze at the Europeans and a silver at the Worlds behind Towler and Ford.

They took over the top of the podium, and ice dancing, in 1970; and through 1976, the only events they didn't win were the 1972 Europeans, when they were beaten by Germans Angelika and Erich Buck, and the 1975 Worlds, which they skipped because of Gorshkov's serious lung illness.

Pakhomova and Gorshkov were enormously popular, especially in their home country where "they were the symbol of art and sport," Moskvina recalled. "Thanks to them, we learned that sport. Before them, there really was no dancing there." So celebrated were they that in 1972, a Soviet astronomer discovered a minor planet and named it 3231 Mila in honor of Pakhomova.

After much internal arm twisting, the International Olympic Committee was convinced to accredit ice dancing as a medal sport, based partly on the momentum created by its Russian champions.

Pakhomova and Gorshkov won the 1976 Olympics handily and, after winning their sixth Worlds a few weeks later, retired from amateur skating. They left behind several memorable performances including their legendary showpiece La Cumparsita. And, ironically, the woman who couldn't master compulsory dances with her first partner invented one with her second. The Tango Romantica is now part of the international rotation.

By the time they left competition in 1976, they had already been married for six years and in 1980 Pakhomova gave birth to their daughter Yuliva. Gorshkov pursued the officiating channel of the sport, becoming an influential judge and referee before being elected to the powerful technical committee and later heading that committee. Pakhomova became a successful coach in Moscow. Oleg Ovsyannikov, who won two world titles with Angelika Krylova, says Pakhomova was responsible for his switching to ice dancing when he was eight years old.

By 1986, Pakhomova had become too ill with cancer to accompany her students to the World Championships, and she died two months later at the age of 36.

"It was a national tragedy," Moskvina says. "Nobody could believe that an Olympic athlete, a champion, could die so young."

"For her and for her life and sports companion, Alexandr Gorshkov, it was the principal objective to multiply the best traditions of the Soviet school of figure skating," the state-run press agency Tass wrote upon her death. "They strove for perfection."

And, in the process, initiated a dynasty that lasted nearly four decades and still has plenty of life in it yet.

Eva Romanova and Pavel Roman

In its first half-century as a world championship discipline, ice dancing was ruled by two culturally opposite dynasties. Each reigned virtually unchallenged, and each established the performance standards that other medal hopefuls were forced to imitate.

In Great Britain, figure skating had been loosely linked to ballroom dancing for decades, so couples from that country had an enormous head start when the International Skating Union finally relented and made ice dancing first a test sport, and then, in 1952, a full medal sport. Theirs was a rather formal style, based on the beauty of control. From 1952 through 1970, British couples won 13 world championships (including the first nine), as well as eight silver and five bronze medals. Three times, the British made a clean sweep of the medals.

Then the balletic and theatrical Russians assumed power, winning every world championship of the 1970s under the banner of the Soviet Union. Between 1970 and 1999, as the Soviet Union, Unified States or Russia, the country captured 24 world championships, 16 silver medals and 10 bronzes. Twice, in 1992 and 1993, Russian dance duos finished 1–2–3.

During each of those long monarchies, only one couple from outside the ruling country won more than a single world championship. The Russian reign was interrupted by the four years of magic from Great Britain's Jayne Torvill and Christopher Dean, who regained the throne for the original ruling country.

And the early British supremacy was interrupted by Eva Romanova and Pavel Roman, young siblings from what is now the Czech Republic.

Romanova and Roman won four consecutive world championships from 1962 to 1965, but their dominance has been little more than a historical

Four-time world champions Romanova and Roman in 1965, the final championship season for the only Czech dancers to have ever won a world title.

footnote. The factors in their relative anonymity are several: no Czech ice dancers had ever won a world medal before Romanova and Roman, and they haven't won one since, so there was no chain of success that would link back to the founding pioneers. Then Roman died in a car accident in 1972, five days after his 29th birthday; and his sister moved to a farm in the U.S. after marrying fellow Holiday on Ice performer Jackie Graham and did not remain visibly active on the world skating scene.

But Romanova and Roman were major stars in what was then Czechoslovkia. They were also well-known throughout Europe and made a major impact on Bernard Ford and Diane Towler, the final champions of the British dynasty. The siblings took up dancing in the mid-1950s at the whim of their father, who called coach Mila Novakova out of the blue and suggested she teach his children the sport.

Romanova and Roman finished third in the 1962 Europeans for their first major podium finish. Shortly afterward, they won the Worlds over heavily favored European champions Christiane and Jean Paul Guhel, their rivals from France. They did this on home ice at Prague, in one of the most emotional World Championships in figure skating history: First, it was the first Worlds after the entire U.S. team was lost in a plane crash on the way to the 1961 Prague World Championships. Second, another Czech-born brother-and-sister team, Maria and Otto Jelinek, won the Pairs title for Canada in their first trip back to Czechoslovakia since their harrowing escape from the Communist regime 14 years earlier. Third, Czech Karol Divin won the men's silver medal, finishing behind Donald Jackson who needed the world's first triple Lutz to win.

And 16-year-old Romanova and her 19-year-old brother won the ice dance championship before a delirious, packed house.

Romanova and Roman won four straight Worlds, but didn't win the Europeans until 1964, after which they never lost another competition.

"They were extraordinarily well-matched, even for brother and sister," recalls Bernard Ford. "To me they were amazing. It wasn't dance-y, like things had been. They skated to the music, but they attacked it. They had a lot of speed."

Ford described Pavel Roman as "a man's man. He did all sports. He cross-country motor biked, he raced cars. He was an all-round jock, which was certainly well outside the ice dance image. And on tour, he'd tow a sports car behind his trailer."

Roman and Romanova don't get enough credit for their impact on a discipline that was about to shed its stylistic handcuffs.

"People always say that we were the ones who introduced athleticism to dance, but they [Romanova and Roman] really influenced me," Ford says. "They made dancing so much more athletic. They changed the direction of the sport."

Diane Towler and Bernard Ford

Diane Towler and Bernard Ford won four straight world championships from 1966 through 1969, just before couples from the Soviet Union put a decade-long vise grip on ice dancing gold. The dynamic British duo also won the unofficial championship at the 1968 Winter Olympics in Grenoble, France, when the top 10 couples in the world were invited to compete in an exhibition event as a precursor to ice dancing gaining official Olympic status in 1976.

"They didn't give us gold medals," Ford quipped. "But they did buy us a meal in a good restaurant."

Towler and Ford were known for their deep edges, speed, athleticism and emphasis on footwork, rather than just the carriage of the upper body.

They are also recognized today as the couple that legitimized dance lifts, twizzles and pairs-like dance spins, which have all become staples in modern ice dancing.

Dance had been essentially a "four-feet-on-the-floor" pursuit until November 1964, when Ford hiked Towler slightly off the ice during the free dance, which won them their first British championship.

"There was only a small space between her feet and the ice," Ford said. "Some people loved it as the new direction, some said the rules might have been made to be bent, but they're not to be broken."

They repeated the lift at the European Championships, and finished fourth without any controversy, and again at the Worlds, finishing fourth there, too. After that, lifts became commonplace, and Towler and Ford proceeded to make them a little higher, and with added variations.

"I guess they were looking for a change in direction, to revitalize the sport . . . which had gone dull," Ford theorized.

Towler and Ford had teamed up almost by accident. Originally in the late 1950s and early 1960s, Ford skated in Birmingham, England, and like many skaters

of that era, competed in more than one discipline. At the time he was a club mate with John Curry, and as Ford explains it, "The great irony is this, I'd beat John Curry in singles skating and he'd beat me in dance."

Thankfully, for the development of world figure skating, the two skaters didn't base their careers on this early evidence, and Curry, of course, went on to have a historic impact on men's singles skating.

Ford meanwhile, still practicing singles, had begun making weekly Saturday treks from northern England to work with iconic coach Gladys Hogg at London's Queen's ice rink in 1960. One weekend, when Ford was 13, his mother asked Hogg to take a look at her son's ice dancing technique. Hogg agreed to do it, but she needed to find a demonstration partner and chose a girl who was nine months older. Towler, a native Londoner, was a club member and had just broken up with her dance partner.

Hogg immediately recognized a natural fit. What began as a casual single-morning exercise evolved into the most accomplished, and competitive, dance team of the late 1960s.

When they were 16 years old, Towler and Ford finished fourth at the British Senior Nationals and were named as world team alternates. As luck would have it, the third-place couple broke up and the teenagers found themselves going to Dortmund, Germany, for the 1964 World Championships. They finished 13th, the lowest a British dance couple had ever placed at the global event, which wouldn't normally have been cause for any great optimism.

But their marks in the compulsory dances ranged so wildly — from 6th to 13th — that the referee needed to summon an on-ice judges' meeting after each of the four compulsories. That furor attracted a lot of attention to the young couple.

"Sometimes bad results produce good things," Ford said. "Everyone was watching us quite closely because of that, and started saying that we were the couple of the future."

They won their first British title the next year, in a rare leapfrog over the defending national champions and European silver medalists Janet Sawbridge and Ken Hickinbottom, and then climbed nine places to finish fourth at the Worlds. The next year, they began their four-year reign as world champions, all the while

Diane Towler and Bernard Ford skating to gold at the 1966 World Championships. The win marked the tenth time a British duo had won gold in the first 14 years of world ice dance competition.

and Ford retired from the amateur ranks.

They performed in a few professional shows in England, Poland and Russia, but Towler did not want to leave London for full-scale touring. So, the couple went their separate ways.

Ford emigrated to Canada in 1971, but even an ocean apart, the partnership continued to influence ice dancing. For their contributions to skating, Towler and Ford were appointed as Members of the Order of the British Empire (MBE) by Queen Elizabeth II.

Towler returned to her old club and guided former rival Janet Sawbridge and her partner Peter Dalby to a European bronze medal in 1972. Three decades later, she coached her ice-dancing twin daughters Phillipa and Candice Towler-Green to international status.

Ford has coached in Toronto, Seattle and Edmonton, and assisted on the International Skating Union's dance technical committee where he co-invented the Cha-Cha Congelado, which is now a compulsory dance. He was the original coach of Canadians Tracy Wilson and Rob McCall, the three-time world bronze medalists who seemed cut from the same inventive, athletic, footwork-oriented cloth as Towler and Ford.

"I think part of Diane's and my success was that I didn't know anything about dance," Ford said. "We were told we were innovative, but we were just doing stuff we consider very basic now. I don't know what the hell they were doing before."

pushed by Hogg's perfectionism.

"Once we didn't say 'Good Morning,' and she wouldn't teach us for three weeks," Towler explained in a 2007 interview. "She made us smart, polite and strong people."

The couple's 1968 free dance to "Zorba the Greek" was named as one of the BBC's 100 Greatest Sporting Moments and marked a turning point in ice dance choreography. Towler described the program and its costuming as a risk because "music like that had never been used before."

In 1969, after their fourth world title, having achieved all that was possible in ice dancing, and finding it financially difficult to continue, Towler

Jean Westwood and Lawrence Demmy

In the first week of March 1950, Jean Westwood and Lawrence Demmy, a new couple from the north of England sat in the audience at Wembley Arena, mesmerized by the International Ice Dance event, an unofficial demonstration at the World Figure Skating Championships.

"Little did we suspect that we'd soon be in the thing," Demmy said.

Not only in it, but winners of it. And, soon thereafter, the first official world champions in ice dancing. And the second, third and fourth.

Ice dancing did not become an accredited world championship discipline until 1952, and only then after much debate. As is still its policy with new disciplines today, the International Skating Union required at least two years of unofficial global competition before sanctioning an official world championship — as was the case with both synchronized and junior skating.

It was no accident that the first demonstration championship should be in England. The earlier British skating style, pushed aside by the Viennese International Style, included a form of foursome dancing around an object like an orange, with a rinkside instruction caller. Ice dancing began to spread extensively throughout England in the early 1930s. A small, inter-rink competition was held at Bournemouth in 1932, and in 1937, the National Skating Association held its first British Ice Dance Competition. The first winners, Reginald Wilkie and Daphne Wallis, had already designed the basic patterns for the Argentine Tango, Paso Doble and Quickstep. In 1939, the NISA even held a professional dance championship.

So when the ISU was ready for ice dancing, England was ready for the ISU, and 13 of the first 17 world championships were won by couples from Great Britain, the first four by Westwood and Demmy.

Westwood, daughter of a well-known Manchester doctor, was educated at Cheltenham Ladies College and began skating at the age of seven. Demmy came from an athletic Manchester family. His father fought four times for the national boxing title and Lawrence himself boxed and played soccer. During the war, with the bombing of Manchester, the family moved to Blackpool for safety reasons and just as the war ended Demmy tried skating for the first time, at the relatively advanced age of 14.

Back in Manchester after the war, Demmy was skating in a public session at the reopened Manchester Ice Palace — which had somehow not been bombed, despite housing a munitions factory — when he noticed Westwood.

"She was a far better skater than I, and I asked her, 'How about a little dance?'" Demmy recalls. "And that's how it started."

They created a formal partnership in 1950 and entered the British Championships, finishing ninth out of 11 couples. So naturally, Demmy never pictured himself as part of the burgeoning international scene.

But when a national skateoff was held to determine which British couple would compete in the second unofficial world championship, Lawrence and Demmy won. And later they won the demonstration event at the 1951 Worlds in Milan, despite Westwood suffering from severe throat injuries due to a car accident, which had kept her in hospital for five weeks and left little time for pre-event training.

When ice dancing was accorded full championship status in 1952, Westwood and Demmy won that historic event over fellow Britons Joan Dewhirst and John Slater. They captured four straight titles before deciding to leave competition.

A half-century after being the first dancers to stand on top of a Worlds podium, Westwood and Demmy were still contributing to their sport.

Westwood emigrated to the United States and spent many years as a choreographer for Holiday On Ice and Ice Follies. She eventually moved to Victoria, B.C., for a lengthy coaching career.

Demmy, whose family ran a clothing business, didn't want to turn professional and began working his way up skating's administrative ranks. He was chairman of the ISU dance technical committee for 15 years, spent 33 years as an ISU officer, lost a 1994 presidential bid to Ottavio Cinquanta, and in 1998 was elected ISU honorary vice-president.

BREAKING THE LIMITS — *Dance Pairs from the 1980s through the 2000s*

Natalia Bestemianova and Andrei Bukin

Although North Americans rarely see them, Natalia Bestemianova and Andrei Bukin still skate and still influence young ice dancers — more than two decades after their amateur career ended.

From a historical perspective, Bestemianova and Bukin will probably never escape the long shadow of the peerless Jayne Torvill and Christopher Dean, whom they succeeded as Olympic, and four-time world champions.

But the eye-catching duo from Moscow scattered their own creative footprints all over ice dancing during their undefeated four-year reign from 1985 to 1988. And since winning the 1988 Olympics, they have been performing in the revue produced by Bestemianova's husband, Igor Bobrin, who was one of the most innovative, interpretive singles skaters of the late 1970s. Bobrin's ice theater is a complex, demanding combination of ballet and theater, which sometimes includes circus acts.

When Torvill and Dean turned professional in the summer of 1984, the hierarchal nature of ice dancing at the time dictated that Bestemianova and Bukin graduate from the runner-up position they'd owned for three straight years. But it was going to be difficult for whomever succeeded the great Britons, because the International Skating Union had promised to crack down on restrictive rules that had been bent, and sometimes mutilated, in favor of artistic impression during the Torvill and Dean era. However, led by the unconventional Bestemianova and Bukin, the next wave of leading dancers actually amplified the dramatic, theatrical side of the discipline instead of returning it to the more formal ballroom style which had preceded Torvill and Dean's artistic reign.

Bestemianova and Bukin were outstanding technicians, which freed them to carry out the avant-garde visions of their coach Tatiana Tarasova, who had put them together in 1977 when Bestemianova was 17 and her partner 20.

Like so many female dance legends, Bestemianova did not begin her career in ice dancing, but had been a singles skater, until her first coach told her directly that she lacked the talent necessary for a productive career. But in Bestemianova, Tarasova found the perfect vehicle for her vision of the sensationally dramatic female dance partner.

When the pair first came together, Tarasova was often away at competitions with her more senior skaters, notably Bestemianova and Bukin's ideological predecessors Moiseeva and Minenkov, so Bukin had to instruct his partner in some of the fundamentals of ice dancing.

Bestemianova and Bukin had the perfect partnership that can only come from a combination of natural chemistry and hours of long, hard training under a demanding tutor like Tarasova. Their footwork was intricate, their lifts startlingly unique and exacting.

A common observation of the mid-1980s was that "nobody dies better than Natalia Bestemianova!" Several of their programs involved her death, with Bukin tragically carrying her limp body in his arms or mourning her as she lay motionless on the ice. As *International Figure Skating Magazine* pointedly noted, Bestemianova "died" four times in one show program. The ISU eventually discouraged death scenes but was unable to enforce a full ban.

What made Bestemianova so convincing at portraying death was its staggering contrast to some of the couple's principal and vibrant assets: she and her partner were full of life and energy on the ice. They emitted a palpable sexuality, and they could deliver sophisticated comedy, as illustrated by their humorous 1987 take on *Cabaret*. (In their professional careers, they easily carried the ironic humor of Bobrin's distinct choreography.)

Many of the couple's amateur programs were choreographed by ballroom dancers Irina Tchubarets and Stanislav Shkliar and involved complex subtleties

Natalia Bestemianova and Andrei Bukin finished on the world ice dancing podium a record-matching eight times.

Bestemianova and Bukin at the 1988 Olympics — their third Olympic appearance, and their first gold medal.

Not only did Bestemianova and Bukin win four world championships and the Calgary Olympics, they created an artistic buffer for the dancers of the next few Olympiads. The anticipated return to a simpler, "just skating" form of ice dancing did not occur after the retirement of Torvill and Dean. Arguably, and like it or not, the discipline became more histrionic than ever.

One of the few criticisms of Bestemianova and Bukin was that their superb harmony, speed and technical gifts were often overshadowed by blatant theatrics.

But that was counterbalanced by the grand scale of the emotions they extracted from their audiences, and the artistic influence they exerted on almost every ice dancer of their time.

Shae-Lynn Bourne and Victor Kraatz

They were a prism through which their generation and, arguably, the entire tangled history of ice dancing was refracted.

In their 12-year partnership, Canada's Shae-Lynn Bourne and Victor Kraatz never medalled at the Olympics and captured just a single world championship in the discipline most riddled with judging protocol and backroom deal making. But their gold at the 2003 Worlds at Washington, the first ever by North Americans, is, to date, the most powerful symbol of skating's new century.

"If they were Russian, they would have been world champions many times," says Nikolai Morozov (married for a brief time to Bourne), who coached them to the world title, and is himself Russian.

With soft knees, outright speed and background in other sports, Bourne and Kraatz were athletic, exciting and always a little dangerous. When they burst onto the world scene in 1992, they were a refreshing antidote to the histrionic posing that had, under the guise of artistry, invaded ice dancing.

as well as the outrageously obvious theatrics.

Entering the international arena with a 10th place finish at the 1979 World Championships, Bestemianova and Bukin, backed by the powerful Soviet Union federation, moved up to third by 1981, and then second behind Torvill and Dean the next year. Because of the incomparable Britons' dominance, the only major title the Moscow couple won in the early '80s was the 1983 Europeans, which Torvill and Dean missed.

But after finishing second at the 1984 Olympics, Bestemianova and Bukin never lost another international event. They were, however, taken down a peg at home in 1985, when they couldn't win a domestic competition because the Soviet federation thought their performances were too dramatic.

They would not be deterred from their love of theatrical dance, however, and their persistence was justified. After four years of British rule, Bestemianova and Bukin regained control of ice dancing for the Soviet Union. Other than the Duchesnays' 1991 Worlds win, Soviet or Russian ice dancers won every world and Olympic title from 1985 to 1999.

"People tell me they enjoyed it because our skating had a feeling of risk and that feeling of jumping without the actual jump," Bourne says.

Along with Elvis Stojko and coach/choreographer Uschi Keszler, they pioneered hydroblading, a dazzling use of edges to defy gravity and keep the couple's bodies almost parallel to the ice, with just Bourne's hand as a support.

Bourne and Kraatz were the most versatile dancers of their era. They set a Canadian record with 10 national championships, and inspired a whole generation of North Americans to take up ice dancing. But until 2003, none of this helped them pry the world title from its Eurocentric grip.

Since it became part of the world championship roster in 1952 and an Olympic discipline in 1976, ice dancing had been dominated first by the ballroom-oriented British, and then mostly by the ballet-influenced eastern European nations.

Shae-Lynn Bourne and Victor Kraatz skate their compulsory dance at the 2002 Games; they placed fourth, but went on to place second at the 2002 Worlds.

Dancing had long been accused of having a pre-arranged finishing order. And those suspicions were borne out in successive Olympic Games: in Nagano in 1998 when one judge recorded another judge telling her several days before the event what the final seeding of medals — without Bourne and Kraatz — would be; and again in Salt Lake City in 2002, when the roots of the pairs-judging scandal were traced directly to ice dancing.

Just 13 months later, in the U.S.A., the very country where the biggest scandal in skating history had occurred, under interim rules and intense scrutiny, the judging panel — which marked under an ISU-supported guise of anonymity in order to avoid the

influence of their own national federations — gave Bourne and Kraatz their long overdue championship.

And a dam broke.

Two years later, right in Moscow, Americans Tanith Belbin and Ben Agosto won the U.S.A.'s first dance silver medal in 30 years and the following season, for the first time in nearly a half century, two North American couples made it to the podium. In 2007, four of the top seven ice dance couples in the world were from Canada and the U.S.

But Bourne and Kraatz did not start out to be the fulcrums of ice dance history. In fact they didn't even start out to be ice dancers.

Bourne was originally a pairs skater. She grew up in Chatham, Ontario, and moved to Montreal with her mother and older brother Chris, who was an accomplished pairs skater. After she finished second in the Canadian novice pairs championship in 1990, she became attracted to ice dancing and switched disciplines.

Kraatz grew up in the mountain lakeside town of Ascona, Switzerland, and was an alpine skier until the early 1980s, when, at the age of 10, he rented skates, fell on his head and ended up in hospital. Undaunted, he began ice dancing in Swiss pre-novice programs. In 1987, when he was 16, Kraatz and his family moved to British Columbia and a year later he began competing. In 1991, both he and the 15-year-old Bourne found themselves without partners. They did a trial skate together in Montreal and immediately clicked.

Before she began ice dancing, Bourne recalls she "had no interest in dance, so I had nobody I was looking up to, or trying to be like. And Victor had a very similar mind. Because we went our own way, it ended up being something interesting."

They won the 1992 Canadian junior title after less than a year together and in 1993, shockingly surpassed the reigning champions and several other veterans to win their first of 10 senior crowns. They debuted at 14th in the 1993 Worlds and rocketed to fourth within two years.

Coming off a disappointing fourth place finish at the 2002 Games, Bourne and Kraatz remained eligible for 2003, the year they won their only world championship.

Then the climb became steeper and greased with injuries and anti-North American politics. They won four straight world bronze medals, but were locked out of the 1998 Olympic podium, despite their memorable Riverdance program, one of the most uplifting free dances of all time.

When they finished a faltering fifth at the 2000 Grand Prix final, they took nearly a year off to regroup, and returned to finish fourth in the world in 2001, and then second in 2002. Bourne wanted to turn professional after 2002 but agreed, at Kraatz's request, to remain eligible for one more year — which turned out to be their one championship season.

As their winning free skate ended, Bourne turned to Kraatz and said, "Thank you."

After their world championship, they were to tour professionally, but Kraatz always preferred the heat of competition and balked at the pro lifestyle, so the partnership dissolved. Bourne skated solo in tours and became a coaching consultant. Kraatz and his wife, Maikki Uotila-Kraatz, became coaches and ice dance directors at the B.C. Centre of Excellence in Vancouver. Bourne and Kraatz reunited in 2007 to promote Canadian skating events, including acting as co-chairs for the 2008 Nationals.

Kraatz once said he wanted their partnership to be remembered as the one that carried on the legacy of Wilson and McCall, the athletic world medal winners of the mid-1980s who inspired thousands of Canadians to ice dance, "and we want to pass the torch on to someone else who might go further than us."

It's skating's loss that Bourne and Kraatz didn't have a prolonged career touring North America as world ice dance champions. They could have been a lyrical reminder that even the most tenacious tyrannies must eventually fail.

Isabelle Duchesnay and Paul Duchesnay

Isabelle and Paul Duchesnay were raised in Canada, trained in Germany, coached by a Slovak and choreographed by a famous Briton. But the results of their mercurial careers were felt most directly in France.

When the brother and sister figure skating

pair from Aylmer, Quebec, exercised their dual citizenship and began competing for France in 1985, the former powerhouse in the sport was drifting in the skating doldrums.

The French had not made an impression at the World Championships in years, and although they were developing some promising youngsters and assembling a politically-savvy federation, there was no lightning rod, no galvanizing force.

The Duchesnays, especially the commanding Isabelle, became that force.

Uncelebrated in Canada, they became the well-supported battering ram of the new era in French skating. When they won a bronze medal at the 1989 World Championships, right in Paris, they not only captured the hearts of French sports fans (in several ensuing polls they were ranked No. 2 among the most popular athletes in the country behind only solo sailor

Florence Arthaud), they began rewriting French skating history.

The Duchesnays' bronze in 1989 was the first medal by French ice dancers in 27 years, and two years later they became the first couple from France to win the world championship, breaking a seven-year stranglehold that Soviet couples had had on the title.

When the Duchesnays won the Worlds in 1991, French skating had its first world title of any kind since 1965 when Alain Calmet won the men's world crown. The confidence and expectation levels rose in France for the likes of singles skaters Surya Bonaly, Philippe Candeloro, and, later, Brian Joubert, as well as ice dancing multi-medalists Sophie Moniotte and Pascal Lavanchy and eventual world and Olympic dance champions Marina Anissina and Gwendal Peizerat.

In fact, in the 10 years after the Duchesnays won in 1991, France, after being shut out for so long, won 12 world championship medals (one gold, eight silver, three bronze), including at least one in every discipline.

But as much as France owed the Duchesnays, Isabelle always said she and her brother were the indebted ones.

"If it were not for the French," she said before the 1992 Olympic Games, "we would not be here."

Paul was born in France, their mother's home country, and Isabelle in Canada, their father's country. They were raised in a Gallic, rather than a Quebecois, home atmosphere and began their skating career as a pairs team. But when Isabelle fell from a lift during a 1978 practice and was hospitalized overnight, they switched to ice dancing.

They finished second in the Canadian Junior Championships in 1982, and that summer began attending clinics in Oberstdorf, Germany, where they caught the eye of Betty Callaway, Torvill and Dean's famous coach.

After they had risen only as high as third in senior rankings, the Duchesnays felt they had become slotted in the Canadian hierarchy behind the renowned Tracy Wilson and Rob McCall, who would win three world medals, and Karyn and Rod Garossino, a team of siblings from Calgary who the Duchesnays sensed were being pushed for their hometown 1988 Olympic Games.

Isabelle and Paul Duchesnay dance the polka at the 1992 Olympics in Albertville to claim the silver medal — their final skate in amateur competition.

The Canadian Figure Skating Association denied the allegations but in 1985 the Duchesnays accepted a financially rewarding offer from the newly aggressive leadership of the Federation Francaise des Sports de Glace to skate for France and help raise the profile of French skating. France was able to provide better coaching and more ice time and Betty Callaway persuaded Martin Skotnicky to train them in Oberstdorf. Three years later, the French association set up sponsors to provide the Duchesnays with an annual budget of two million francs.

"The French offered them a lot of training support," said David Dore, who was then director-general of the Canadian Figure Skating Association. "It was more than we could give them."

Artistically and financially liberated by the move to France, the Duchesnays began pushing the limits of ice dance regulations, which had been tightened

The Duchesnays perform their compulsory dance at the 1989 Worlds in their adoptive home country, France; they placed third.

after the reign of Torvill and Dean. They hired Dean as their choreographer in 1987, and he and Isabelle Duchesnay were married briefly in the early 1990s.

As siblings, the Duchesnays were shut out from the vast repertoire of romantic themes which other dance couples could use, but Dean still created explosive groundbreaking routines for them.

In 1988 they arrived back in their home country for the Calgary Olympics, and received a standing ovation for their Tribal Rites dance, an African rhythm skated mostly to percussion, which was far more performance art than ballroom dance.

Although triumphant artistically, the Duchesnays were rejected by the judges, and were ranked eighth in a suspicious competition, during which the top 14 couples stayed in the same order from the first compulsory dance to the end of competition.

Undaunted, the Duchesnays continued to unveil exciting programs, often being accused of illegal moves, including "two-foot skating" and certain lifts and maneuvers which would not be used on a ballroom floor. Despite Isabelle's three knee surgeries before and during the 1988–89 season, they won world bronze under intense national pressure in 1989 in Paris. They moved up to silver in 1990 with the heralded Missing routine, an athletic free dance from the movie of the same name about South American peasants longing to be free of oppression.

A more avante-garde piece the next season didn't work and was scrapped midway in favour of Missing II — which gave them the 1991 World Championship over Marina Klimova and Sergei Ponomarenko, and set them up for the 1992 Olympics in Albertville, France.

But a string of misfortunes dogged them during the Olympic season. Isabelle required surgery for a broken right foot, which kept her off the ice for six weeks, and a recurrence of Paul's old thigh muscle injury forced them to miss the Europeans. In between, they were emotionally devastated by the death of their older half-brother Gaston.

As advised by the French federation, Dean chose a more conservative program for the Albertville Games, with the Duchesnays playing Maria and her brother Bernardo from *West Side Story*. Later, both Dean and Paul Duchesnay said that not continuing to push the technical frontiers was a mistake. "Chris [Dean] felt tied down by the rule book," Isabelle said at the time.

It was an extraordinarily high-energy program, without a true slow segment, but even before the free dance, the Duchesnays were too far behind to catch Klimova and Ponomarenko and had to settle for silver.

They turned professional immediately afterward, but their touring career was truncated by Paul's back injuries, incurred while rollerblading. They moved on to coaching positions in the United States.

But what they created lived on, as dancing became increasingly theatrical and athletic and France became the most powerful and successful skating nation in continental Europe.

Oksana Grishuk and Evgeny Platov

They were at the epicenter of ice dancing for more than half a decade, but history's jury has yet to pass full judgment on Oksana Grishuk and Evgeny Platov.

Chances are that the sheer weight of their competitive achievements will outlive the raw memories of their volatile reign.

Controversy and melodrama may have walked like a shadow with the fiery Grishuk, as her wry and balanced partner tried to steer a steady course, but the Ukrainian-born couple were unbeatable in the middle of the 1990s.

When they won at the 1998 Games at Nagano to become the only couple ever to repeat as Olympic dance champions, Grishuk and Platov extended their string of major victories to a remarkable 22, which included four world championships and three European titles.

"They really had the basics," recalled their contemporary, Shae-Lynn Bourne. "Everything was so together, so held, so technically good. Textbook. They were always competitors and they had that edge."

Yet within two months of their second Olympic gold they were no longer partners, ultimately defeated by their long-term, off-ice soap opera and the stress of fending off an increasing pool of talented contenders.

Grishuk sought the bright lights of a Hollywood career, which never blossomed, and the winningest dance team in history did not skate together again until eight years later, when they hastily put together a once-only program for the smash Russian TV show *Dancing On Ice*.

In the interim, Platov had forged a peaceful five-year performing partnership with Maia Usova, who with then-husband Alexander Zhulin, had been Grishuk and Platov's chief rivals in the early 1990s. Usova, Grishuk and Zhulin had once comprised a notorious love triangle, which, in combination with her unpredictable behavior, resulted in Grishuk being expelled from Natalia Dubova's training center in 1992.

During this time, Platov actually remained training with Dubova for three months and teamed with

Tatiana Navka, who would, fittingly, eventually marry Zhulin.

But Platov knew that he and Grishuk were a winning combination, and soon re-joined her with coach Natalia Linichuk. Less than two years later, they were the 1994 Olympic winners, upsetting reigning world champions Usova and Zhulin and returning legends Torvill and Dean.

Grishuk and Platov contemplated leaving amateur skating after winning the 1995 Worlds. Platov's recurring knee injuries were a serious consideration, but as he recalls, "then we started to feel that we were a young team, we had just got to the top, and not many people recognized us. We said we needed more popularity, and we thought we could probably make a record by winning a second Olympics.

"We came close to breaking up several times. My injuries. The craziness. There was so much pressure on our shoulders. If you're in second place in your second Olympics, for us we would be losers. This pressure

that we had to be first stuck in our heads and we could not get over it."

In 1997, worried that Linichuk was more concerned about her other students, they changed coaches again, to the legendary Tatiana Tarasova. Under increasing stress to repeat as Olympic champions, and attempting more daring and difficult elements because of it, Grishuk and Platov tumbled to the ice a couple of times during their final year of competition, including during the Olympics, which prompted new rule changes for mandatory deductions for falls.

They managed to keep it together to win a second Olympic championship at Nagano, receiving two 6.0s for presentation. But weeks later, they split.

Platov hadn't been sure the partnership would

Oksana Grishuk and Evgeny Platov pose at the beginning of their gala performance at the 1995 Trophée Lalique, where they were the gold medal winners.

Grishuk and Platov are the only ice dancing couple ever to win back-to-back Olympic Games (Lillehammer, 1994; Nagano, 1998).

They were fifth at the 1990 Worlds and moved up a place every year to enter the 1994 Games as world silver medalists.

"I never thought I could win an Olympics," Platov recalled. "I was five times Ukrainian champion and I thought if just once I could make the Soviet team for Junior Worlds, I'd quit and become a sailor, like my father."

Instead, he and Grishuk charted their own rough waters, personifying the course of Russian skating at the end of the 20th century. They had started skating in a Soviet republic; competed for the USSR, then with the "unified team" after the fall of the communist state and then a re-formed Russia; followed their coach Linichuk to the U.S. during the retooling of the Russian economy; and still extended the dynasty of Russian Olympic ice dance champions.

"There was so much going on, so many victories," Platov explained. "In the end, you never remember the bad stuff, you only remember the good stuff."

ever get off the ground in the first place, despite their impressive résumés.

Put together by Dubova in August of 1989, after each had won a World Junior Championship title with a different partner, they were soon ranked third in the talent-deep USSR, but it still took a year for the couple to mesh their contrasting styles: Platov had been trained by Dubova, whereas Grishuk, originally a singles skater, had been brought from Odessa to Moscow and had been trained by Linichuk.

Platov recognized his new partner's excessive theatricality — "In life, I am exciting and I try to be exciting and funny when I skate," Grishuk once said — but he respected her work ethic and her willingness to train six or seven hours a day. She had grown up in relative poverty and had an incredible drive to succeed.

"It was very hard right from the beginning," Platov conceded. "Most people as talented as Oksana have very strong personalities and sometimes it's hard to deal with. But you make a decision: if you want to be at the top, you have to eat some things. You don't think about it. You have a goal, and you just go there."

Marina Klimova and Sergei Ponomarenko

It was the *other* great Russian love story of their era.

The final moment of their unprecedented Olympic careers was spent prone on the ice locked in an emotional embrace, in front of millions of TV viewers, husband telling wife how much he loved her.

On that February evening in a French Alpine valley, Marina Klimova and Sergei Ponomarenko knew they had just won the 1992 Olympic ice dance championship with their steaming interpretation of Bach and Chopin.

"This is not news," commented one columnist, "but in France, sex sells."

"I think only a man and wife could skate to that program," Ponomarenko agreed later, in reference to the Duchesnay siblings, whom they'd beaten right in their adoptive home country.

The gold medal gave Klimova and Ponomarenko

an Olympic figure skating record: medals of all three hues in successive Games. They had won bronze in 1984 at Sarajevo and silver in 1988 at Calgary.

The next month they won their third world championship, to go along with five runner-up finishes. Over their last seven seasons, they never finished lower than second in any competition. And after spending nine seasons among ice dancing's elite, the couple turned professional in 1992. With her thick red hair, their expressive faces, and their powerfully assertive lines and edges, Klimova and Ponomarenko skated like a sweeping Russian romance novel.

Their obviously loving relationship and competitive dominance was not as well known, nor as celebrated as Ekaterina Gordeeva and Sergei Grinkov's story — considered *the* love story of 20th century skating — because of several factors. Klimova and Ponomarenko faced a thick language barrier during their amateur careers, which kept the nuances of their personalities from the public eye. They spent their last two years of eligible skating fighting off rising domestic and international rivals. There was also a sense that their classical mode was passé. And they were in ice dancing, which always aroused suspicions of a permanent hierarchy, a criticism that always irked the hard-training Klimova and Ponomarenko.

Klimova started skating in Sverdlovsk. In 1978 she and partner Oleg Volkov accepted an offer to move to the demanding program in Moscow run by Natalia Dubova. Ponomarenko, who took up the sport because doctors thought it might help his spine curvature, had already skated singles and spent a year in pairs before combining with Tatiana Durasova to win the 1978 and 1979 world junior ice dance championship.

Both partnerships folded and Dubova teamed Klimova with Ponomarenko for the 1979–80 season. He was 19 and she just 13, so he was the natural teacher and leader, but she was a quick study.

In later years they would reveal that they both felt romantic stirrings from the beginning.

They were eighth at their first nationals in 1980 but by 1983 had moved up to the national team, debuting at fourth at the Worlds. They won the Olympic bronze in 1984, the same year they were married.

Klimova and Ponomarenko moved up to silver

Marina Klimova and Sergei Ponomarenko in 1995, three years after turning professional.

at the Worlds for four straight years behind the energetic and expressive Natalia Bestemianova and Andrei Bukin, before finally taking over the top of the podium in 1989 and 1990.

But they began to feel out of favor in their home country and Europe. Dubova began treating Maia Usova and Alexander Zhulin as her leading students. After the rising, raw energy of the Duchesnays defeated the classic style of Klimova and Ponomarenko at the 1991 Worlds, they left Dubova for Tatiana Tarasova. There was also the "leak" of a report that Klimova had a positive drug test at the 1991 Europeans, which was proven false but had a major negative effect on the pair. At the same time their homeland was radically changing, and with change came less access to resources and funding.

But, with each other's support, they prevailed. The pair led at the 1992 Olympics from start to finish, and went on to win the Worlds that same year. But, with limited opportunities in Russia, they turned professional in the U.S.A. After touring for eight years, they became coaches in California.

Skating to Bach and Chopin, Klimova and Ponomoreko give their most memorable performance at the Winter Games in Albertville, where they placed first.

They were always there for each other. "I could have skated with my eyes closed without any hesitations," Klimova told a Russian radio program, "because I was absolutely sure that Sergei would be exactly where it was necessary."

Jayne Torvill and Christopher Dean

It seems ludicrous that one-half of history's greatest ice dancing team was originally bound for a lifetime of police work.

"But I like to think there would have been some very creative arrests," Christopher Dean has often quipped.

Because Dean and his partner Jayne Torvill danced their way through figure skating to become nearly as popular as the British Royal family, it's hard to remember that they had been just two working-class kids from Nottingham, England, forced to hold down full-time jobs just so they could afford to practice for a couple of hours — after midnight.

Dean began skating at the age of ten and eventually won the British novice and junior dance championships with partner Sandra Elson, but constant bickering broke the pair up.

Torvill had been a pairs skater with Michael Hutchinson and the two won the junior and senior national titles before running into reality with a last-place finish at the Europeans. She then skated singles for a year and took some dance lessons.

No one envisioned Torvill as the new partner for the much taller Dean, except coach Janet Sawbridge, who liked the athleticism, speed and skating skills Torvill had developed as a pairs skater. Sawbridge put the pair together and in 1976, their first summer together, they won an international competition in St. Gervais before they'd even competed in Britain. They progressed steadily, but were hindered by limited practice time.

Five years into their partnership, and with a fourth-place finish at the 1980 World Championships on their résumé, Torvill was still working as a clerk in an insurance company and Dean as a constable with the Nottingham police. Then, in 1980, Nottingham

City Council awarded the pair a grant, which finally enabled them to train full time.

The returns were immediate and stunning. Great potential became even greater achievement. Given time to hone their already formidable technical strength, and tap into a wealth of creative ideas, Torvill and Dean soon had no peers.

In winning the 1981 European and World Championships in convincing fashion, they vaulted over two two-time world champion Russian couples — Irina Moiseeva and Andrei Minenkov and Olympic gold medalists Natalia Linichuk and Gennadi Karponosov — and herded them toward retirement.

In 1982, they changed the ice dancing world forever. Rather than build the traditional four-segment program, Torvill and Dean gambled on one piece of music for their free dance. Dean had found, and loved, the overture from a failed 1971 Broadway musical about the tumultuous romance between silent movie producer Mack Sennett and his leading lady, Mabel Normand.

Mack and Mabel became the seminal program in modern ice dancing. It told a story and underscored the narrative with exceptionally difficult moves. Visually stunning and technically sublime, it was the entry point to Torvill and Dean's 20-year tradition of harnessing the incredible. It received a record eight out of a possible nine perfect 6.0s for artistry at the Europeans in 1982, and added five more 6.0s at the Worlds. The Mack and Mabel routine pushed succeeding generations of dancers into choreographic invention for which most of them were not quite ready.

The routine also made the next two years of ice dancing more coronation than competition.

"They were way ahead of their time," said Betty Callaway, the iron-willed British skating legend who was their coach in the late 1970s. "People looked to them for inspiration, and ice dance witnessed a revolution."

Jayne Torvill and Christopher Dean salute the crowd with a reprise Bolero performance during an exhibition at the 1994 Games. The routine originally earned them gold at the 1984 Olympics.

Torvill and Dean had become nobility, hounded by a posse of British paparazzi who monitored their every move and who speculated the couple would eventually marry. (They did, but not each other.)

They were now skating against only their own accomplishments, and in 1983 the duo unleashed a free dance taken from the stage musical *Barnum*. They transported the audience right into a circus, both overtly and subtly, evoking all the pageantry and sleaze of the Big Top. There were elephants and jugglers, and at one point, Dean played the trombone using Torvill as the slide. Some said it was mime, but the judges said it was perfection. All nine judges awarded Barnum artistic merit of 6.0, a first in world championship history.

Torvill and Dean topped even that innovative program with their 1984 farewell to amateur skating. They won Olympic gold and their fourth world championship with their mesmerizing, intense interpretation of Ravel's *Bolero*, which earned a total of 12 perfect 6.0s at the Sarajevo Olympics, including a clean nine-judge sweep of the artistic marks. Including their comeback for a bronze in 1994 at Lillehammer, through a one-time special exemption to allow professional skaters back into amateur competition, Torvill and Dean recorded 22 perfect marks at the Olympics, the most in any skating discipline, with the next highest being four. They had 56 sixes in their world championship appearances, nearly doubling the next highest total of 29.

When Torvill and Dean turned pro, the ISU acknowledged, by formally tightening the regulations and insisting that all programs be danceable on a ballroom floor, that some of their moves had indeed been beyond the boundaries. But they had also had the good sense not to inhibit the great Brits by enforcing the rules during their spectacular reign when ice dancing gained millions of new disciples.

As professional skaters, Torvill and Dean grew even more creative and expressive. They toured Australia, Europe and the U.S. with their own show, bound by a single theme throughout. They did a turn with Stars on Ice, made several tapes and films, most notably *Fire and Ice*, assembled a troupe of touring Russian skaters, and provided opportunities for talented, but

Torvill and Dean pose with their Olympic gold medals from the Sarajevo Games. The duo completed 1984, and their amateur careers, with a world championship gold medal, their fourth.

OPPOSITE: Torvill and Dean skating at Sports Aid in 1986. The event, similar to Live Aid, raised money for Africa.

unknown, performers. As in their amateur career, Dean would conceive the general idea and his partner would help refine it.

"Chris has a more aggressive nature; everything has to be done quickly and now," Torvill said. "I sort of sit back and do things thoroughly. We get to the same place at the same time, but in different ways."

That tension between mood and methodology produced some of the world's great on-ice masterpieces. But, despite their championships, honors and perfect marks, only those who saw them skate can ever truly understand their timeless grandeur.

"Watching them caress the ice," four-time world champion Bernard Ford said in Torvill and Dean's autobiography, "It's like watching God skate."

LEGENDS IN THE MAKING

Jeffrey Buttle's surprise retirement from eligible skating six months after winning the 2008 World Championships underscored how difficult it will be for skaters of the modern era to ascend to legendary status.

Only the sixth Canadian man to win a world title, Buttle said he found it hard to mount the motivation and commitment to continue his intense training and competition schedule.

Buttle is a complex, all-round skater who, had he gone on to master a consistent quad jump, would have been the prototype for the International Judging System's ideal champion.

Only five weeks after Buttle's unanticipated declaration, an even greater shock hit the international skating community. Two-time world champion Stéphane Lambiel of Switzerland announced that he, too, would retire from competitive skating, mostly because a recurring adductor muscle injury was limiting his training and performance capabilities. A rival coach once said Lambiel could "be as good as he wants to be," and he had already won the 2005 and 2006 world titles and a silver medal at the 2006 Olympics.

At the time of his retirement, Lambiel possessed more natural talent than any man in his global skating class, and when he combined his artistry and physical skills with the right practice and work ethic, he was almost unbeatable. Accomplished artistically, he was a good jumper who landed quad-triple-double combinations, and could do every jump up to the triple Salchow in both directions and, in the long tradition of Swiss skaters, Lambiel also was a magnificent, creative spinner. He is just the third Swiss skater in any discipline ever to win a world championship (the other two are Hans Gerschwiler, 1947 and Denise Biellmann, 1981).

Yu-Na Kim performing in the short program at the 2009 World Championships. Kim won the short program and the gold.

But even before Jeffrey Buttle found his motivational well had gone dry, Lambiel experienced the same problem. He withdrew from the European Championships in the middle of the 2006–07 season, citing a loss of inspiration and hinting he would not return. But he came back on just five weeks' training to finish third at the Worlds.

So, in the important season before the 2010 Olympics, the men's division faced the unprecedented retirement of two skaters who had won three world championships and two Olympic medals. The primary factors in their departure, injuries and emotional burnout, are the flip side of the current competitive figure skating coin: fields today are full of more all-round talent than in the past; there is far more high-level competition coming from younger skaters who are mastering tough, body-punishing tricks at an earlier age than in previous eras; there is wider access to better coaching; and the new scoring system dictates far more difficult and draining programs.

Either Buttle or Lambiel might have repeated as world champion, and won the Olympics, but the well-coached fields are now extremely deep. So, realistically, any given competition — including the Olympics — has a large number of potential winners.

It has become much harder today for any skater or team to "own" an era as so many of the skaters featured in this book did in the past. That may be conducive to a robust competitive atmosphere, but it's also a potential roadblock for creating legends. Additionally, according to many critics, the second-by-second monitoring used in the new marking system has made skaters and their routines start to look more alike. Yet one of the prerequisites for becoming a legend is individuality.

Conversely, the increased competition, the required attention to detail, improved coaching and training methods, and better nutrition are producing better skaters, and more of them.

From that deeper pool it's possible that any one, or more, of the following modern stars could join the pantheon of figure skating's greatest stars.

MIKI ANDO

When she finished a depressing and humiliating 15th at the 2006 Winter Olympics in Turin, Italy,

Miki Ando could not have imagined that she would be world champion within 13 months. And neither could her critics in Japan.

But with great consistency, and under terrific pressure in her home country, Ando held off two 16-year-olds, Yu-Na Kim of South Korea and Mao Asada, her national rival, to win the 2007 Worlds in Tokyo, and become only the third Japanese woman to wear the global crown.

Ando is among the leaders of the Asian wave sweeping through women's skating in the 21st century. She entered the history books at the 2002 Junior Grand Prix Final by becoming the first woman in history to successfully land a quadruple jump. In fact, she had landed that quadruple Salchow three times as a junior, but fell on her attempt during the free skate at the Turin Olympics, part of an overall meltdown that night. A controversial addition to the Japanese Olympic team in the first place, after finishing sixth at the Nationals, Ando was subsequently left off the team for the 2006 Worlds just a month after the Olympics.

"There were people who criticized my selection to the Olympics and I had a very hard time with that," said Ando.

Broken, Ando had contemplated quitting skating, but instead switched coaches — from Carol Heiss to Russian wunderkind Nikolai Morozov. Morozov rebuilt her confidence, as he had done with similarly undone Shizuka Arakawa just before she rebounded to win the 2006 Olympic Championships.

"Miki is the best skater," Morozov says. "We just had to bring it out of her and rebuild her confidence. She had had great results in the past."

Ando won a bronze medal in 2002 and a silver in 2003 at the World Junior Championships, before capturing the 2004 title. Many skaters would have graduated to senior ranks after their first world junior medal, but Ando didn't feel she was a senior-caliber skater because of the depth of competition in Japan. She won back-to-back national titles in 2004 and 2005, but then was second to Asada in both 2007

Miki Ando skates at the ISU's new World Team Trophy event in 2009; competing nations field skaters in all disciplines and vie for points in a cumulative, total-team score.

Mao Asada, the 2008 world champion, performs at the Grand Prix Final in 2008. Asada won the gold.

with what stood for eight months as a world free-skating record points total, and missed the gold medal (won by Miki Ando) by less than seven-tenths of a point.

Asada was bound for skating stardom almost since the day she and her older sister Mia left gymnastics for a lifetime on ice when Mao was five. Three years later, at age eight, she was hitting triple jumps. At 12, she was the first "woman" to land a triple-triple-triple combination when she combined a flip and two triple toe loops at the Japanese Novice Nationals, which she won twice in a row. When she was 14, she became the first junior woman to land a triple Axel in an international event, winning the Junior Grand Prix Final. She landed another triple Axel to win the World Junior Championships the same season.

Because 14-year-olds are allowed to compete on the Grand Prix Circuit (but are ineligible for the Worlds and Olympics, where the age minimum is 15 by the July previous to the event), Asada graduated to senior for the 2005–06 season and was the surprise winner of the Grand Prix Final by a whopping eight points over veteran Irina Slutskaya. A few weeks later, her free skate at the Japanese Nationals contained two triple Axels, a first for a woman. She finished second to Fumie Suguri, but her age made her ineligible for the 2006 Olympic team. Instead, she went to the Junior Worlds and landed the first short-program triple Axel by a woman, finishing second to fellow youthful sensation Yu-Na Kim.

Asada left California-based coach Rafael Arutunian in January 2008, and without a formal coach won the 2008 Four Continents and, a month later, the World Championships. She joined forces with legendary Russian coach Tatiana Tarasova for the 2008–09 season, and trained extensively in Moscow. Despite this, Asada finished fourth at the

and 2008 in one of the world's hottest domestic rivalries. Injuries forced Ando out of the 2008 Worlds a minute into her free-skate program, which she had entered in eighth place, but she rebounded to win a bronze medal at the 2009 Worlds, buoying her elusive self-confidence.

MAO ASADA

The performance everyone remembers most is the one that put Mao Asada of Japan in second place, not first. She won her first world championship in 2008 by being consistent, finishing second in both the short program and free skate, good enough for first overall.

But in her world championship debut at Tokyo in 2007, 16-year-old Asada unleashed a dynamic free skate for the ages, leaped from fifth place to second

2009 Worlds after she fell on her second triple Axel of her free skate. The fall cost her the bronze medal, which went to Miki Ando by a margin of just 1.29 points.

Asada has made the triple Axel, plus a difficult variation of the Biellmann spin, her calling cards. Paradoxically, she has admitted to struggling with the two triple jumps that lesser skaters master easily: the toe loop and Salchow. And when the ISU began judging takeoffs more critically, she was often penalized for turning her Lutz into a "flutz" for taking off on the wrong edge.

But Asada's advanced footwork and spins, and her ability to camouflage her entries so that her triple jumps look like they occur spontaneously, make her a good candidate for multiple world championships.

YU-NA KIM

Yu-Na Kim is already a legend in her homeland. Her back-to-back, third-place finishes at the 2007 and 2008 World Championships were the first world medals ever won by a South Korean skater.

And when she won the 2009 world title with a stunning 207.71 points — the first time a woman had broken the 200-point plateau — the 18-year-old Kim became the most popular athlete in South Korea.

But Kim has been putting the previously lightweight skating nation, now agog over the sport because of her, on the international map since before she hit her teens.

At 12, she was the youngest national champion in South Korean history. She won the gold medal in her second international event, a novice meet at Zagreb in Croatia, the first international medal and championship ever won by a Korean skater. She was second at the 2005 World Junior Championships,

Yu-Na Kim performs at the 2007 Grand Prix Final, where she took the gold. Kim and Asada are the only two skaters to win the Final since 2005–06.

Joannie Rochette skates to a bronze medal at the 2007 Four Continents. Rochette's 2009 silver marked her third successive Four Continents podium finish.

losing to Mao Asada. But the next year, Kim outdistanced Asada by an astounding 24.19 points to win the 2006 world junior title.

The high-octane rivalry they began on the junior circuit moved immediately onto the senior international scene. Kim and Asada have both benefited from acting as foils for each other; Kim had tended to fare better during the "regular season,"

winning the Grand Prix Final in 2007 and 2008, while Asada's silver and gold topped Kim's pair of bronzes in their first two world championships. But that changed in the 2008–09 season, as Kim lost the Grand Prix Final to Asada, but then at the Worlds, she broke Asada's old points mark (199.52) to win the championship, while Asada finished fourth.

Kim is a terrific all-round skater. One of her signature moves is a layback Ina Bauer spin, which moves directly into a double Axel or double-triple combination. She has power, precision and grace, and showed a fighter's spirit when she battled the pain from a herniated disk in her back. The injury threatened to force her to the sidelines during the 2007–08 season, but she persevered to win the Grand Prix Final and a bronze at that year's Worlds.

She moved to Toronto full-time in 2007 to work with coach Brian Orser, and also to escape the intense fandom of the South Koreans. "She is," Orser surmised after working with Kim for just a few weeks, "simply unbelievable."

JOANNIE ROCHETTE

At the start of the 2008–09 season, Canadian Joannie Rochette announced that she was taking dead aim on the world championship podium.

"Not many people believed I would do it," Rochette admits. "And I didn't believe, myself, I could win a medal until that season."

But Rochette made good on her prediction, nailing two impressive Grand Prix victories before earning a solid second-place finish in the very competitive women's division at the 2009 Worlds, launching her into the elite handful of medal contenders for the Vancouver Olympics.

It had been a long, hard climb for the native of tiny Ile Dupas, Quebec, a French-speaking village with a population of about 600, located on an island in the lower St. Lawrence River northeast of Montreal.

Rochette, the only woman to win the Canadian novice, junior and senior titles, was 17th at her first World Championships as a 16-year-old in 2002. She ping-ponged from 8th, to 11th, 7th, 10th and 5th over the next five years and seemed to have settled into a permanent home in the middle of the top 10.

Fast and athletic, she struggled to maintain

THE AMERICAN WOMEN

KIMMIE Meissner is the most recent American woman to win a world championship. Yet her chances of sustained stardom at the world level won't be challenged by just her international rivals, but also by an armada of rising young stars on the U.S. domestic scene.

Although U.S. women qualified for only two Olympic berths for Vancouver and came out of the 2009 Worlds without a medal for the third year in a row — the longest such drought since 1964 — the American Nationals have regained some of their traditional depth in the women's division. Four different champions reigned from 2006 to 2009: Sasha Cohen, Kimmie Meissner, former world junior medalist Mirai Nagasu and upset 2009 winner Alissa Czisny who, at 21, was the elder stateswoman of the top contenders.

Caroline Zhang and Rachael Flatt, who both won world junior championships, have also medaled at the U.S. Nationals. Nagasu and Zhang were born within 34 days of each other in 1993, and Flatt is only a year older, so this trio could still be around to challenge for the 2014 Olympic podium in Sochi, Russia.

Meissner was a precocious 16-year-old herself when she won the 2006 World Championships a month after finishing sixth at Turin, Italy, where she was the youngest member of the entire U.S. Olympic team. Only six women have won the Worlds at a younger age, and she was the first since Oksana Baiul to capture the world title in her debut appearance. Meissner won the world title before she won the U.S. crown, an omission she corrected in 2007, when she became the first woman in 46 years to complete the U.S. triple of novice, junior and senior champion. She is also the only female to simultaneously hold the U.S., World and Four Continents Championships.

The Maryland native excels at jumps, and at the 2005 U.S. Nationals became just the second American woman, after Tonya Harding in 1991, to land a triple Axel. Like many technical-based skaters, Meissner has had to work hard to develop a mature artistry so she doesn't need to rely on the inconsistencies of a jump-dependent image. After winning the Worlds in 2006, she was fourth the next year and just seventh at the 2008 Worlds, after finishing a shocking seventh at the Nationals. In 2009 her season ended early because of injury.

The reduced number of available berths for the American women at the 2010 Olympics will make it even harder for a U.S. skater to medal, given the fierce competition, which will

include the past three world champions: Miki Ando, Mao Asada and Yu-Na Kim.

The unstable, if multi-faceted, state of U.S. women's skating even provoked the comeback of Sasha Cohen for the 2010 Olympic season and has fueled talk about a possible return to eligible skating by national icon Michelle Kwan.

performance consistency, and rarely was able to put two good programs together in the same competition. She was dominant domestically, winning five straight national titles through 2009, but as her opponents became younger and younger, her chances at a medal seemed farther and farther away.

But, encouraged by Manon Perron, who has coached her most of her career, Rochette didn't give up. She kept getting physically stronger and was becoming a mature artist aided, she said, by frequent appearances with the Canadian leg of Stars on Ice.

Rochette beat world champion Mao Asada at Trophée Eric Bompard in France in the fall of 2008, which injected a new confidence into her approach.

Brian Joubert concluding his short program at the 2009 Worlds. His third-place finish placed him on the podium for the fifth time in six years.

She put the difficult, and (for her) inconsistent, triple-triple combination aside and concentrated on performance and a clean delivery for the World Championships. She was second in the short program and third in the free skate and, at 23, she finally had her first world medal.

It was the first world championship medal by a Canadian woman since Elizabeth Manley's silver 21 years earlier, and Manley was waiting near the Kiss 'n' Cry to congratulate Rochette after her free skate. It was only the second world medal for a Canadian woman in 36 years.

While Rochette's medal may have come as a surprise, there had been strong hints of its possibility. She is a half-decade older than most of the other major players in the women's division, but she's always had the skill, technique and choreography to challenge for the podium. She lacked consistency,

which was mostly a function of confidence, and her self-belief took a quantum leap upward in 2008–09.

And so did Canadian women's skating, which has long been the family embarrassment in one of the world's great skating nations. For many years, the task of the national champion was to analyze not her own victory but the mediocrity of Canadian women's skating. Rochette's long and steady effort to become an "overnight success" changed all that.

"I just hope to inspire some young girls to want to achieve big things in skating," Rochette beamed. "Through hard work I think anything is possible and I think I just proved that to myself and hopefully to all the other Canadian ladies."

BRIAN JOUBERT

Once France's Brian Joubert got those butterflies flying in formation, they lifted him to the top of the podium.

Joubert had a chance to win the 2005 World Championships, but anxiety butchered his free skate and he finished sixth. The following year, he admitted that he could not withstand the season-long pressure of being an Olympic medal favorite and finished sixth at the Turin Games.

But in 2007, Joubert overcame his "fear of flying," performed well, but without excessive risk, in the free skate to win his first world championship, and France's first men's global title in 42 years. Alain Calmat, who had won France's last men's world title in 1965, was in the audience when Joubert won at Tokyo, He was also present when Joubert took the European title in 2004, France's first since Calmat had triumphed 40 years earlier.

Joubert prides himself on being a "masculine" skater and is often compared to Alexei Yagudin, the 2002 Olympic champion. Yagudin, Joubert's favorite athlete, was also his mentor for part of the 2003–04 season. His critics say he sometimes patterns himself too closely after Yagudin.

With a forceful, erect bearing and muscular jumps, Joubert commands attention on the ice. He is adamant that a championship program must contain at least one quadruple jump and at the Cup of Russia in 2006, he became the first skater to land three quads in the same program. His critics say that his focus on the quads leaves him less time and mental energy to

practice and develop a more complex artistry — his major shortcoming.

Joubert had lost a kidney to serious illness when he was 11 months old, and for this reason, took up skating because there wasn't the physical contact that other sports involved. He didn't excel as a junior, finishing 14th at the 2000 Junior Worlds, before moving to senior. But two years later, he finished third in the tough French Nationals to grab a berth in the European Championships, where he was the unexpected bronze medalist. He won the 2004 and 2007 European titles, the latter being part of an undefeated season.

Just a few weeks before the 2007 Worlds, Joubert spiked himself in the foot during practice, which forced him to avoid certain triple jumps until right before the Championships. He overcame that injury and his demonic butterflies to claim his first world championship. The next year, he was beaten by a near-perfect but — as Joubert rather undiplomatically pointed out — quadless Jeffrey Buttle. He still finished second and was third in 2009 for his fifth Worlds medal, the most among his current peer group.

EVAN LYSACEK

Entering the 2010 Olympic season, the only men's skater other than Brian Joubert who had collected more than one world championship medal was American Evan Lysacek.

Yet, until March of 2009, few figure skating insiders, including many American experts, gave the Illinois native much chance to win a major title, let alone ascend into all-time status. He had always struggled with consistency on his quad, which forced him to think too much about the element rather than skating right through it. And injuries always seemed to crop up at the wrong time: hip injuries forced him to miss both the 2005 and 2006 Grand Prix Finals; an infection had him occasionally coughing up blood at the 2006 Worlds; he missed the 2008 Worlds after he was injured when a blade broke performing a triple Axel in practice; and in 2009, he skated the latter part of the season with a stress fracture in his left foot.

But Lysacek's stock soared significantly in the early part of 2009. Lysacek, the two-time defending national champion, finished third at the 2009 U.S. Nationals,

Evan Lysacek celebrates victory on home soil at the 2009 World Championships. His win ended a personal two-year world podium drought.

but went on to win the Four Continents Championships for the third time, and then won the free skate at the World Championships by a four-point margin to climb from second place to the top of the podium. And even though no reigning men's world champion has won the Olympics since 1984, Lysacek instantly became the gold-medal favorite for Vancouver in 2010.

With his world title, the first by an American man in 13 years, and the first by a U.S. man on American ice in 28 years, Lysacek has returned to the massive expectations that accompanied his arrival on the senior scene in 2004 after three world junior championship silver medals.

The injuries, and his struggle to land a consistent quadruple jump, often shunted Lysacek off the fast track to stardom. At times, such as the 2007 Four Continents Championships, his only goal was to land the four-rotation jump. He had landed his first one (a quad toe loop) to help him win the bronze medal at the 2006 Worlds. He had also finished third, without a quad, at the 2005 World Championships when his stated goal was merely to get beyond the qualifying round.

Lysacek and his coach Frank Carroll decided to take the quad, and its attendant pressure, completely out of the equation for the 2009 World Championships in Los Angeles, permitting Lysacek to concentrate only on skating a complete program. The move paid off handsomely with what was virtually a hometown championship for Lysacek, who trains in nearby El Segundo.

Tall (6-foot-2) for a singles skater with a commanding presence on the ice, Lysacek has the technical skills and artistic sense required to become an Olympic and multiple world champion. But the quadruple jump is still one of the delineation marks between the really good men skaters of the 21st century and the great ones.

Patrick Chan at the 2009 Worlds where he placed second; Canada's second men's world medal in as many years.

PATRICK CHAN

When Elvis Stojko retired in 2002, Canadian skating fans worried about the future of their men's program. But within a couple of years, Jeffrey Buttle starting capturing medals and went on to win at the 2008 World Championships. When Buttle retired later that year, there was more collective anxiety about Canadian men's skating, but it didn't take long for Patrick Chan to allay those worries.

Just three months after his 18th birthday, Chan won the silver medal at the 2009 World Championships, capping an incredible sophomore season in which he won two Grand Prix events, the Four Continents Championships and his second Canadian title (by an astonishing 48.52 points).

Inside Chan's young body resides an old skating soul — perhaps because his two coaches have been Osborne Coulson (in his 80s when he took Chan on) and the venerable Don Laws (who guided Scott

Hamilton to the 1984 Olympic title) — and he possesses a sophisticated sense of artistry and nuance far beyond his years.

Chan, like Buttle before him, is hardwired for the International Judging System. In fact, as a proponent of the well-rounded program he got into a very public debate with Brian Joubert at the 2009 Worlds over Joubert's assertion that quadruple jumps should be worth more points.

Chan finished the 2008–09 season without a quad, but his spins, footwork and other elements are performed at such a high technical level that he harvests points in great bunches. Should he start landing quadruple jumps, there is no one among his peers to rival his potential.

Chan won the national novice and junior titles before he upset Buttle to win his first Canadian senior title in 2008, just weeks after his 17th birthday. He debuted at ninth in the Worlds that March, and the next year he stepped boldly into the void left by Buttle to become the second-youngest Canadian man ever to medal at the Worlds. (Don McPherson was two months younger when he won the 1963 Worlds title.)

"It's a big shock," Chan said. "I didn't expect to get this far in just my second Worlds."

Chan is young enough that he could make two Olympic appearances and most veteran skating analysts agree that he's got the potential to become an Olympic and multiple world champion.

DAISUKE TAKAHASHI

Coach Nikolai Morozov recognized that there was a huge difference between being famous in Japan, and being famous worldwide. "I want to make Daisuke [Takahashi] part of the history of skating," the young but renowned Russian-bred coach said. "Not just part of the history of Japanese skating."

However, Takahashi left Morozov in 2008 despite an incredible career turnaround that he attributes directly to the New Jersey-based choreographer/coach. Morozov had had disagreements with Takahashi's new agent. He also had taken on Nobunari Oda, and Takahashi couldn't abide sharing a coach with his chief national rival.

Takahashi returned to Japan to work with Utako Nagamitsu, who had coached him most of his career and also helped during Takahashi's Morozov years. But a knee injury and subsequent surgery forced Takahashi to miss the entire 2008–09 competitive season, a major setback at the beginning of an Olympic campaign.

But in the three years after he joined Morozov as a confidence-lacking 19-year-old ranked 15th in the world, Takahashi regained his self-belief and unleashed the promise he showed in 2002 when he emerged from obscurity to become the first Japanese man to win a world junior championship.

A 13th place at the 2003 Four Continents and ragged 11th- and 15th-place results at his first two world championships in 2004 and 2005 had filled Takahashi's conversion from junior to senior skater with self-doubt. But after he moved to the U.S. in the autumn of 2005, Takahashi steadily grew more confident: Morozov taught him proper technique, worked him into excellent condition and choreographed well-suited programs, which made him more comfortable on the ice.

Under Morozov, Takahashi was in contention for a medal at the 2006 Olympics after the short program, but a poor free skate dropped him to eighth. And in 2007, in front of a raucous audience in Tokyo for the Worlds, he ignited the partisan audience with a stirring free skate to Phantom of the Opera. It won him the silver medal, the highest world finish ever by a Japanese male. The following year, he lost the Grand Prix Final by just 0.16 points to Stéphane Lambiel and Takahashi's hip-hop routine was called one of the best short programs of all time. But he dropped to fourth at the Worlds after a sixth-place free skate.

Takahashi has a spectacular work ethic that, Morozov says, has pushed him beyond the limitations of his natural talent. An explosive, dynamic skater who is committed to two quads per free skate, Takahashi combines with Nobunari Oda and Takahiko Kozuka to give Japan its greatest depth ever in men's skating.

NOBUNARI ODA

Nobunari Oda is a passionate and pensive contrast to his explosive Japanese rival Daisuke Takahashi. But he shares certain things with Takahashi including the world junior title (Oda won in 2005) and coach Nikolai Morozov, whom Oda joined in the spring

Daisuke Takahashi celebrates his silver-medal winning performance at the 2007 Grand Prix Final.

of 2008, hastening the departure of Takahashi from Morozov's New Jersey training center.

After a stirring head-to-head contest with Takahashi at the 2005–06 Japanese Nationals, Oda was announced as the champion, but a glitch in the computer program failed to take into account that he had completed too many combination jumps. When the error was caught, the title reverted to Takahashi. Faced with having only one berth at the Worlds and the Olympics that season, Japanese skating authorities decided to split the two major assignments and sent Takahashi to the Olympics and Oda to the Worlds. Oda stunned the federation with a fourth-place finish in his first Worlds, and was seventh the following year, while also earning a bronze medal at the Grand Prix Final.

It's been difficult to accurately assess Oda's progress and his potential for future stardom because he lost a whole season of competitive development in 2007–08. In July 2007, he was arrested in Osaka for driving a moped while under the influence of alcohol. The federation suspended him for the Grand Prix season and, embarrassed, he decided to sit out the rest of the year as well. That meant he didn't gain qualifying points for the following Grand Prix season, and was limited to one major international competition — the NHK in Japan — on a host's invitation.

He made the switch from Canada's Mariposa club to Morozov in New Jersey before the 2008–09 season. Like so many Japanese skaters who switch to Morozov, Oda's immediate results were impressive as he won the NHK, his only Grand Prix event, and won his first national senior title. But he finished a disappointing seventh at the Worlds.

Oda is wildly popular in Japan, partly because he is the 17th direct descendant of Oda Nobunaga, a famous samurai who conquered much of Japan during the country's "Sengoku" period. This present day Oda is always a threat to medal at the Worlds, but lags behind Takahashi and others in the development of a reliable quadruple jump, a must in today's high-tech market.

TANITH BELBIN and BEN AGOSTO

The most decorated ice dance team in American history, Tanith Belbin and Ben Agosto seemed destined to become the first U.S. world champions in this traditionally European-dominated discipline. But in 2008, that feeling stalled after the duo missed the Worlds podium for the first time in five years, and Belbin and Agosto switched coaches from Igor Shpilband's dance factory in Michigan to Natalia Linichuk and Gennadi Karponossov. They were being seriously challenged, and sometimes beaten, by younger training partners Tessa Virtue/Scott Moir and Meryl Davis/Charlie White and felt they needed a change.

The strategy worked. Despite Agosto's chronically sore back (which had forced them to miss both the Grand Prix Final and their national championships), Belbin and Agosto returned to the podium at the 2009 Worlds, with the second silver medal of their careers, to go with a pair of bronzes and the 2006 Olympic silver.

They finished just 1.22 points behind Russians Oksana Domnina and Maxim Shabalin, who had also switched coaches to work with Linichuk and Karponossov at the start of the season.

"There were mixed emotions," said Belbin. "There were so many different options for how Ben could

Tanith Belbin and Ben Agosto performing their compulsory dance at the 2009 Worlds. The duo finished second, their fourth world podium finish in five years.

have gotten through this injury and he could have been defeated by it, but instead he fought through it. I don't know anybody else who could have stood such pain."

Virtue/Moir and Davis/White owe a huge debt of gratitude to their former clubmates. It is impossible to overstate how difficult it was for Belbin and Agosto to force their way into the upper echelons of the sport's most American-resistant division. For every place they rose in the standings, they had to be demonstrably superior to those they passed in the Eurocentric discipline.

And for the most part, they have been demonstrably superior.

Dancers Tessa Virtue and Scott Moir display their 2009 World Championship bronze medals, their second straight medal finish at the Worlds.

They started at 13th in the world in 2002, but their talent was too obvious to keep them far from the podium: they jumped to seventh in 2003, and were fifth in 2004. But they often didn't get the marks for their compulsory dances, or in the "artistic" and, later, component scores that some of their lesser-talented European competitors did.

Belbin is a Canadian, but felt stymied by her lack of progress in her native country and moved to the U.S. to join Agosto in 1998. The new couple began to have immediate success, winning the Junior Grand Prix Finals and World Junior Championships in 2002,

and ascending to the U.S. Championships in 2004. Their silver medal at the 2005 Worlds matched the highest U.S. dance finish of all time, and was the first American world dance medal of any hue in 20 years.

Because Belbin was not a U.S. citizen, the couple was ineligible for the 2002 Olympics in Salt Lake City, and only the fast-tracking effort of a determined local senator three years later landed Belbin her U.S. citizenship on New Year's Eve in 2005, just six weeks before Turin. When they won silver at the Turin Games, it was the best-ever Olympic result for American dancers.

Following hard on the heels of Canadian pioneers Shae-Lynn Bourne and Victor Kraatz, Belbin and Agosto helped to create a worldwide acceptance for North American dancers. They are entirely capable of winning an Olympic championship, a world title, and more.

TESSA VIRTUE and SCOTT MOIR

There was a time, not long ago, when Tessa Virtue and Scott Moir would have waited years to get on the world ice dance podium — and maybe not have got there at all.

They are from North America, which didn't have a world champion until 2003; they are young; they are not cut from the taller, classical eastern European mold; and they generally eschew cheap theatrics for a purer artistry.

But when fellow Canadians Shae-Lynn Bourne and Victor Kraatz broke the European domination with their world title in 2003, and the new International Judging System — which forces ice dance judges to look more objectively at what's being skated, without reference to reputation — followed closely thereafter, it created the perfect milieu for Virtue and Moir.

Virtue and Moir were teamed up by Moir's aunt, a skating coach in western Ontario, when they were just 8 and 10, respectively. Progressing through the earliest dancing instruction through to the world podium together, they've developed a unison that other couples will always struggle to achieve. They skate lightly, but with incredible speed.

The partners' 2006 World Junior Championships win was the first ever by Canadian ice dancers, and the following year they made a spectacular sixth-place debut at the Worlds. In 2008, they were world silver medalists, winning the free dance and missing gold only because of a mistake in the original dance.

The Canadians' ascent was slowed slightly by surgery that Virtue had in September 2008 on stress fractures in both her shins. That kept the couple off the ice until December, and limited their competitive season to the Nationals, which they won for the second time; the Four Continents, where they won a silver medal; and the 2009 Worlds, where they hung on to the bronze medal by .04 points over their close friends and Michigan training partners Meryl Davis and Charlie White of the U.S.

Virtue and Moir are leaders of the second wave of North Americans enjoying global success in a division that until recently was a European stronghold. Bourne and Kraatz, Marie-France Dubreuil and Patrice Lauzon, and Tanith Belbin and Ben Agosto all won silver or gold early in the 21st century. Virtue and Moir and Davis and White have arrived near the top far more quickly, and with greater expectations of becoming and remaining world champions, than any North Americans in ice dancing history.

ALIONA SAVCHENKO and ROBIN SZOLKOWY

Despite a long and successful history, elite pairs skating in Germany was virtually dormant until Ukrainian Aliona Savchenko, a former world junior champion, arrived in Chemnitz in 2003.

Coach Ingo Steuer teamed Savchenko with Greifswald native Robin Szolkowy, who had been without a partner for 18 months, and had even taken up synchronized skating to maintain his skills.

The new partners clicked immediately because of their speed and athleticism, and within a year they won the 2004 German Nationals. After a sixth-place Worlds debut in 2005, Savchenko was granted German citizenship in late December, allowing the pair to compete at the 2006 Olympics, where they finished sixth.

In 2007 they broke through to a bronze medal at the Worlds. A couple of months earlier they had won their first European title, ending an 11-year Russian hold on the continental championship, and becoming the first Germans to stand on top of the podium since

Aliona Savchenko and Robin Szolkowy soar to a second straight World gold medal at the 2009 World Championships in Los Angeles.

coach, Steuer, himself and Mandy Woetzel won the Europeans in 1995.

The next year Savchenko and Szolkowy were almost unbeatable, and their only loss was to Dan Zhang and Hao Zhang of China at the 2007 Cup of Russia. Otherwise, they were perfect, winning three Grand Prix events, the Grand Prix Final and the Europeans (setting a new short-program points record). Then, to top it off, they won the 2008 World Championships, the first pairs title for Germany since

THE BIGGEST TEAM IN SKATING

IT IS figure skating's growth industry, and if it ever gains the Olympics status that the ISU seeks for it, synchronized skating will dwarf the rest of the sport in participation numbers.

Known until the early 21st century as "precision skating," synchronized is skating's ultimate team game. There are 20 skaters (down from the original 24) skating in unison, but this isn't the same sport that began as an off-shoot of American college marching bands in the early 1960s.

The skating is fast and there are now lifts and other high-risk moves, and the best teams require nearly as much commitment as national-level singles skating does.

Mass routines have been part of club carnivals for over a century, but the acknowledged creator of formalized synchronized skating is Dr. Richard Porter of the Ann Arbor Skating Club in Michigan. In the early 1960s, he was concerned about the number of skaters leaving the sport in their teens after they no longer had the time, or the talent reserve, to compete at a high level in singles. So he founded the world's first team, and called them the Hockettes, a double pun on the famous Radio City Rockettes and on the team's own appearances during intermissions at the University of Michigan hockey games.

The concept spread quickly and by the early 1980s both Canada and the U.S. had national championships, and routines became more ambitious and dangerous. After a couple of years of informal events, synchronized skating got its own official world championships in 1998.

As coaches and choreography have become more sophisticated, the sport has evolved toward mass ice dancing, with emphasis on speed, edges and creativity. In more developed synchronized skating nations such as Canada, the technical demands are so high that competition has been split into elite and recreational streams.

While the sport has clear North American origins, the early legends of synchronized skating are Scandinavian. Team Surprise, based in Gothenburg, Sweden, has won all but five world titles and finished second in four others. Finland's Marigold Ice Unity has won three world championships and in 2008 the Rockettes of Finland won their first title with Team Surprise second.

Canada's superstar team is southern Ontario's NEXXICE which finished third at the Worlds in 2007 and 2008, and took gold in 2009. Other perennial strongholds are Quebec's Les Pirouettes and Toronto's Black Ice. The Haydenettes, the most consistent U.S. team, is usually hovering close to the podium, too. But the sport's founding nation didn't win its first world medal until 2007, with a silver going to the RedHawks from Miami University, the first American school to accord synchronized skating varsity sport status.

Steuer and Woetzel 11 years earlier. They repeated, with ease, the following year.

Each victory gave the relatively new team more and more confidence, and they are now skating like champions. Quick afoot, with blinding pairs spins, Savchenko and Szolkowy have set themselves apart from the rest by the difficulty of their programs and with some unorthodox entries into jumps and lifts. They have also mastered the triple twist, which has become imperative for championship hopefuls, and have huge, interesting throws. If they remain injury-free and continue their soaring career arc, they could become one of the pairs for the ages.

QING PANG and JIAN TONG

Qing Pang and Jian Tong of China spent so long in the lengthy shadow of compatriots and international icons Xue Shen and Hongbo Zhao that whenever they had a chance to emerge into the spotlight, the brightness sometimes unnerved them. The talented pair are always in contention, but have rarely showed long stretches of maximizing their vast potential. They did win the 2006 World Championships, a month after narrowly missing the Olympic podium. But even they were shocked that they had won the Worlds after a less-than-stirring performance, which included a fall by Pang on the triple Salchow.

Both partners were singles skaters and Tong also trained as an ice dancer for two years, before coach Bin Yao teamed them up in 1993 in their hometown of Harbin. But Yao then left for Beijing for four years, leaving them essentially coachless, partly explaining why they never finished higher than eighth in the world junior rankings. As seniors, they began to make their mark. In the absence of Shen and Zhao, they won the National Championships in 2000, 2004, 2007 and 2008. The pair also captured a trio of Four Continents titles, the most recent being in 2009.

Pang and Tong overcame serious problems to win a silver medal at the 2007 Worlds. Pang was recovering from a kidney ailment and Tong was wearing a headband to hide the 12-inch scar he suffered when he was hit by a car earlier in the season. With their 2004 World Championship bronze medal, the silver gave Pang and Tong world championship medals of all three hues.

Qing Pang and Jian Tong skate to a gold medal at the 2008 NHK trophy in their first appearance at the tournament in four years.

Over time, Pang and Tong have sanded off their rough edges and become an all-round pair. But the duo still has consistency issues as evidenced by their 5th and 4th place World finishes in 2008 and 2009. Until they can find consistency in the most difficult technical and artistic elements, they will continue to operate in the shadow of the retired Shen and Zhao.

DAN ZHANG and HAO ZHANG

Zhang and Zhang, who are not related, teamed up in 1997 when he was 13 and she 12 and coming off a national junior women's gold medal. Because of their physical contrasts (he is looming and muscular, she slight and slim) they've been labeled by less sensitive fans as "Beauty and the Beast." The pair debuted as stars on the ISU's junior pairs international circuit where they executed a rare quadruple twist to win the 2001 World Junior Championships, and won the

Dan Zhang and Hao Zhang perform during the ISU World Team Trophy. Zhang and Zhang have won four world medals but have yet to claim gold.

global Juniors again two years later. They also took two Junior Grand Prix Final titles.

By 2009, Zhang and Zhang had already won a Worlds bronze medal (2004) and three silvers (2006, 2008, 2009), and had finished on the Grand Prix Final podium four times.

Pushing the envelope was not new to Zhang and Zhang, who'd always been third in the Chinese pairs' pecking order, but could one day emulate the accomplishments of the great Xue Shen and Hongbo Zhao. They'd gained notoriety around the world for Dan Zhang's horrific fall early in the free skate of the 2006 Olympics, as they were attempting to complete history's first throw quadruple Salchow. Her feet splayed gruesomely as she hit the ice, her partner had to help her to the side boards and their Olympics appeared to be over. Zhang had sprained ligaments in her knee, but after consulting with coach Bin Yao, the pair decided to continue. They sailed through the rest of their program and finished to a standing ovation and a seemingly impossible silver medal. "We were challenging the extreme

power of human beings to handle pain," she said afterwards with her knee and thigh wrapped tightly with a tensor bandage and ice.

As Zhang and Zhang continue to hone their skills under Yao, cynical fans will be forced to admit that the pair exemplifies more beauty than beast.

YUKO KAWAGUCHI and ALEXANDER SMIRNOV

Yuko Kawaguchi is already a historic figure in Russian figure skating. Mostly because she is not Russian.

The native of Aichi, Japan, had already become the first Japanese pairs skater to win an international medal when she and Russian Alexander Markuntsov finished second at the 2001 World Junior Championships, representing Japan. And when she and Alexander Smirnov, representing Russia, finished ninth at the 2007 Worlds, it was the first time in the century-plus history of organized skating competition that Russia (or the former Soviet Union) had been represented by someone outside the country.

Kawaguchi started as a singles skater in Japan but wanted to skate for legendary Russian coach Tamara Moskvina, who said she only coached pairs. So Kawaguchi came to the U.S. in 1999 to work with Moskvina, and followed the coach when she returned to St. Petersburg in 2003. Along the way, she was paired with Markuntsov (2000–03) for Japan, with American Devin Patrick in the U.S. Championships (2004–06) and Smirnov, starting in 2007, for Russia.

Kawaguchi and Smirnov surged to fourth at the 2008 Worlds and confirmed they're made of podium material by moving up to claim the bronze medal in 2009 (just .13 points off the silver). With Kawaguchi gaining Russian citizenship in December 2008, she is now able to represent her new country at the Olympics. But what she and her partner represent most are the shifting sands of international skating. Aside from coaching, Russia's most important skating export in the previous two decades had been pairs and dance partners, but with Kawaguchi, the Russian federation has become an importer.

Yuko Kawaguchi and Alexander Smirnov skate to a second place finish at the Cup of Russia in 2008.

ACKNOWLEDGMENTS

The author would like to thank the staff of the World Figure Skating Hall of Fame, especially Karen Cover and Linda Famula for their help and encouragement; Ben Wright for his meticulous and usually solitary dedication to maintaining the threads of figure skating history; Beth Davis; authors James Hines, Ellyn Kestnbaum and Joy Goodwin for their extraordinary additions to figure skating's bibliography; and to Steve Cameron and Michael Worek at Firefly Books for their belief and patience.

As always, my life-long gratitude to my inner circle: Jess, Toby, Michelle and mom, Thumb and the four T.G.'s — particularly T.G. Smithy.

Further Reading

Bass, Howard. *Skating*. London: Chartwell Books, 1980.

Cranston, Toller, and Martha Kimball. *Zero Tollerance*. Toronto: McClelland & Stewart, 1997.

Goodwin, Joy. *The Second Mark: Courage, Corruption, and the Battle for Olympic Gold*. New York: Simon & Schuster, 2002.

Hamill, Dorothy. *A Skating Life: My Story*. New York: Hyperion, 2007.

Hines, James R. *Figure Skating: A History*. Chicago: University of Illinois Press, 2006.

Kestnbaum, Ellyn. *Culture on Ice: Figure Skating and Cultural Meaning*. Middleton, Connecticut: Wesleyan University Press, 2003.

Milton, Steve. *Skate*. Toronto: Key Porter Books, 1996.

Milton, Steve. *Skate Talk: Figure Skating in the Words of the Stars*. Toronto: Key Porter Books, 1998.

Smith, Beverley. *Figure Skating: A Celebration*. Edited by Dan Diamond. Toronto: McClelland & Stewart, 1994.

Stevenson, Sandra. *The BBC Book of Skating*. London: BBC, 1984.

Waldman, Frank. *Famous American Athletes of Today*. Boston: L.C. Page and Company, 1949.

Additional resources include www.isu.org, www.goldenskate.com and www.ruvr.ru; select issues of magazines: *Blades*, *International Figure Skating*, *Skating*, *Sports Illustrated*, *Spotlight on Skating* and *TIME*; archives from the World Figure Skating Hall of Fame, as well as the United States Figure Skating Association 2008–09 Media Guide.

CREDITS

INDEX